Human Behavior
and the Social Environment

Human Behavior
and the Social Environment

A Perspective for Social Work Practice

Grace Ganter and Margaret Yeakel

Columbia University Press
New York   1980

Library of Congress Cataloging in Publication Data

Ganter, Grace.
  Human behavior and the social environment.

  Includes bibliographical references and index.
  1. Social psychology.   I. Yeakel, Margaret,
joint author.   II. Title.
HM251.G228   302   80-470
ISBN 0-231-04620-0

Columbia University Press
New York   Guildford, Surrey

To Helen Ganter Kribel (1918–1975),
in celebration of her courage

Acknowledgments

Many encounters have shaped and sustained the inception, development, and completion of this work. We take pleasure in gratefully acknowledging the contribution of Norman A. Polansky, our mentor and friend, who first brought to our attention the concepts which we have elaborated in this book. While he may not subscribe to all we have said, we thank him for the encouragement he gave us to pursue our own ideas.

It has been our good fortune to have the interest of a number of colleagues in professional social work education. We recognize with gratitude the help of the members of the faculty of Temple University School of Social Administration. In particular, our special thanks go to Albert E. Wilkerson for his sustained encouragement of this project; to Marcella Sawyer for her creative and stimulating responses to the content and her assessments of its usefulness for teaching graduate students; to Zita Attinson for her appraisal of its appropriateness for undergraduate learners; to Audrey Pittman for sharing with us her knowledge and insights on the black family; and to Zelda Samoff and Philip Jaslow, whose perceptive observations enriched the chapter on older adults. Similarly, we thank Willard Richan, who reviewed portions of the work, and Dean Ione Vargus, who provided continued encouragement toward its completion. Appreciation goes, too, to Asha Verma, librarian, for her assistance with bibliographical details and to Barbara Brocklehurst for typing and retyping our numerous drafts.

Among colleagues in other schools, we wish particularly to

recognize Marion Wijnberg for her clarifying suggestions and John Main for his ongoing interest in the progress of the work. To our students, whose responses to the material as it developed helped us understand the kind of knowledge they could use, we are much indebted.

Dorothy Yeakel Hall's lively, intelligent, and enduring interest sustained us on more occasions than she knew. For seeing us through the vicissitudes of the writing we also thank many friends, with special appreciation to Dorothy Christopher, Lucia Irons, Effie Warren, Claire Ness, Opal Jacobs, Jean Brooke, June MacDowell, Miriam Druckman, and Irene Gibson.

Nancy Bergman, who read the early drafts of several chapters, gave us invaluable suggestions and confidence to continue the work. For editorial encouragement and counsel in bringing the book to fruition, we are grateful to John D. Moore and Columbia University Press.

Finally, we acknowledge and thank the following authors and publishers who gave us permission to quote excerpts from their work: William E. Cross, Jr., "The Negro-to-Black Conversion Experience," copyright © 1971, by *Black World* and reprinted by permission of Johnson Publishing Company and William E. Cross, Jr.; Erik H. Erikson, *Identity and the Life Cycle, Psychological Issues*, vol. 1, no. 1, used with the permission of W. W. Norton, New York, copyright © 1959 by International Universities Press, Inc.

Grace Ganter
Margaret Yeakel

Contents

Contents

Human Behavior
and the Social Environment

Introduction

This text has its background in earlier efforts of the writers to discover ways in which undergraduate and beginning graduate students process knowledge about human behavior and the social environment for use in their practice. In it we identify and discuss a selected number of concepts linked to provide a conceptual framework that can serve as a useful guide to social workers as they examine the life stream of human experience, regardless of the practice field or setting in which they choose to concentrate.

The nature of social work practice requires practitioners to confront and to respond to complex human events and situations. Social workers are expected to act to influence human events, and what they choose to do depends on what they see to do, on how they perceive the situation. What social workers see to do is informed by aspects of behavior to which their attention is drawn. Social workers' attention is directed by the knowledge of human behavior they use to explain human events. This is to say that social workers are actors and that what they select to do depends on taking in and processing a great deal of stimuli so that they can consciously attend to particular aspects of the situation to which they are responding, without being overwhelmed, or immobilized, by it.

Social workers' knowledge has been drawn from many sources. The level of complexity of social phenomena with which they work has always required a broad-ranging knowledge of human behavior. Their responses require that they select, out of many possible explanations, those that best explain the situation they are confronting at any one point in time. What they elect to observe, then, is guided by the explanations they choose.

An important goal of education for social work is to provide students with the opportunity to organize the knowledge on which they will draw and from which they will choose explanations which inform their actions. Generations of social work educators and practicing social workers have made efforts to select, out of the increasing body of explanations of human behavior, those that improve the ability of social workers to understand human events. The organizing conceptions which social workers have chosen have evolved from a number of sources. These have included, for example, explanations of individuals' motivations, behavior, and development provided by a variety of psychodynamic theories; explanations of human learning drawn from the work of learning theorists; explanations, provided by sociological theories, of the group life of individuals, of the complex social structure, and of the systemic human relationships in which groups are involved; insights about the nature and processes of socialization and acculturation provided by social anthropologists. Social workers have drawn on the work of educators, physicians, and other disciplines, and they have also drawn on the experience and wisdom of practicing social workers, many of whom have recorded, with varying degrees of rigor and precision, the explanations they have gleaned from their practice.

Many good collections of knowledge and wisdom about human behavior and social events are currently being developed. Indeed, educators, students, and practitioners find themselves bombarded by stimuli from many sources, and the question frequently arises: What of all of this is critical? Questions have been raised about whether there is at present a body of organized and codified knowledge that can be clearly identified as necessary for social work practice.[1] Our own efforts to identify, in an increasing volume of knowledge, that which is most critical have led us to a partial answer. There is a social psychological framework that links enough critical concepts from both social and psychological theories to provide social work students with an identifiable body of knowledge which we believe is necessary for social work practice. We view the framework as a partial answer because it suggests to us that if students have, at a minimum, the knowledge which this framework organizes to which to refer their interventions, they will be able to examine other theoretical formulations and to deepen their understanding of human behavior as they define their professional practice.

Efforts of earlier social work educators and practitioners, as well as our own, have contributed to the evolution of this framework. We have concentrated our attention on these social and psychological explanations of human behavior which link individuals to the organizational and institutional arrangements within which they live out their lives. A critical premise of this book is that the organizational and institutional arrangements within which people live largely determine the ways in which their human energies are directed. Therefore, the knowledge we have selected as fundamental to the social work practice for which students are preparing is weighted on the social determinants of human problems and their psychological implications. Such knowledge is fundamental to the definition of social problems in social terms, and to the understanding of their impact on human development.

We have, then, drawn heavily on social psychological theory, concentrating on the need to link knowledge about the individual and knowledge about the social environment. The concepts which we have lifted into the foreground reflect our view of the nature of concepts needed by practitioners. The following discussion will help to clarify our view of the significance, for social workers, of the concepts they use.

The Nature of Concepts Needed by Practitioners

The structure of knowledge includes, as its basic building blocks, verbal symbols that are known as "concepts." To have a conception of something means to have images and feelings about it; when one associates a word—a name or verbal symbol—with these images and feelings, one is using a concept to organize them, to put them into order. We use the term "concept," then, as a symbol that is applied to a range of experiences that have something in common. We conceptualize by abstracting, from a welter of impressions of events and experiences, those that are like each other and different in some crucial way from others. When we identify some set of experiences by a word, we are symbolizing, that is, using a verbal signal to call attention to, and bring to consciousness, that set of experiences.

The aim of conceptualizing is to give a reasonably simple and efficient picture of what is happening. The verbal symbols we use become, then, a description of some recurring set of events or experiences in the phenomenological world. The concepts we use serve us as a guide to what to look for, or bring into view; thus, the concepts we entertain direct our perceptions of human behavior. It is important to be aware that since we form concepts by abstraction, we block out other ways of looking at the same events when we use them.

When relationships are found between one concept and another, we are on our way to developing a theory. Theory grows as predictions are checked in practice. Predictions are based on statements that link several discrete concepts in a way that asserts how one set of events or acts influences, and is influenced by, other sets. A fully developed body of theory embraces many such statements, linked to each other in such a way that they form a network of interlocking propositions. Each proposition becomes a unit in a theory, in the same way in which concepts are the units out of which each proposition is constructed. This network of propositions sensitizes us to what we take to be recurring patterns in the experience of many human beings, and helps us to recognize meanings that frequently may not be apparent in the immediate manifestations of behavior which social workers seek to influence.

The need for theory arises from the nature of a professional practice. Social work is goal-directed work, and social workers' commitment is not solely to the advancement of their own knowledge. Social work practice requires that practitioners view and respond to human events both compassionately and effectively. The extent to which one can respond effectively depends on the way one conceives of what there is to respond to, and what one perceives depends on those concepts that structure one's knowledge.

Propositions and theories provide explanations of events; concepts identify events. The concepts that social workers select to use derive their meanings in part from the bodies of theory in which we find them. The question of whether there is a body of knowledge that can be identified as necessary for social work practice must be joined with the question of whether social workers have consciously examined the assumptions about behavior that are implicit in the theories from which they draw the concepts and propositions they use. For example, social workers have drawn on a number of psychological concepts from traditional depth psychologies which direct them to look for the causes of human problems within individuals. They have also drawn on concepts from traditional sociologies which direct them to look for the causes of human problems in environmental forces outside the individual's control. Each of these perspectives orients social workers to a different set of causes. Psychological explanations frequently rest on the assumption that differences among individuals derive from their internal dynamics and that individuals make their own environments. Sociological explanations frequently rest on the assumption that differences among individuals derive from environmental variations which determine their behavior. Such psychological explanations tend to neglect environmental forces, and such sociological explanations tend to neglect forces within the individual. The implication is that when people have learned to conceive of human events from one point of view, they will block out the other point of view. This will occur if knowledge is organized solely by concepts which have been linked in propositions providing explanations of either social factors or individual factors as causes of behavior.

Many educators and practitioners, dedicated to changing social, economic and political forces which prevent individuals from reaching their human potential, despair when they see people concentrating on internal dynamics as explanations of human misery. There is no question that some psychological explanations of human behavior encourage social workers to work to change the victims of dehumanizing social conditions rather than to change the conditions that dehumanize them.

In our view, commitment to changing dehumanizing conditions requires an understanding of how such conditions are
maintained and of the psychological implications such conditions have for individuals.

A social psychological perspective offers a way to bridge
the gap between the psychological and the sociological streams
of theory. When social workers can learn to draw selectively on
social psychological concepts, they have a better chance to
account for critical social and psychological implications of
human behavior. We have chosen for elaboration in this text
four concepts, drawn from social psychological theories, which
we believe are necessary to the social worker because of their
bridging potential. These four constructs illustrate the kinds of
terms which we believe can alert social workers to what it is
important to pay attention to in their practice, and to aspects
of experience which they might otherwise overlook. They are
the self-concept and the concepts of reference groups, social
reality, and social role. The human events to which they direct
the social worker's attention include social and psychological
influences on the self-concept; the impressive influences of
social definitions by groups which individuals use for appraisal
and judgment of their behavior; the comparative group
references underlying human liberation movements; the emotional anchorages of social attitudes and common human
defenses; the effects of yielding to pressures to conform; the
micro, mezzo, and macro systems within which behavior is
institutionalized; the psychological pain of social role foreclosure; and the function of social role behavior in system
maintenance.

We have, by singling out these concepts, foregone a
number of other ways in which human behavior can be viewed.
We believe that the concepts which form the framework within
which this text is written will bridge enough critical knowledge
to provide a perspective for practice that will be useful to
students of social work and to many practitioners. But what
we present here does not encompass all the knowledge needed
by social workers. Students will find that there are many
sources which they can explore in greater depth. In addition,
we have not dealt with that line of theory which has led to
behavior modification technology; we have not dealt with

explorations such as those represented by Paul MacLean's work,[2] into the structure of the brain, nor have we dealt directly with recent advances in biological research. These exclusions are not intended to suggest that such directions of thought need be, or should be, neglected by social workers. As we have suggested, the framework presented here represents knowledge at a minimum. We have emphasized the social psychological perspective for the reasons we have advanced, and because it seems to us to provide an integrative theoretical grounding that has not yet been elaborated in this way for social work use. We think that students who have this framework will want to increase their knowledge of other theoretical approaches as they continue their education and their practice.

The book is so organized as to present, first, the four concepts which make up the social psychological framework. Later chapters take up a descriptive analysis of stages of human development from the point of view of issues which highlight the application of these concepts.

Chapters 1 through 4 present, in sequence, the self-concept, reference groups, social reality, and social role. Chapter 5 reviews premises underlying psychological theory and premises underlying social theory and presents the need for linking the four concepts in the subsequent chapters on the life stages. Chapters 6 through 10 discuss the life stages from infancy through old age, with emphasis on those human events which are defined by the conceptual framework developed in earlier chapters.

Chapter 1

Social Influences
on the Self-Concept

The term "self" is an abstraction, a mental construct. We use the concept to represent a whole range of experience that everyone has. It suggests the way we conceive of the human experience which it represents. At first glance, we might assume that it would bring the same images to everyone's mind, and that pressed to define what is meant by "the self," most people could define it without difficulty. This is not usually the case. The way we conceive of what we call the "self" remains at a fairly impressionistic and somewhat disorganized level, until we find the words that belong to our feelings and thoughts about it. The concept is only as good as the preliminary order which it brings to our images and thoughts about the experience to which it refers.

It is in efforts to understand this experience that social workers come to know who they are in relation to those with whom they work. Social workers must learn the answer to the question, "Who am I?" Our ideas of who we are, our conception of ourselves and other selves, our ideas of where oneself ends and others begin, all refer to social experience. We cannot conceive of ourselves unless we also can conceive of other selves. This "self," (which is interpreted by the most purely personal of words, expressing an inward, individual experience), is formulated out of groups to which we belong and to which we have belonged.

Observers and students of human behavior have been curious about the consciousness of self for as long as human beings have yearned to move humanness ahead. Philosophers, social scientists, psychologists, social workers, poets, and novelists have all brought some insights to bear upon the experiences of individuals as they attempt to find a sense of self and of belonging with others in the world. Contemporary society is caught up in self-conscious labels which attest to concern for an identity of one's own and an anchorage in society. The questions, "Who am I?" "Where do I belong?" have been faced by all of us in our search for identity. This is reflected in our fears of loss of self-determination, of dehumanization, and loss of control over our environment. Social workers, perhaps more than any other human service group, work with these fears in themselves and in those they serve. Indeed, the human problems that underlie the development of social agencies and social movements of all kinds might be described in terms of alienation, estrangement, depersonalization, isolation, and loneliness.

Students who choose to be social workers often enter this field with critical concern about these human problems. This concern is usually born out of a motivation to change social and psychological conditions in the affairs of life which cause such problems. And all social work students need to make some choices as to which set of causes makes the best sense to them. In the researcher's terms, this translates into the question: Which set of givens produces which outcomes? For example, if we know what causes people to regard themselves as worthwhile, we can accentuate those conditions which make for positive self-regard. If we take as a given the premise that all individuals have the human potential to think well of themselves, to have faith or confidence in themselves, to believe in their essential worth, we can speculate about what causes people to lose faith in themselves.

Our speculations will be determined by what we understand about how a sense of self evolves. Social workers need to understand as much as possible about this process. We begin then, by turning our attention to some of the ways in which social and psychological theorists have described the self.

Early Development
of the Self-Concept in Theory

How do individuals come to have a sense of self? What are the sources and nature of the self? What are the conditions that foster or interfere with its development and maturation? What knowledge can we draw on to clarify our understanding of the self and make our thinking about it more precise? What is the import of such knowledge for social workers? Questions like these may serve to focus the present part of our exploration for ways that others have viewed, and formulated their views, of this aspect of human experience.

Early Theorists of the Self

In the early part of this century, a number of theorists contributed insights which have been influential in the development of thought about what it is that the self refers to. Among social theorists, the self, as a concept, developed from the work of William James, first, and later from that of Charles Horton Cooley. Neither James nor Cooley dealt with the process through which the self develops in interaction with the environment, but their explanations led to more precise work on the matter. Subsequently, George Herbert Mead did present a detailed description of the process through which a sense of self evolves for the individual.

1. *The social self according to William James.* Among the first of American psychologists, James dealt with the phenomenon of the self somewhat philosophically. His analysis of the "stream of consciousness" led him to focus on "self-consciousness" as a fundamental psychological fact. In exploring this fact, James discriminated between two aspects of an individual's awareness of personal existence: the self as known to the individual, which he called the "me," and the self as knower, or the "I." The "I" or knower was basically, for James, the person's thoughts; his analysis brought him to this conclusion, and he left the question at that. "The thoughts," he concluded, "are the thinker."[1] The "me" he viewed as including three elements, or classes: these constituent parts were the material me, the social me, and the spiritual me. His view was

that the "social self" had its origins in the recognition by others of the individual, and the individual has as many selves as there are others who recognize and carry an image of that individual in their minds. A person has as many different selves as there are different groups about whose opinions the person cares.

A man's social me is the recognition which he gets from his mates. . . . Properly speaking, *a man has as many social selves as there are individuals who recognize him*, and carry an image of him in their mind. But as the individuals who carry the images fall naturally into classes, we may practically say that he has as many different social selves as there are distinct *groups* of persons about whose opinion he cares.[2]

James's conception of the person's self as rising initially from others' recognizing the person as a person, as being a "self," opened a vista for a number of theorists who followed him, and in the next chapter we shall follow out additional lines of exploration that his ideas helped to stimulate. Close to James in historical sequence was another observer on whose notions of the self and its origins James had a strong influence.

2. *The "looking-glass self" of Charles Cooley*. When Charles Cooley discussed the self, he picked up James's notions of others "recognizing" and "carrying an image" of the individual in their minds. Cooley admired James's treatment of the conception of the self, and in the contribution for which he is now best remembered he traced out something of the thinking process involved in the individual's self-idea, or image. Cooley sought to avoid metaphysical thinking, and he was concerned with social rather than psychological facts. He regarded the "imaginations which people have of each other" as a primary social fact, and these imaginings were, for him, the central and most important objects of study for the sociologist. It was through such imaginings that persons became socially "real."

Cooley is remembered for his concept of the "looking-glass self." Following James's notion, he believed that a person's idea of self always involved, in varying degrees of clarity and specificity, a reference to other persons. "There is no sense of

I . . . without its correlative sense of you, or he, or they."[3] Further, he thought,

In a very large class of cases, the social reference takes the form of a somewhat definite imagination of how one's self—that is any idea one appropriates—appears in a particular mind, and the kind of self-feeling one has is determined by the attitude toward this attributed to that other mind. A social self of this sort might be called the reflected or looking-glass self. . . . in imagination we perceive in another's mind some thought of our appearance, manners, aims, deeds, character, friends, and so on, and are variously affected by it.[4]

Cooley did not advance any other explanation of the self-concept, which to him had its origins in a "self-feeling" which he postulated as an instinctive given. The person, then, is a reflective image of what that person sees in other's eyes; one sees oneself in the eye of the beholder.

Both theorists viewed the self as involving a focusing of attention and energy, and both viewed the source of the self as the people in one's environment. James did not deal with the issue of how the individual comes to care about the opinion of others; Cooley did not deal with the issue of how the individual comes to develop any basis for forming the imputed judgments which were a crucial element in the looking-glass self. If, as Cooley proposes, people are dependent on what they see as other people's views of the self, then they would be somewhat overdetermined, overdependent on others. Without more knowledge of how this might come about, the reader is left to speculate whether the beheld and the beholder interact in any way to test the reality of their views of each other.

3. *The development of self-conceptions according to George Herbert Mead.* George Herbert Mead did present a detailed description of the process through which the self develops. One of the last traditional scholars to combine philosophy and psychology, Mead was not only influenced by Darwin's theory of evolution but also identified with the nineteenth-century belief in pragmatism, that is, that the truth of a proposition is to be found in its practical consequences.[5]

Mead saw the development of language as the *sine qua*

non of the mind, and explained this development as part of the evolutionary process. The human being's ability to communicate symbolically, then, he explained in terms of the interaction of the person and the environment; and learning, according to Mead, takes place through this interaction. Mead differed from the learning theorists of the first half of this century, who tended to explain feelings about the self as a specific response to a specific stimulus in interaction between one individual and another.[6] He differed as well from other early social psychologists in his pragmatic emphasis on the role of reason and rationality in man's evolution, in contrast to theorists like Cooley, who postulated instinctually determined social processes such as suggestion and sympathy to explain social behavior, learning, and communication.

Mead was interested in the organizational behavior of people, in more complex social organizations than the interaction of one person with another. He did not ignore the inner experience of individuals, which indeed he took as needing to be explained, but he explained it in terms of observable, external behavior.

According to Mead, the self is not present at birth, but evolves through social experience.[7] Observations of children's play and games formed, in large part, the base of this explanation of the process through which the individual comes to a consciousness of self, and constructs a self-conception. Through play, children take the role of another person and learn to respond to themselves from another's perspective. By taking the roles of many others, children can explore the attitudes held by others toward them and respond to the self from the perspective of others; in this way, the child can become an object of himself or herself.

There is an important difference in the way Mead views the development of the self and the way others view it. In Mead's view, the child is an active explorer at an early age. According to Mead, play is the first stage on which the child begins to develop consciousness of self.* The second stage engages the child as an actor in organized social activity with a number of other players. Mead used games—for example,

---

* Plays, after all, happen *on* stages!

baseball—as an illustration of organized social activity in which the child must be aware of the attitudes of all the other players.

The attitudes of the other players, which the participant assumes, organize into a sort of unit, and it is that organization which controls the response of the individual. . . . Each one of his own acts is determined by his assumption of the action of the others.[8]

In this way the child goes further than the particular attitudes of specific others. The game is not the only example of this, of course. The child gradually becomes conscious of many constellations of others, of rules and regulations and expectations of behavior which bring approval or disapproval, harmony or disharmony in groups including and beyond the family. The notion here is that the child can learn about the self in more and more complex role relationships. This is the process through which the child learns to hold in mind a number of factors in these relationships at the same time, and to generalize from them.

Mead referred to "the generalized other" as the organized community or group which gives the individual a kind of self-integrity. Perhaps Mead is reflecting, here, on what later theorists refer to as personal identity. He does not attempt to explain more than the cognitive development of the child; this implies an explanation of how people come to know and to judge their own and others' behavior. Although Mead does not say so, his work suggests that the child is not only aware of others' attitudes toward the self but is also aware of his or her own attitudes toward others. The self is formulated out of groups to which the child belongs.

Mead observed that "each individual self has its own peculiar individuality, its own unique pattern."[9] Mead's explanation of this uniqueness suggests that the social process is experienced somewhat differently by each self. At this point, we could wish that Mead had been more concerned with emotional development, or that he had the time to be, since the question of uniqueness is more complex. One is left with questions about whether Mead's developmental theory contains insights which go beyond the learning processes of an individual, presumed to be an average, expectable individual;

whether individuals with fairly similar life experiences are
more alike in their self-conceptions than those of dissimilar
experiences, and whether some individuals are more likely to
be products of their social learning than others.

Early Psychodynamic Contributions

Mead's theory, as suggested, was not primarily concerned with
emotional development or with maturation, and was not based
on assumptions of an individualistic nature. That is, he was
not essentially interested in dealing with the separate individuals that make up social relationship arrangements. A different slant on the self-concept derives from a group of theories
that are concerned with the emotional development of individuals. In contrast to the premises of Mead's theory,
psychodynamic theories, among them those known as psychoanalytic theories, emphasize forces internal to the individual as the most powerful determinants of behavior. Individualistic assumptions do characterize early theories from the
psychoanalytic school. Such assumptions deal with individuals
as though there is nothing beyond the individual, who is seen
as subject to the fate of his instincts. These assumptions leave
the impression that understanding human behavior begins and
ends with the individual and does not go beyond the individual's coping ability.

The theorists of the psychoanalytic school did not, insofar
as they were concerned with elucidating general principles by
which to explain behavior, require themselves to take explicit
account of the kind of phenomena to which such terms as
"social," "societal," "human group," or "organizational
behavior" refer. We turn to them, however, for a glimpse of the
way in which they approached the answer to the question of
how it comes about that the human individual may begin to
experience a self.

1. *Self-differentiation in infancy and adolescence according to Sigmund Freud.* Freud, the originator of the theory of
psychoanalysis, directed his earliest work to explaining the
unconscious and psychic determinism. (The concept of events,
ideas, feelings, and the like as being unconscious was not
unknown to other theorists, but they did not have the conception of *the* unconscious, nor did they try, in any systematic

fashion, to relate what was unconscious to consciousness.) Based on his work with what he came to call the unconscious, Freud later described stages of development of the individual and the conception of ego defenses. Freud did not directly address the social implications of the self-concept; indeed, he did not quite answer the question as to whether or not human-kind is inherently social. As we shall see, he arrived at the question of how the individual comes to care what other people think through a route quite different from that of the social theorists, and he dealt with this question in quite different terms. Freud, and most of his followers, described intrapsychic dynamics that propel the individual to engage with others in social interaction and to differentiate the self from other selves. The currency of exchange in this line of theory deals solely with psychological determinants.*

A critical premise associated with the formation of the self is that the infant experiences itself as the center of the universe, then learns otherwise as first, typically, the mother and then other significant family members are recognized, either as able to meet the infant's dependency needs or as hav-ing to be dealt with in some way if such needs are to be met. This recognition occurs on a continuum from the most to the least critical caretakers. The infant is in a position of having to compromise infantile omnipotence, which Freud called infan-tile narcissism. The infant projects its "center of the universe" feelings onto the one or ones closest to it, usually the mother, who becomes the center of the infant's world. The infant does not distinguish the self from the mother. What is projected onto the mother is self-love; it is as though very young children love themselves in the most significant caretaker.

According to this explanation, the same process is impli-cated in the later separations of young people from their parents, which are sometimes experienced as very painful. In adolescence, for example, the individual is expected to become a person of his or her own, and frequently finds others to idealize en route to this goal. Here, the process is easier to understand. Adolescents sometimes tend to blend into other

* The discussion here of self-formation describes only that material from this theory system which relates to infant behavior and the beginning of the differentiation process. It appears to be repeated, in part, during adolescence.

people, to project their self-love onto selected others, and to love themselves in these others, forgetting where they themselves end and where others begin. In these terms, then, the ideal person, beginning with the mother, is endowed with one's own sense of being ideal. According to Freudian theory, some people seem repetitively compelled to endow others with characteristics of either a positive or a negative quality and to react toward these others as they reacted to the early significant caretakers.

Dependence on early life experience, then, is critical to ongoing social relationships within which one defines oneself more or less as a separate person. The implication of such dependence is that the sense of self is dependent on the earliest of life relationships, on the ability of the mother, and in many instances on the ability of the father, to separate themselves from the growing child, and to accept the child's disappointment when it discovers that they are not ideal people capable of meeting all of the child's growth needs. Self-differentiation is also dependent on the child's ability to risk new relationships, to withstand the stress that is often involved in social learning with new adults and with other children.

The formulations on which this somewhat oversimplified summary of Freud's position on self-development is based include the concept of the superego. This part of the unconscious and conscious mind develops as the growing child internalizes values, beliefs, and standards of behavior, based on identification with the significant parents and their substitutes. Gradually, the child takes in enough knowledge of the world of others to regulate responses to the self and to other selves. Beyond the import, for this self-differentiation process, of the immediate and significant others, Freudian theory does not explicate the social process through which the young child goes in internalizing standards for behavior. It is clear that the child learns by differentiating responses of approval and disapproval associated with pleasure and pain; inner controls are developed as a consequence of reality testing. It is not clear how people view themselves as actors in larger organizations.

2. *Rank's position on individuality and self-differentiation.* Originally a disciple of Freud, Otto Rank gradually

developed his own position. In Rank's view, the self begins to develop through physical separation from the mother at infancy. The process of differentiation from the mother goes on during childhood and is transcendent at adolescence. This is the life stage in which the young person has to assert the self negatively against the parent in order to become a person with a separate self-identity. Such negative assertion—a clash of wills—is needed less as a means of getting free of the parent's self than as a means for the adolescent to define herself or himself as a separate person. Being still dependent on the parent, experiencing continued attachment despite the assertiveness, the young person in consequence feels ambivalence, and the self-assertion brings up feelings of guilt. The guilt, which has its beginnings in the child's relationship to the parents, is often carried over into other relationships. Until it decreases or ceases to be transferred to others, the person cannot begin to experience a positive regard for the self, or to find social anchorage. The struggle is based on acceptance of the need to be different from others, to be a person of one's own. When this difference becomes acceptable to the person, then differences between others also become acceptable.[10]

Definitions across Frames of Reference

A later chapter elaborates the notion of "frames of reference," and the phrase is used here relatively impressionistically. The frames of reference of the various theorists vary more or less widely. Each thinker toils in the prism of his own thought, and sometimes without access to that of others. While some concepts cannot be truly compared because the frames of reference of the users are entirely different, attempts to clarify their meanings and the inferences that can be drawn from them can give us, at times, a more precise sense of their connections.

Self and Ego
Both Freud and Rank tend to describe the self as a group of active processes such as thinking, perceiving, and remember-

ing. Mead's use of the self-concept defined the person's attitudes and feelings about the self, specifically in reference to the ability of the person to evaluate the self as an object. These two meanings have continued to be used in modern psychology. According to Calvin Hall and Gardner Lindzey, the self

has come to have two distinct meanings. On the one hand, it is defined as the person's attitudes and feelings about himself, and on the other hand it is regarded as a group of psychological processes which govern behavior and adjustment.[11]

In the past, a group of writers used the term "ego" to refer to psychological processes that govern behavior and adjustment. What Rank refers to as the self, Freud would refer to as the ego. Are "ego" and "self" interchangeable words? Can they be distinguished?

Percival Symonds defines the ego as a group of psychological processes "for developing and executing a plan for attaining satisfaction in response to inner drives" and the self as the ways in which one reacts to oneself. According to Symonds, the self consists of four aspects: (1) how one perceives oneself; (2) what one thinks of oneself; (3) how one values oneself; (4) how one attempts through a variety of actions to enhance or defend oneself.[12] Thus, individuals who might describe themselves as hard workers and individuals who might describe themselves as dreamers think up and carry out designs for making themselves comfortable when they are uncomfortable. In this example, individuals' reactions to themselves form the self-conceptions, and their inner needs to be comfortable with themselves push them to find ways of expressing their conceptions of themselves.

More important, Symonds calls to our attention that the self may be energized by stimuli from sources other than "inner drives"—when, for example, one's self-boundaries are threatened in some way. The source of the threat may come from within or from outside the self. The self, Symonds suggests, encompasses more than the faculties engaged in striving for some goal, and the idea of "enhancing or defending oneself" brings us back to the proposition that individuals ordinarily care what some others, at least, think of them. Self-evaluations, perceptions, and qualifications are not static, immobile, or unchanging, but may vary from situation to situation and from group to group in the individual's life.

Defenses and Self-Reference
The description of the processes concerned in self-differentiation referred to the notions of risk and stress, which on the feeling side we may describe generally as the experience of vulnerability. This vulnerability extends to the self; the developing self-sense is vulnerable to loss of its own boundaries, or to change in the feelings associated with the self-image. The individual, we say, can experience anxiety, a sensing that somehow all is not right with the world, a sensing of ill-being or the possibility of ill-being. Becoming social, as a human being, implies continuous vulnerability and experiencing of differences in states of being as well as of anxiety. The compromise that is involved, in the Freudian sense, in the infant's dependency implies the necessity of choice between a mode of experiencing that includes self-consciousness and a mode that does not. To maintain the former implies continuous choice of consciousness that includes the possibility of anxiety associated with awareness of vulnerability. In Freudian theory, the compromise is an ego process, which subsumes defense mechanisms. These processes become part of the coping abilities of the individual and are thus implicated in all the individual's dealings with the self and with the "not-self." Growth involves continuous risk of the self-image and self-feelings, and the person copes with this risk through successive compromises and choices between knowing and not knowing, using available knowledge to secure more knowledge while at the same time reducing anxiety.

A great deal of Freud's interpretation of human behavior is based on unconscious processes; he deals with the unconscious as a basic concept. For these reasons, the self-reference in Freudian concepts is often difficult to detect, and it is frequently also difficult to find a way to make a juncture, conceptually at least, between psychoanalytic formulations and those of other theorists. Ernest Hilgard, a psychologist who wrote about human motivation and the concept of the self, dealt with this problem. He believed that the study of the self is critical to understanding the defense mechanisms, which imply a self-reference. Discussing the phenomenon of self-blame, a feature of self-evaluation, he observed that

To feel guilty is to conceive of the self as an agent capable of good or bad choices. It thus appears that at the point that anxiety becomes infused with guilt-feelings, self reference enters. If we are to understand a person's defenses against guilt-feelings, we must know something about his image of himself.[13]

In this sense, the way in which Freud perceives the mother-child relationship and its residuals, and the way in which Rank perceives guilt as the residual of the will of the child to separate from the other, implies a self-reference.

Hilgard further discusses the general misconception that behavior is completely self-determined in the sense that one is conscious of one's intentions to behave in this way or in that way and can consequently hold oneself responsible for one's actions. He believes that we cannot simply assume that what anyone knows about the self, whether one's own or another's can safely include only that which is accessible to one's own or another's conscious awareness. "Awareness includes the not-self as well as the self. . . . Some items . . . remain in awareness, but are not part of self-awareness."[14] Moreover, awareness is a relative state; that is, there are various states of awareness. Social workers not infrequently find themselves invited, or pushed, to assent to views of other human beings which require the social workers to encourage those others to blame, or belittle, themselves for their differences in exchange for obtaining something they want. Self-blame as an aspect of self-criticism, Hilgard suggests, may tap a more pervasive source of vulnerability than the residuals of the person's past life experiences, or the supports of self-valuing in current life experiences, can absorb. For example, there are life circumstances in which people are confronted with conditions they are powerless to change, and for which they are blamed, and for which they may blame themselves.

It is important to consider that behavior is implicated in a complex of both social and psychological processes of which the person is largely unaware. Hilgard's reference to guilt feelings and to ego defenses reflects a blending of psychoanalytic and nonpsychoanalytic approaches to the question of motivation; the latter have been developed by observers of various theoretical persuasions, including some whose thinking is cast within the broad framework of behaviorism. When we are willing to consider that the individual's development of a self-concept implies both psychological and social processes, it becomes possible to raise the question of repercussions in later behavior of early experiences in self-formation without implications of pathology at either time.* Mead's theory of learning from organized social activity might well occur, for instance, as Mead describes it, and then be part of the experience of the adult individual but not readily accessible to consciousness, except through symbolization in the maneuvers adults use to manipulate their social relationships. Thus, learning from social experience, as well as organic needs, instincts, or drives, can become an unconscious directive. Behaviors which are learned in early socialization experiences happen again and again until they are below our psychological sights, as it were, and we need not necessarily impute pathology to behaviors that are so motivated.

Motivation and the Self-Concept
Some of the theorists who struggled to explain the factors that produce behavior preferred to concentrate on the idea of personality, to develop a body of knowledge about persons that is sometimes called "personology." Many of them believed that psychoanalytic theories failed to furnish concepts and a perspective that was adequate to take account of what was unique about each human being. They wanted to work out an approach to understanding behavior, and a way of explaining it, that stressed each person's individuality, or uniqueness, as well as what each had in common with all individuals.

Gordon Allport was an influential spokesman for those psychodynamic theorists who broke with the instinct theories

---

* The development of psychoanalytic theory was related empirically to the practice of diagnosing and treating pathology. Freud was originally a biologist, then a physician who specialized in neurology and eventually developed the practice of psychoanalysis. Psychoanalytic theory is the conceptual model that guides such practice. The interpersonal model associated with the practice is a medical one, of doctor and patient.

of the psychoanalytic school. His starting point was the analysis, not of the "stream of consciousness" but of the "stream of observable behavior," from which tendencies toward action, or predispositions, or individualized "patterns of tension" were inferred. These highly personalized mixtures of pleasure and pain, which he called traits, were organically based, but became very far separated from their origins as the individual grew. Furthermore, Allport stressed that the human personality was an open system, and he believed that while such personalized systems of tension included biological drives that were common to all human experience, such drives themselves were not the motives of human behavior. In his view, human motivations could not be

divorced from the images, goals, past experience, capacities and style of conduct employed in obtaining the goal. . . . If biological drive plays a part (thirst, hunger, sex), it does so not as *the* motive, but merely as an irritable state of bodily tissues set within an intricate and personalized psychophysical system.[15]

Allport argued forcefully for the conception of the "functional autonomy of drives," that is, the idea that individuals' unique configurations of tensions, and modes of expressing them, could be observed even in the absence of organic tensions. Allport also stressed planning and future orientation as a major characteristic of human, as distinguished from other animal behavior. He thought that the need to reduce excitation and restore an equilibrium only partly accounted for human motivation; human beings also strove to maintain tensions and experienced pleasure in the state of striving for modes of being that they had not yet realized.

Allport thus emphasized individuality, human personality as an open system, and growth itself as the motivation for further growth. He did not formulate an explicit self-theory, but his work was part of the matrix out of which Abraham Maslow's self-actualization formulations developed.

The Self in Contemporary Thought

James, Cooley, and Mead did pioneering work on the concept of the self and its social reference; Freud and Rank were theorists of a psychodynamic school whose creation of conceptual schemes widened the vista of the interior of the person. Their view limited itself to "psychological causality, motivation and goals."[16] Many of the most powerful observers of social and of psychological events have struggled to make connections between social and psychological factors that influence our understanding of the self-concept. They have recognized that "human events," as individual lives manifest and are manifested in them, are not experienced in terms of actuarial tables, or computer programs, or even of television documentaries. Most practitioners of the social and behavioral sciences have tended, in one way or another, to be concerned about the motives and intentions of people, whether they have been thinking of individual persons or of large or small collectivities. There has been general concern about the forces that keep individuals and groups of individuals going in a direction, in the sense of the kinds of experiences that such words as "aspiring," "hoping," "developing," and "discovering" suggest.

There is a variety of ways to describe and report discoveries about the self-concept, not always clearly identifiable in the works of those who have contributed a great deal that is useful in understanding it. For the most part, the work of developing knowledge about the self-concept has tended to be regarded as the province of ego psychologists, social psychologists, philosophers, and students of values and attitudes.

Within the discipline of psychology, Abraham Maslow has identified three general prevailing frames of reference. One he identifies as the "orthodox Freudian" orientation; another he calls the "objectivistic, behavioristic (mechanomorphic)" orientation; the third he describes as a group of theories with an orientation identified by the term "humanistic psychology."[17] At the core of humanistic psychology has been an interest in individual autonomy and the "idiographic," as well as in what is nonautonomous and in what is general, or species-wide. This has included a striving to explain the nature of choice, of psychological freedom, and of the individual as the chooser.

Mead, it will be recalled, had observed the uniqueness of the self, the particular individuality of each person's self-pattern, but he did not elaborate on the source or nature of the uniquenesses. He conceived the individual as active and exploring, but he did not elucidate the processes of constructing the self-pattern or deal with the question of the self as a guide to action, or as providing information about its own nature to the environment as well as taking it in. It was clear, in Mead's view, that the self was a product, but the question lingered of understanding the self as a maker. Yet such conceptions as self-mastery and self-motivating imply something to do with what prompts individuals to deal with the self in one way or another, not in the sense of the self as an object composed of an "I" or a "me" but in the sense of the self as an initiating force.

1. *Abraham Maslow's concept of the self.* The theories that comprise Maslow's "third force" are themselves quite disparate, and many of them are relatively narrow in scope. Maslow became the major integrator, conceptualizer, and interpreter of this frame of reference for understanding the self. Many influences played in his work. He was influenced by, and drew on, both the practice and the thinking of many other students, observers, and theorists. Most of them had found themselves in the position of having to account for observed patterns of activity in their own and others' lives that could not be accounted for by the explanations already available to them as practitioners.

These thinkers were carrying on their work in the mid-decades of our own century, and a great deal of their effort concerned individuals and groups whose behavior was defined, not only by significant others in the environment, but by the individuals and groups themselves, as "deviant," or "sick," or whose lives had encompassed cataclysms of a more or less violent or overwhelming nature. Maslow gives credit to the previous work of Kurt Goldstein, who worked with brain-injured soldiers and who invented the concept of self-actualization to explain what guided the way individuals reorganized their lives and capacities after such injury.[18] Taking account of the cultural context of growth and behavior had also brought many theorists to recognize that each individual is at once in some respects like all other individuals, like some other individuals, and like no other individuals.[19]

Working, then, with such sources, Maslow formulated a wide-ranging and comprehensive theory; his ideas can stand as a major example of the "third force" approach.

Maslow views human beings as having a natural tendency toward self-actualization, or the fulfillment of basic potentialities. His formulations begin with a basic premise that people are growth-oriented, forward-moving, and concerned with the nature of existence.[20] He believes that human beings not only learn from the environment, they have natural inclinations to reshape it, and they may change it.

This calls for another explanation of self-potential. If the person is not simply shaped by the environment of significant others, then the person must bring something to those outside influences on the self-conception. Maslow discusses the existence of a selfness that has characteristics antecedent to any interactions with the environment. He calls this an "essential inner nature . . . an inner core [which] shows itself as natural inclinations, propensities or inner bent."[21] He observes that

Even though "weak," this inner nature rarely disappears or dies. . . . It persists underground, unconsciously, even though denied and repressed. Like the voice of the intellect (which is part of it), it speaks softly but it *will* be heard, even if in a distorted form. That is, it has a dynamic force of its own. . . . Effort must be used in its suppression or repression from which fatigue can result. This force is one main aspect of the "will to health," the urge to grow, the pressure to self-actualization, the quest for one's identity.[22]

Maslow discusses this self-propelling force as a creation of the person, in part. He suggests that it grows and can be gradually discovered by acceptance of it. Awareness of this original self-potential is engaged in life decisions.

Life is a continual series of choices for the individual in which a main determinant of choice is the person as he already is (including his goals for himself, his courage or fear, his feeling of responsibility, his ego-strength or "will power," etc.). We can no longer think of the person as "fully determined" where this phrase implies "determined only by forces external to the person." The person, insofar as he *is* a real person, is his own main determinant. Every person is, in part, "his own project" and makes himself.[23]

2. *Carl Rogers's self-theory.* Among contemporary practitioner-theorists who have dealt specifically with the self-concept, Carl Rogers has formulated a well-developed presentation of self-theory and growth. While Rogers's thought is not so broad-ranging as Maslow's, his conceptualizations provide a useful example of a concept of the self and its development that is in the same tradition.

Rogers takes it as axiomatic that the individual is valuable, values the self positively, and struggles to maintain and fulfill its potential. He views it as given that the self exists and develops in interaction with the environment of others. Prominent in his approach to understanding human life is the assumption that basic human nature is positive, that there is nothing inherently negative or destructive in it, that human beings do not have instincts which can undermine them. According to his view, the self originates out of, and exists in, the phenomenal field defined by all human experience. "Every individual exists in a continually changing world of experience of which he is the center."[24]

The most critical human motive, in Rogers's view, is the self-actualizing tendency; he believes that the human being inherently tends to maintain a self and to strive for actualization. The concept of actualization in Rogers's thought is reminiscent of Maslow's conception of growth and fulfillment. As Rogers views human development, the infant is inherently driven to grow toward fulfillment, and individuals continue to be forward-moving, toward productivity and creativity, although they may be interrupted in this growth course, or restrained by environmental conditions including, most potently, interactions with significant others.

Rogers thinks of the self as a differentiated portion of the phenomenal field of human experience, consisting of a pattern of conscious perceptions and values of the "I" or "me." Everyone, in Rogers's view, has the propensity for developing self-knowledge. In a discussion of Rogers's theory, Hall and Lindzey review his conception of the nature of the human organism.

The organism possesses the following properties: (*a*) it reacts as an organized whole to the phenomenal field in order to satisfy its basic needs; (*b*) it has one basic motive: namely, to actualize, maintain and enhance itself, and (c) it may symbolize its experiences so that they become conscious, or may deny them symbolization so that they remain unconscious, or it may ignore its experiences. The phenomenal field has the property of being conscious or unconscious, depending upon whether the experiences that constitute the field are symbolized or not.[25]

Rogers thus views consciousness as anything that can be symbolized, for example, or talked about. This consciousness is the figure in the field defined as human experience; the background for this figure is the unconscious or relatively unconscious experiences. Unconscious material, he believes, can be brought into consciousness when the need for this material is strongly felt by an individual.

According to Rogers's view, if people are not forced to conform to rigidly constructed, socially institutionalized behavior and are accepted for what they are, they will live their lives to enhance themselves and society. Inflexibility of social structures define minimal conditions of personal growth; a principle of unconditional positive regard from others defines, for Rogers, the optimal conditions within which people can grow.

Self-actualization is not simply accomplished without struggle, of course. Individuals engage in some painful struggle and tolerate painful feelings because of the impulse to grow. Rogers suggests that growth takes place only if the choices people have to make are perceived clearly and symbolized accurately. These are conditions that allow the growing individual to be able to differentiate between productive and unproductive behaviors, between regression and mastery.

Rogers, then, defines the actualizing tendency as the motivating force of human life; the self-actualizing process reflects itself in the development of a self-concept and continues to enhance and encourage actualization of the human organism's self-potential. His conceptions of self-development include the notion of the possibility of an alienated state, in which dissociation develops between the person's self-concept and his or her inner experience.[26]

Another level of knowledge, directed toward understanding a critical problem that affects many people at this time in our world, derives from a group of thinkers who have concerned themselves directly and extensively with the issue of existential choices and the problem of alienation. The frame of

reference of this group of theorists, which includes Soren Kierkegaard, Jean-Paul Sartre, and Martin Heidegger, reflects
Maslow's and Rogers's concern that human beings have many
choices to make which critically influence their existence.

Existential Views of the Alienated Self

Alienation is associated with estrangement from the self and
from other selves. Stanley Rosenberg and Bernard Bergen
characterize the feelings that belong to such estrangement:

In the alienated experience one comes to feel like an object under the
control of alien forces. These forces can be as general as values or
institutions and as specific as the demands of a parent. By capitulating, the self feels transformed into an object. Instead of feeling free,
alive, and the agent of one's own choices, he may feel an oppressive
deadness.[27]

The proposition that one does not have to capitulate, that
one is always clear on one's choices, which is often suggested as
a way out of the dilemma of alienation, is not supported by
human experience. People often find themselves unable to
withstand pressures to conformity. It is, after all, very
threatening to hold opinions which differ from most others.
The struggle to believe that one always has options is extraor-
dinarily complex if one does not have support from others.
When the self loses touch with itself, in this sense, one feels
alienated. The existential theorists describe the deep sense of
despair over giving up the right of choice in surrendering to
such pressures. This is the meaning of dealing in bad faith
with oneself. Efforts to distort the meaning of such despair disguise perceptions of the self as alienated.[28]

In the modality of bad faith, the self may bemoan the fact that the
other does not adequately see one's "objective" attributes: his
strength or his righteousness. The despairing self may act on these
assumptions, trying to alter its objective relationships until it finds a
pattern that erases its inner disquietude. In the impossibility of this
pursuit, the self often begins to experience its alienation. . . . The self
longs for a new mode of being in the world. One wishes not to be in
the mode of object, but rather to become his own human self.[29]

According to Kierkegaard, despair can be expressed in
defiance, when people cannot be the selves they consciously

want to be, or in weakness, a state of conscious despair in which they do not feel in touch with themselves.[30]

The bad faith stance presents considerable restraint on the self and has many implications for self-realization. Perhaps an example of the bad faith position, and the way in which it affects self-regard, or what many people call self-respect, may help to clarify this point.

Kierkegaard's sense of the significance of defiance is reflected in the controversy over whether or not to accept the right of young people to refuse to serve in the armed forces during the Vietnam war. The question is posed, by many, as to whether or not they should be pardoned for their defiance of the law. The response from the defiant is often stated in terms very close to those we are discussing. It was not so much a matter of increasing self-esteem in the eyes of others, most of them could not engage in that war in good faith with themselves. These were not young people applauded as heroes. They did not join the system of relationships designed by the military complex. They were not prototypes of Yassarian in *Catch 22*, or of Hawkeye Pierce, who "fought . . . against being caught up in the madness and brutality of collective institutions"[31] within those institutions. In the aftermath of that war the last vestiges of disapproval are likely based on contrasting the motives of those who refused to join the armed services and those who did join. The issue in this controversy is not who did and who did not, it is whether people should have the right to choose to engage their energies in war. If people are to make decisions according to those internal forces which propel them forward to the realization of their human potential, then their options must be clear to them. The internal force referred to by Maslow and Rogers is available to the individual, but choices are not predetermined for the individual by this force; the choosing gives direction to the force, but the force does not govern the individual's choices. Social workers need very much to deal with the freedom of choice issue, to come to understand it from a number of points of view, and to work to clarify options for themselves and for those whom they serve.

In the beginning of this chapter it was suggested that the questions Who am I? Where do I belong? are dealt with in the search for identity. It would be logical to present a theorist whose contribution takes account of all those who have come before, and whose frame of reference synthesizes disparate views of human behavior, or whose formulations we could regard conclusively as definitive of the self-concept. The state of theory has not yet produced this overarching definition. We turn, then, to Erik Erikson, a contemporary theorist, whose original contribution (despite his reliance on traditional psychoanalytic theory) deals with the concept of identity in terms of those questions: Who am I? Where do I belong?

The Search for Identity according to Erik Erikson

Erikson did begin to build some bridges between psycho-analytic theory and social influences, but in the creation of a developmental theory of human behavior his work remains, for the most part, so closely aligned with psychoanalytic premises that its usefulness for describing the growth potential and drives to self-realization tends to narrow our view to the unconscious as determined by destructive instincts. Erikson, however, was a sensitive observer whose identity formulations were not overly influenced by such an assumption, and his views on the connections of the self-concept and identity, in the form in which he elaborated them, include a sense of the blending of social, cultural, and historical forces in the individual's strivings for a place in his society. His way of conceiving the nature of the question "Who am I?" gives us a feeling for consciousness of identity. Indeed, according to Erikson, the "Who am I?" strivings are the consciousness of identity. In his view, "Identity is an unconscious striving for continuity. . . . A striving within to bring together the self that one is with the self that one was, with the self that one wants to be. . . . It is a criterion for the silent doings of ego synthesis."[32] It includes a feeling of being "at home in one's body . . . a sense of knowing where one is going and an inner assuredness of anticipated recognition from those who count."[33]

In these terms, Erikson introduces the concept of continuity, gives equal significance to the past, present, and future self. He deals with the sense of knowing where one is going and the importance of social support.

Implications

Social workers direct their attention to the interface between the individual and those human relationship arrangements which express the expected behaviors of the society into which the individual is born. In following chapters, the transactions that characterize these social expectations are presented. The implications of knowledge of the self-concept are better understood as knowledge of the group life of the individual in the society is broadened. However, the material presented this far has some implications, in itself, for work with individuals.

In order to work with individuals, social workers need to develop a perspective that allows them to view behavior of others through the eyes of those with whom they work. Their work with individuals is guided by their understanding of self-development.

The application of such understanding is illustrated in the following premises. These premises were articulated by three social workers to guide their efforts to design and implement interventions which might alter, for a number of very troubled children and their parents, the outcomes of their struggles to learn to draw their self-boundaries, and to get more and more in touch with their potential for valuing themselves as constructive human beings who could make choices about how they wanted to live their lives.[34]

The capacity for self-observation requires the ability to learn to formulate a conception of oneself-as-actor influencing, as well as being influenced by, situations of which one is a part, and to perceive patterns in one's behavior and experiences. To see such patterns, one must be able to abstract certain common elements from concretely diverse instances. Children who cannot abstract cannot generalize and integrate. They frequently cannot find the words that belong to their feelings, and, therefore, they cannot stand behind their words . . .
        . . . Many people appear to be unable to make the distinction between self and non-self. They have great difficulty discerning where they begin and other people end . . .
        . . . Self-observation requires the ability to . . . perceive and evaluate or compare what is perceived about one's own functioning.

The part of the self that conducts this operation is a set of identifications and partial identifications with others that have already meant
something in the person's life.[35]

Social workers experience others in relation to themselves,
and the more able the social worker is to draw self-boundaries,
the more the social worker will give others freedom to do the
same. There are instances in which individuals can be
overwhelmed by life circumstances in their transactions with
others. They may think, feel, and act in ways that block their
drive to growth, and they may be destructive to themselves
and to others. In such instances, their behavior may best be
understood within a framework that directs attention to
pathology. The assessment offered here depends very much on
accurate perception of such behavior, and as we shall see in
subsequent chapters, this perception is heavily influenced by
the evaluators and the evaluated in the social reality within
which such assessments are made. A perspective that
delineates pathology narrows the view of the social worker to
pathology, and eliminates from view other explanations that
may be critical.

Perhaps the first set of choices with which the social work
student has to deal are implied in the questions: Who am I?
Where do I belong in relation to beginning work with other
people? Self-definition is important for social workers to
understand. It is in such efforts at understanding that many
social workers initially encounter those with whom they work.

In this connection, consciousness of self is associated with
awareness of other selves, who help in self-definition. This is
not a one-way street. Social workers do not simply define those
with whom they work: they are also defined by these others.
To understand who we are and where we belong we must
engage in self-observation enough to maintain a sense of our
own self-conceptions, and enough to be willing to change these
conceptions. Social workers are sometimes endowed with
characteristics they simply do not have by people whose self-
boundaries are only vaguely defined. Social workers may also
endow people with whom they work with characteristics which
do not belong to them. The pressures toward conformity to
labeling types and categories of people are very strong, and

they tend to influence the ways in which people perceive each other. Understanding such pressures requires us to examine more closely the groups within which the individual struggles to find and define a self. The following chapter begins this examination.

Reference Group Behavior

The conceptions that people have of themselves and of others are formulated out of their social responses to each other. What we become, what we are, and what we do can be conceived as developing, in large measure, from the nature of relationships we have and have had with other people. There is no self without other selves, and we are all dependent upon social response to formulate our conception of who we are.

The notion that groups of which people are members influence them is not a new one; neither is the idea of a nonconformist who does not represent group expectations, who hears a different kind of music and marches in a different direction. What is new is that "in the process of self-appraisal, from many possible groups available as a framework . . . individuals make their own particular selection."[1] This selection is not always a conscious one, especially in early life when children are most impressionable and dependent. But we cannot make arbitrary assumptions about *which* groups and individuals will be most influential in people's lives simply from the study of their earliest human relationships. People's self-esteem, their self-acceptance and self-worth, is associated with groups and individual members of groups that influence them throughout their lifetime.

Interpretations of Socialization

The Society Preceding Individuals and Groups

Just as it is not possible to make arbitrary assumptions about the groups and individuals that will be most influential in a person's life, we cannot assume that the self the individual becomes is solely a result of the individual's own continuing free choices. The society into which human beings are born precedes any existing individual or group, and the general pattern of beliefs and values that characterize that society at any particular time will determine the ways in which human experience is interpreted by individuals. For example, in the nineteenth century quite different views of the world prevailed than those that are common in this century. Although these views overlap from one century to the next and are not equally influential for all individuals in either century, they represent quite different influences on self-definition.

Being Defined by the World: the Society in the Individual

The nineteenth-century view is illustrated in the writing of Franz Kafka,[2] who dramatized the phenomenon of guilt. Kafka writes of a character who dreamed that he was on trial for his life. He describes the terror and despair of the dreamer, who was convicted of some crime for which he was to be executed. During the trial the dreamer wanted to defend himself, but he could not. Somehow, he felt such a dreadful burden of guilt that he knew he would be convicted. In his dream Kafka's subject never knew what crime he had committed.

Characteristic of Kafka's description of the trial of his overwhelmed dreamer was a view predominant in nineteenth-century Western societies, that the world defined human kind. It was as though many people expected to be judged by others who had set the rules and regulations by which they were to live. The common suspicion was that people would somehow fail to keep the rules, and that they would be found out. In the form of self-reproach, guilt and shame characterized many people's responses to themselves. This emotional state included a constant apprehension that they would not follow some rule or live up to expectations of which they were unaware. Fear of disapproval, of how one might appear in the eyes of others, was more characteristic in the nineteenth century than it is in the twentieth century.

The notion that human beings are controlled by the rules, regulations, and subsequent expectations of the existing society and that the individual is a product of the demands of the society is discussed by Dennis Wrong as an "Over-

Socialized Conception of Man."[3] He contrasts his own view as a sociologist with those of colleagues who tend to view the individual as a product of society without consideration for the propensity of the individual to realize the self otherwise. Wrong cites the following declaration by Francis Sutton as an example of the explicit statement of more traditional sociology: "People are so profoundly sensitive to the expectations of others, that all action is inevitably guided by these expectations."[4] In contrast, Wrong's own view takes account of uniquely human characteristics:

"Socialization" may mean two quite distinct things; when they are confused an oversocialized view of man is the result. On the one hand socialization means the "transmission of the culture," the particular culture of the society an individual enters at birth; on the other hand the term is used to mean the "process of becoming human," of acquiring uniquely human attributes from interaction with others. All men are socialized in the latter sense, but this does not mean that they have been completely molded by the particular norms and values of their culture.[5]

The extent to which persons can experience their own human attributes depends upon interaction with others and upon the nature of that interaction.

Deprivation and Conformity

The search for self-definition is intricately interwoven with the responses one elicits from others. Social response is a basic human need. It underlies those needs identified as "safety, belongingness, love, respect and self-esteem."[6] Social response deprivation, over prolonged periods, leads to great human suffering. When social response is blocked, emotional hunger for responses from others arises, and if this human need is long denied to people, such denial may also lead to disorientation, or to obsession with such feelings as hate and guilt to the exclusion of other human feelings.

A basic need is more often identified by its absence than by the evidence that it has been met. Students of human behavior generally agree that, given the choice of meeting basic needs for human responses or meeting needs for other satisfactions, people will prefer responses which confirm some aspect of their self-esteem. Some personality theorists suggest both that people grow through complex social stages which require increasing amounts of inner control and synthesis of life experience, and that growth in itself is resisted. In their view, the individual is required to conform more and more to increasingly intricate webs of social structures, to grow. The traditional psychoanalytic position tends to be rooted in this explanation. Thus, Freud tended to see the demands of the society as countering the raw drives of the individual. The ego, conceived by Freud as that psychic structure which mediates the fate of the instincts in relation to the society's expectations, has more or less strength in such negotiations according to whether or not basic needs are met. Unmet basic needs, according to this view, lead to mental illness which becomes apparent by formation of symptoms, which are built at great cost in energy and which do not allow for the individual's continued growth. Treatment, then, often relies on the provision of a human experience as well as on uncovering the fact of unmet need, or of distortions of the need-meeting experiences one has had. In many instances, the interventions defined as treatment rely upon providing "insight." Given such an expectation, the question then arises: On what strength do people draw in achieving insight into themselves?

Many people who follow a model of personality derived from the psychoanalytic tradition are now questioning the source of ego strength. Few believe that such strength is in direct proportion to the extent to which the individual's needs have been met. Such strength may well manifest a more basic drive to self-actualization. As we have seen in the previous chapter, this explanation suggests that an inner strength is the major determinant of nonconformity, a strength, that somehow defines both the individual and the world.

Defining the World: the Individual in the Society

The twentieth-century writer Albert Camus is associated with the view that individuals define their world; they are not defined by it. The characters in Camus's novels are concerned with courage which they require of themselves, but which does not seem to effect change in others or to be a response to the expectations of others. Camus's subjects engage in claiming human worth beyond that designated by the rules and regulations of their society. It is described as

the act of courage, seemingly useless, that one may nevertheless require of oneself. In its assertion of human values and human dignity beyond those of any particular social code, such an act of courage is the counterpart of shame. It demands action that has no discernible pragmatic outcome but is an affirmation of belief in oneself and of meaning in the world. The choice between doing and not doing an act that may effect nothing but is nevertheless crucial for maintaining the sense of one's own humanity.[7]

Camus's subjects make conscious choices between acting and not acting in ways that are critical to their own sense of humanness. His writing represents the view of the European existentialists who describe essential existential choices in a world perceived as providing no resources for survival of humannesss; it is a view which emphasizes an ultimate aloneness of the individual. According to this view, the person is not determined by others.

This heroic, individualistic view of human beings who define their own behavior in a harsh, nonsupportive world raises questions not yet raised by traditional sociological or psychoanalytic views of the individual and society. According to Maslow, existential writers

speak of the "self as a project" which is wholly created by the continued [and arbitrary] choices of the person himself, almost as if he could make himself into anything he decided to be. Of course in so extreme a form, this is almost certainly an overstatement.[8]

The "overstatement" is illustrated in the lives of people who are subjected to exploitation through severe discrimination, unyielding poverty, and other forms of dehumanization, whether or not major basic needs are met.

The phenomenon of unexpected yielding to physical and mental torture has been observed in the extreme conditions of concentration camps when persons felt the shame of being helpless and defeated, of being betrayed by their own bodies and minds.[9]

What was betrayed for these human beings, and in some measure for all people who were victims of the Nazi terror under Hitler, was their will to make human choices. Not yielding under these conditions can be conceived as choosing to give up the self entirely, to forego self-actualization in life, unless one views the self as existing in others, in which event one is not alone, but determines something for others. Under such dehumanizing conditions, the feeling of helplessness and shame may also be a clue to whether or not one is simply giving over to overwhelming forces outside the self or whether one is judging those forces.

Does the feeling of shame imply an acceptance of the validity of the values or standards of the society in relation to which one feels ashamed? Or, may there be personal or widely human values (if not standards) not wholly derived from the culture, in terms of which one judges not only oneself but one's society as well?[10]

If we answer the second of these questions affirmatively, we give credibility to the proposition that human beings are not only defined by society, not only judged and determined by it, they also define it, judge it, and may in the long run determine it.

Some Implications for the Social Worker's Perspective
The social worker is in the unenviable position of having to hold all these views in mind and to generalize from them those factors which explain the individual's impact on the society and the society's impact on the individual. It is as though the psychologist concentrates on the individual's search for self-actualization by walking alone beside the individual, noticing every milestone along the route, paying special attention to the detours. The sociologist, in this metaphoric sense, maps the route, lays out the most likely roads to the goal in consideration of everyone taking the journey, paying special attention to the likelihood of traffic hazards. Both are concerned with the weather: one with the inner and one with the outer climate conditions. The social worker takes an interactionist position. There are times when social workers may bind wounds incurred on rough roads encountered in the detours; there are times when the special attention of the social worker is focused on those groups of individuals who make the trip together; and there are many more times when the social worker inspects the whole route and revises the map.

Social workers make the bridges between explanations that individuals determine what society can be and explanations that society determines what individuals can be. This is the view that those internal determinants in individuals, whether they are called "instincts" or "drives" or "inner human nature," are not fixed dispositions to behavior in the world of others. These inner forces,

far from being fixed dispositions to behave in a particular way, are utterly subject to social channelling and transformation and could not even reveal themselves in behavior without social molding any more than our vocal cords can produce articulate speech if we have not learned a language.[11]

Social workers learn to understand the language of human behavior from the study of individuals and of the society in which they are joined in the process of socialization. There are both restraining and propelling forces to growth in the society of which the individual is a part, and individuals interpret their search for self-realization in terms of these forces. They are signals by which the individual formulates social identity. These signals begin with the development of standards of judgment; they include the internalized audience of others; they lead to the formulation of frames of reference; and they are reflected in social attitudes.

Recognizing the Points of Reference

All these social forces can be recognized as points of reference for the development of self-actualization.

The Development of Standards
by Which Behavior Is Judged

The first step in the process of acquiring human attributes is the development of standards of judgment. As human beings develop in their social world, the expectations of the social environment become internalized as values and beliefs. One's responses to others and to oneself are guided, or may be controlled, by the processes through which this internalization takes place. Over the course of a lifetime, groups of others and significant individuals become the sources of socialization. These others are agents through whom one learns behavior which is valued and approved or devalued and disapproved, and they serve as anchoring points in the development of notions of what is good and right or bad and wrong. Such notions tend to be absorbed by the individual, initially, without conscious evaluation. Later, they become assumptions and serve as standards of judgment on the basis of which one's own and others' behavior is subjectively evaluated. Many standards of judgment are developed in early life when people are most impressionable. They become the first boundaries within which the individual perceives human behavior, and whether or not individuals expand these boundaries and develop new ways of perceiving themselves and others depends upon the nature of their continuing experiences with others who count.

The Internalized Audience
Young children tend to assimilate notions of how to behave which will assure them of recognition from those who count. Those who count most in early life are the child's family, beginning play groups, and the neighborhood of elders. These are the child's first important set of groups; these are the others from whom the child will first generalize its perform-ance as an actor. Mead's concept of "taking the role of the other" described an important part of this process. He presumed that the person symbolically considers other persons and takes the perspective of others in the socialization process.[12] The individual then, learns to refer to the self that has adopted the perspective of others; in a symbolic sense, the person becomes his or her own audience.

The human actor can examine behavior, can experience meaning through thought. It is in this sense that the reference group theorists define thinking as

an internalized conversation among the self and the internalized others. And the meaning of internalization is simply the covert seg-ment of the general communicative process. The figures of speech differ—an internal audience, an inner forum, a covert conversation of gestures—but the meanings coincide. They all make the other crucial to the self and to meaningful action.[13]

Although the first significant others may make up the internalized audience to which the child plays, the audience changes as the child's life goes on. The more significant the group, or other individuals, become as life goes on, the more the individual will internalize new perspectives, new audiences to which to play, new parts of the self to which to refer the judgment and evaluation of behavior.

Traditional psychoanalytic theory refers to the internalization process as the superego. The functions of the superego are customarily viewed as reactions, internalized in early life, which subsequently become largely automatic and unconscious and are no longer susceptible to modification by continuing influences.

The superego develops through the child's identification with its parents' attitudes, opinions, and judgments, which is one of the most important factors in the learning processes. . . . Expressed structurally, parental attitudes are taken over by the personality, one part of which assumes the same attitude toward the rest as the parents did previously toward the child.[14]

There is a finality in this conception of the superego. According to Erich Fromm, this concept was totally authoritarian and relativistic. He did not agree that parents determine how the child will eventually view the world, or that all significant others will be seen to have the characteristics of one's parents, or that one will expect of the self only what the parents expected. Fromm's argument with the classical notion of the superego was based on his belief in a kind of conscience, intrinsic to the human being, defined by the drive toward self-actualization.[15] There is little evidence to support the notion that Freud believed in an essential goodness, or drive to fulfillment, which could counter or be at odds with wishes, demands, and prohibitions of parents, when these blocked growth of the individual. The people to whom Freud and his early followers directed their attention were people who often seemed compelled to repeat patterns of behavior demanded by such parents. It was as though the earliest influences of parents were so impressive that therapists, whose goal was to cure the problems associated with the rigid superegos of their patients, became members of patients' internalized audience of parents and were defended against as the cause of painful experiences in early life. From this patient-physician context, the theory emerged and became generalized to all human beings.

Ego psychologists who are oriented by psychoanalytic theory, but who have benefited from studies of patients and cumulative experiences since the original theoretical considerations were published, tend to expect to be endowed with some of the characteristics of significant others in the individual's early life. However, depending on the extent to which their patients transfer these characteristics onto them, they take account of additional influences as more or less important.

Many problems are associated with the application of the concept of the internalized audience in practice. In the past, social workers were often preoccupied with applying classical Freudian theory in work with individuals. Their expectations of individuals with whom they worked tended to be the same as those which guided the physician who diagnosed and treated mental illness from a more limited point of reference. The work of social workers is no longer characterized by intensive, long-term treatment of individuals in this psychoanalytic tradition, although some social workers continue to be significant reference individuals for those with whom they work. Social workers do recognize the influence of early others, the yearnings for self-actualization that may have critical influence on behavior, the influences of continuing relationships which are often more impressive than the earliest relationships in life, and the influences of the society through which standards of judgment are continually mediated.

Frames of Reference

Groups and significant individuals whom the person internalizes become part of the person's frame of reference. The frame of reference has to do with the context that influences the individual's standards of judgment, perceptions, and the way the individual acts and feels.[16] A number of examples of human behavior show misjudgment of the context of the situation, as in instances in which "the situation of the other person is silently presupposed to be the same as the situation of the

observer."[17] Most people remember the example of Marie
Antoinette who, "upon being told that the people were hungry
because they had no bread, asked why they did not eat cake
instead."[18] It is sometimes supposed that children who have
learned that to be worthwhile is to live in a wealthy suburban
community, to attend private schools, and to become staff
members of large corporations will, when they grow up, take
conservative stands on social issues concerning equality of
opportunity. But the reverse is more often true. Unlike Marie
Antoinette, these children are more likely to change the
context within which they judge human worth. Given the
opportunity to evaluate the life conditions of those who are not
wealthy, who live in crowded, inadequate. housing, attend
ghetto schools, and learn to value labor unions, such children
frequently change their standards of judgment and perceptions
in the course of becoming adults.

One's frame of reference serves a number of functions. It is
critical to one's need to make sense out of what is happening in
one's life. It guides the individual's expectations and it serves
as an anchoring point for making predictions about other
people's behavior. Everyone has a tendency to perceive human
events in some frame of reference. Throughout life, people get
many different pictures of the world, but at any particular
time in the process of growing and changing from one view to
another, what one has viewed before is used as a way of understanding what one sees next. Anyone who has been a stranger
in a group will recognize the need to refer to earlier group
experiences to predict the consequences of one's own behavior
and to interpret the behavior of others. One begins to look for
signals and cues that the new group is similar to others one has
known. Without some frame, or boundaries within which to
perceive human events, it would be difficult to understand the
meaning of others' responses and to organize one's own.
Boundaries function to organize the person. The likelihood
that one will remain a stranger in a new group depends as
much upon others' evaluation as on one's own evaluation of
others. This interaction provides the opportunity to confirm
one's predictions or to disprove them. The person's need for
others is involved in the striving to realize the self as well as to
maintain a past frame of reference. The individual needs the

opportunity to search for knowledge beyond the limits of that frame.

As the person grows and changes, the frame of reference to which behavior is referred provides a kind of screen through which external stimuli can be sifted and understood. It is in this sense that a frame of reference can be understood as a boundary, since boundaries serve to organize the person. Most human beings seek more and more understanding of behavior as they mature; most experience behavior in an increasing number of contexts and search for more and more knowledge before settling on a final set of beliefs about the world. Given the opportunity, most people can engage in critical thinking about the contexts within which they perceive the world and enlarge the boundaries of their perceptions of themselves as influencing and being influenced by others.

The Function of Attitudes

The extent to which people are able to grow and to change as their life context changes is reflected in their attitudes. Attitudes are firmly held beliefs which are anchored in feelings. They are not the same as standards of judgments or perceptions, although they are derived from both. Attitudes are interpretations of definite situations; they are evaluations placed on specific instances of human behavior, on identifiable other people or groups of others, on issues and proposals which affect human behavior.

Attitude is the predisposition of the individual to evaluate some symbol or object or aspect of his world in a favorable or unfavorable manner. Opinion is the verbal expression of an attitude, but attitudes can also be expressed in nonverbal behavior. Attitudes include both the affective, or feeling core of liking or disliking, and the cognitive, or belief elements which describe the object of the attitudes, its characteristics, and its relations to other objects.[19]

Attitudes differ in intensity; "intensity" refers to the feeling part of the attitude. Some people may "see red," or become visibly upset, when they witness certain behavior, while other people may take such behavior in stride, or feel only mildly dismayed. The same individual may have attitudes which vary in intensity. The television character

Archie Bunker is portrayed as having extremely predictable attitudes toward almost all aspects of difference in others. He is easily overwhelmed by emotional forces and appeals to self-interest, and he has little or no interest in facts.

Attitudes toward others reflect a number of motivations; the same attitude may be motivated differently for different individuals. For example, we cannot make arbitrary assumptions about the origin of attitudes which are destructive of productive human relationships. They may be motivated by frustrations encountered in early life experiences, by strivings to gain acceptance from an important peer group, by the need to disguise some disability one suspects one has, and by a number of other things.

Daniel Katz discusses four major functions which attitudes serve from the point of view of their motivational base.[20]

1. *Adjustment to gain rewards.* People are often motivated to evaluate specific instances of behavior in particular ways in order to gain approval and reward. They may adjust or adapt their responses to obtain need satisfaction. The more other people perceive an individual's behavior as correct, the more the individual is assured of approval. The closer the objects of the individual's needs are "to actual need satisfaction and the more likely they are clearly perceived as relevant to need satisfaction, the greater are the probabilities of positive attitude formation."[21] This is the basis of learned responses in human behavior, as described by behaviorist learning theory.

2. *Avoidance of facing "truth."* At times, people defend themselves against whatever it is they compromise by adapting their behavior to the expectations of others in order to gain approval. At times, they simply defend against the harshness of the environment: "The person protects himself from acknowledging the basic truths about himself or the harsh realities in his external world."[22] These defenses, which are psychological maneuvers occurring within the person who avoids reality by blocking out knowledge of what is actually going on, include denial, rationalization, and projection. Many attitudes operate to defend the self-image. Ego defenses are

the basis of critical conceptions of Freudian theory, and they are emphasized by ego psychologists.

3. *Value expression.* Attitudes may also serve to give positive expression to a person's basic values, often with regard to the person's conceptions about the self. These attitudes "stress the importance of self-expression, self-development and self-realization."[23] Self-theorists focus on this motivational aspect of attitudes. Behaviors which express these attitudes are not directed toward eliciting positive sanction from others: they may accentuate one's difference from others in the service of confirming one's own identity as a separate person from others.

4. *Knowledge-seeking.* People tend to develop attitudes according to their need to structure and to give meaning to their relationships with others. "The search for meaning, the need to understand, the trend toward better organization of perceptions and beliefs to provide clarity and consistency for the individual"[24] describe this motivation. People want knowledge so that they can give order and meaning to situations which are otherwise incomprehensible and chaotic. In this sense, attitudes may directly reflect the person's frame of reference with regard to specific situations and events. This motivation is emphasized in theories of perception which are associated with gestalt theorists.

Implications for the Social Worker
Knowledge of attitude motivation is important for social workers because this is the level of human behavior most frequently observed and to which social workers' judgments are directed. Although our discussion has been presented in terms of the individual, it is important to consider that attitudes are shared by groups of people, that they are derived from the content of the society, and that they are reinforced by forces as broad as those which define economic and political structures.

Later chapters will discuss the implications that attitudes have for social functioning in the human relationship arrangements defined by social systems. At this point, we turn to material which describes those groups that link the individual to the larger society.

Reference Groups

Critical to an understanding of how individuals come to evaluate and appraise their own behavior is the proposition that others, outside the self, are the source of one's self-appraisal. The perspectives of others who are significant to the person are internalized by the person, and these perspectives become the source of the person's frame of reference. Sociologists, psychologists, and social psychologists have examined this proposition from the view of groups to which individuals refer their behavior for judgment and appraisal.

Types of Groups to Which People Refer Their Behavior

Reference groups have two major functions. They function as standards of comparison for self-appraisal and as a source of the individual's value preferences, norms, and attitudes.[25] Reference groups may be groups to which the individual relates as a part or aspires to relate psychologically. They may be composed of persons in the immediate environment who have direct and identifiable influence upon the individual, or groups with which the individual is not communicating but whose imagined or actual judgments influence that individual's self-judgment. They may be groups which are present in the person's awareness, by which one sees one's behavior observed and evaluated, or they may be groups of whose influence the person is not aware. Reference groups may be designated membership groups. They may be groups to which the person is positively attracted without being accepted as a member. They may be groups of aspiration. Groups to which people refer their behavior may be positive or negative; they may be groups in which the individual desires membership and whose rules and standards of behavior are accepted or groups whose norms the individual rejects. They may be used for normative or comparative evaluation.

Normative Groups of Reference

The normative function of reference groups is to define and enforce standards of behavior for the individual.[26] The group works to maintain standards for action whether or not these standards are objectively appropriate as judged by people outside the group. If individuals are motivated by a desire to maintain, or to secure, membership in the group they will accept the enforcement of its standards. The individual has real contact with the normative group, and is aware of it and of his or her interest in belonging to it. The person is in face-to-face contact either with the group members or with group representatives. The group of normative reference has the power to enforce its standards, and the individual internalizes them. The group becomes part of the individual's internalized audience.

"Norm" or "normative" can be defined in terms of the word "expectations," which is generally viewed as meaning the way a person is expected to behave in any given situation. "Norms" refer to what "ought" or "should" be done according to social standards. Sometimes norms are clearly expressed. For example, a fourteen-year-old may be told, "As long as you are a member of this family, you will come to the table with everyone else. That is how we eat here. We do not get stuff out and eat it when we please. Now sit down and behave yourself." By this explicit family rule, "behaving one*self*" means getting oneself in line with what is expected by those in charge of the family. Clearly, the young person in the example was being admonished, in very concrete terms, for failing to remember the rules. It would be hard to imagine that the boy or girl was unaware of what was expected. There is no objective reason to believe that eating is done better sitting down, or that eating when one pleases, or eating with everyone else in the family is more satisfying to the individual who apparently does not want to do it. Therefore, it is obvious that this family norm expresses one of the ways in which the family organizes its need-meeting activities. The family divides the labor of cooking and cleaning up, and expects individual members to contribute to the conversation about how the world looks to them.

Demands on family members reflect parental authority rules which are rules about superior-subordinate relationships. These same kinds of rule relationships exist in a number of life situations. For example, occupational groups, or work groups,

are frequently designed by a strict hierarchy of relationships with exact job descriptions from top to bottom of the
group. One goes along with these explicit expectations if one
wishes to remain in the group. Since the choice of occupation
is often limited, normative behavior of this sort may be
engaged in unwillingly. Normative behavior of people attending school, becoming members of athletic teams, or of groups
of peers whose goals are less task-oriented is characterized by
the enforcement of common standards of behavior.

Many norms are not explicated, and at times people feel
apprehensive as they wonder whether or not they are doing
what they "should" be doing. In the illustration of being
defined by the world, Kafka describes the bewilderment and
unpreparedness of the character who is on trial in his dream.
At one point, the dreamer says, "I don't know this law" and he
becomes aware that "one day—quite unexpectedly—some
Judge will take up the documents . . . and order an immediate
arrest."[27] In this century, perhaps people do not tend to have
such dreams; nevertheless, we can all identify with the dread
and terror of that dreamer. The accumulated wisdom of
centuries may simply be laid down in a kind of collective
unconscious that we all share, or we may still be subject to
some inner dread when we find ourselves wanting, in the face
of others' disapproval, and catch ourselves saying, "I didn't
know . . ."

The attitudes of people are reflected in their normative
behavior, in their expectations of themselves and of others in
those groups which make up the relationship arrangements of
that part of the social order with which one is expected and
expects others to identify. All expectations do not run counter
to the actualization of the self, to the realization of yearnings
to move humanness ahead. In large measure, this depends
upon one's frame of reference at any particular time during
life. There is an essential sadness in the tendency of some
people to draw the boundaries of experience so narrowly as to
select to view themselves and others in rigid, moralistic terms.
And there is an intrinsic joy in the tendency to widen the
boundaries of one's view in order to take in the transcending
wonder of one's own and others' human potential. Most people

internalize audiences which take both kinds of perspectives. And this is "normal." The search for self-definition is implied in the locating of groups of others like oneself who serve as the source of one's self-judgments and self-appraisal.

Normative behavior, and the groups to which it is referred, reflects the knowledge function of attitudes. This function is motivated by the individual's need to give meaning to, and to make sense of, human relationships. One cannot decide to conform or not to conform to social norms unless one understands what they are. The search for the sense of the meanings of human events, the need to understand what is going on, is expressed in exploration of what the norms are to which one is expected to conform. This is essential to the process of belonging to groups to which one wants to belong, or to maintaining oneself in groups to which one needs to belong, for one reason or another. One also joins others in setting and enforcing normative behavior as one interacts with others on the basis of explicitly or tacitly agreed-upon patterns of behavior, defines oneself as a group member, and is defined by others as belonging to this or that group.

Comparative Groups

Comparative reference groups are either real or imagined groups or categories of people to which individuals compare themselves in regard to characteristics they themselves consider important. Unlike groups from which individuals internalize norms, or with which they become identified, comparative reference groups usually do not require one to be a member in face-to-face contact with other members. But some similarity in attributes between the person and the group of reference must either be imagined or perceived, for comparison to be made.[28]

Many questions relevant to a person's sense of well-being are answered in comparative terms. While most people who are asked if they feel good do not answer by asking, "Compared to what?" their answer often reflects some comparative considerations which reveal a group or an individual referent. People tend to locate themselves on a continuum of some sort in relation to others in the social structure. Those things to

which individuals aspire are determined by knowledge of the
achievements of groups whose status or ability, compared to
the individual's own, can be assessed.

Early studies of comparative behavior concerned the concept of "relative deprivation." Samuel Stouffer studied the
perspectives of soldiers during World War I and found that
many soldiers experienced a great deal of deprivation.
However, the sacrifice these men felt was more intense for
some than for others, depending upon the standards used for
comparison.[29] For example, the sacrifice they felt was greater
when they compared themselves to men not in service who
stayed at home with their families than when they compared
themselves with others who were also servicemen. Subsequent
to this and other findings of the original Stouffer study, sociological theorists became interested in the relative aspects of
such comparisons; that is, people felt more or less deprived
with reference to whom? Interest in this question placed
emphasis on the "others" with whom people compared
themselves as well as on people's reaction to the comparison. It
became clear that in order to compare oneself to others, one
must know something about these others, and that the social
structure was a major determinant of comparison.[30]

The notion that people compare themselves by social
aggregates or categories is illustrated in the way many people
view behavior which deviates from what is considered
"normal." During the sixties, the surge of young people who
challenged the society's established patterns of behavior
refused to commit themselves to the adult world of their
society. They refused to accept conventional definitions of success and achievement. They compared themselves with others
like themselves rather than with traditional models, and they
experienced difference. "Though their goals are often confused
and inarticulate, they converge on a passionate yearning for
openness and immediacy of experience, on an intense desire to
create, on a longing to express their perception of the world."[31]

It was noted earlier that we cannot make arbitrary
assumptions about the groups to which an individual refers.
Some predictions, however, can be made about which kinds of
groups are likely to be referred to by which kinds of individuals
under certain kinds of circumstances. It is generally supposed

that young people of college age may not yet be committed to the goals of their society and may choose to examine them. The young people who challenged society's goals were in the general social category labeled "students," who challenged the materialistic values of a society dedicated to a military-industrial orientation. They did more than examine the standards of judgment by which they were expected to behave, and they were subsequently subject to considerable, if not final, repression.

The degree of freedom with which one can choose groups of significance is relative to one's position in the social structure. Any significant changes in normative behavior are dependent upon groups of supportive others with whom people can share common goals. People tend to compare themselves to what, in the opinions of most significant others, seems to be the consensus. In general, students have somewhat more freedom to compare themselves with others like themselves and to obtain more consensus.

Leon Festinger is associated with important work on social comparison. Based on his studies of which other people most frequently chose to compare themselves with, under what conditions and with what consequences, he was able to predict that

a person will choose to evaluate his opinions and abilities by comparing them with his peers or near peers. For example, a college student will choose other college students for comparison rather than prison inmates; teenagers will choose other teenagers rather than adults . . .

Given a choice, a person will choose someone close to his own opinion or ability for comparison. . . . If only a divergent comparison is available, the person will not be able to make a precise evaluation of his opinion or ability.[32]

According to Festinger's prediction, then, people tend to compare themselves with others like themselves in making their self-appraisals, unless the pressure to compare with others unlike oneself cannot be overcome. If such a "divergent comparison" is all that is available, one may not be able to make an accurate evaluation of one's own opinion or ability. It is often suggested that students will change their opinions "when they get out into the real world," for example. The term "real" appears to suggest that students are likely to change their views when they no longer have the support of others like themselves. Most people accept the notion that if groups that hold similar, but unpopular, opinions can be divided, they can be conquered. The same notion underlies the efforts made to separate individuals from certain groups which appear to influence them in ways that make those with the power to enforce such separations uncomfortable.

Shared goals and group support for action are characteristic of all social liberation movements. Support for equality of opportunity is generated by increased group efforts of women who have organized a movement toward this goal. The shift in many women's opinions of themselves is reflected in their increased interest in examining the extent to which they perceive deprivation of their human rights as compared to the rights accorded to men.

People who have made a homosexual choice tend to be viewed by many others in society as either "sick" or "sinners." Therefore, they are in danger of being discriminated against in housing and occupation. Only in the last decade has there been any concerted effort on the part of homosexuals to mobilize group support in the face of considerable pressure of opinion against homosexuality. The general consensus of the society was against their sexual choice; those who made it tended to carry on a somewhat secretive life, and supportive referents were relatively few. The controversy over discrimination has brought the issue of homosexual choice to public attention. It is likely that this controversy has mobilized homosexuals to greater mutual support. More knowledge is available on the basis of which people can compare themselves with others like themselves. Homosexuals can compare themselves with homosexuals who speak out for freedom of choice.

The extent to which certain internalized norms of the society can be changed depends upon the amount of group support to which people have access. People who experience certain social norms as blocking self-actualization can make more precise evaluations of their opinions and their ability to change those norms when they can compare their views with others like themselves.

Although people are not entirely determined by their comparative reference behavior, their need for others who view them as equals on some important dimensions is highly influential. It is as though a person sees himself reflected in the eyes of the beholders who are closest to him. Assertion of self takes place in groups of others who are the closest beholders.

Assertion of self for many black people in this society has been extremely complex in the face of normative expectations held by a majority of white people for a minority of black people. The struggle for a black identity, separate from the destructive characteristics with which most of the expectations of the majority group were associated, is the essence of black liberation. William Cross has discussed the process of achieving liberation and identified it as "the Negro-to-Black Conversion Experience."[33]

According to Cross, the process is divided into five stages:

Pre-Encounter

In the pre-encounter stage a person is programmed to view and think of the world as being non-Black, anti-Black, or the opposite of Black. . . . the content of the preliberation Black experience within the class system differs, but the context is similar since both [lower- and middle-class Black people] think, act and behave in a manner that degrades Blackness.[34]

Encounter

The encounter is a verbal or visual event, rather than an "in-depth" intellectual experience. For example, the death of Martin Luther King, Jr., hurled thousands of pre-encounter Negroes into a search for a deeper understanding of the Black Power movement.[35]

Immersion-Emersion

In this period the person immerses himself in the world of Blackness. . . . Regardless of the opinions of others, the person actually feels that he is being drawn toward qualitatively different experiences as he is being torn from his former orientations. The immersion is a strong, powerful, dominating sensation constantly being energized by Black rage, guilt, and a third and new fuel, a developing sense of pride. . . . The first half of the third stage is immersion into

Blackness; the second is emergence from the dead-end. . . . during
the emersion phase of the Black experience the individual begins to
gain awareness and control of his behavior.[36]

Internalization

[Individuals] . . . internalize and incorporate aspects of the
immersion-emersion experience into their self-concept. They achieve
a feeling of inner security and are more satisfied with themselves.
. . . Feeling "Black and beautiful" becomes an end in itself rather
than a source of motivation for improving one's skills or for a deeper
understanding of the Black condition. . . . Generally, the self-concept
modifications do make the person receptive to meaningful change in
his world view.[37]

Internalization-Commitment

Assuming the person is able to continue his development . . . he
or she will eventually *become* the new identity. The shift is from
concern about how your friends see you. . . . to confidence in one's
personal standards of Blackness; from uncontrolled rage toward
white people to controlled, felt and conscious anger toward
oppressive and racist institutions; from symbolic rhetoric to quiet,
dedicated, long-term commitment; from unrealistic urgency to a
sense of destiny; from anxious, insecure, rigid inferiority feelings to
Black pride, self-love. . . . attitudes toward white people become less
hostile . . . and pro-Black attitudes become more expansive, open,
and less defensive. . . . he or she is committed to a plan. He is
actively trying to change his community. His values, like the stage-
four person, will probably still have a decidedly Western overtone.
He is going beyond rhetoric and into action, and he defines change in
terms of the masses of Black people rather than the advancement of
a few . . .should the person develop a comparative reference (non-
Western and Western insights) we have the "ideal" Black person.[38]

Other groups of people are struggling to maintain or to
develop different comparative reference groups in order to
liberate themselves from oppressive normative expectations
that deny their human worth and restrain them from reaching
their potential. For example, the struggles of Chicano, Puerto
Rican, and Asian American people for equality of opportunity
and social justice in our society are all characterized by an
awareness of pressures to compare themselves with members of
the dominant group in society in making self-appraisals. It is
difficult for the members of these minority groups to make
accurate evaluations of themselves as long as the dominant

group remains the comparative reference. The assertion of their own worth requires that they compare their views with others like themselves and liberate themselves from the negative characteristics with which they are frequently endowed by the dominant group.

The struggle for an identity which celebrates the unique cultural differences of Chicanos is the essence of Chicano liberation. Many Chicanos reorient themselves through consideration of their history as a "colonized minority in their own conquered land."[39] They come to view the responses of the dominant Anglo society as rooted in that society's distortion of its history of conquest of those parts of the United States where the majority of Mexican people have settled, and which were at one time part of Mexico.[40] Comparison of themselves with others who share a similar history and identity underlies their pride in difference from the dominant Anglo group and leads to mobilization of energies to work for changes in the Chicano condition.

The Puerto Rican experience on the mainland United States illustrates further the complexity of changing comparative reference groups. Puerto Ricans who have lived on the mainland most of their lives, those who are recent arrivals, and those born and reared on the mainland tend to have different reference groups.[41] Attitudes toward the preservation of the Spanish language among these groups appear to differ according to their level of accommodation to the normative expectations of mainland society. From the point of view of some, the loss of the language would have many adverse implications for a people for whom use of Spanish is a traditional mark of identity. Language has been seen as "an unusual public symbol of identity, of the solidarity of Puerto Ricans in a group of their own kind . . . of the strength they can have if they remain together."[42]

Although there does not appear to be consensus among mainland Puerto Ricans on the issue of language, there is increasing agreement that they must maintain or develop a sense of pride in their difference from the dominant group. There is a movement to create solidarity among Puerto Ricans in groups of others like themselves who value the culture which gives them their identity. This group support underlies the

effort to organize their resources in order to change those institutions that restrain the realization of the human potential of
Puerto Ricans in mainland society.

There is a popular belief that Asian Americans do not
experience discrimination in this society. As a result, their civil
and human rights have "largely been ignored by governmental
agencies, educational institutions, private corporations, and
other sectors of society."[43]

Asian Americans are a heterogeneous group. The tendency
to assume homogeneity among Chinese, Japanese, Korean,
Filipino, Samoan, Vietnamese, native Taiwanese, and other
Asian groups leads to misconceptions which ignore their
uniqueness. While these diverse groups may serve the individuals who constitute them as standards of comparison for
self-appraisal, they do not necessarily serve as sources of value
preferences and attitudes. The identity struggles within these
groups are further complicated by their need to develop coali-
tions characterized by group support to strengthen their position as a political force.

Some Implications for Social Workers

Social workers often find themselves, in their work with
people, responding to the "shoulds" and "oughts" defined by
social norms simply from the standpoint of approval or disapproval. Acceptance of the behavior of others is not the same as
approval or disapproval. Seeing the world through the eyes of
those with whom they work, which social workers learn to do,
requires a great deal of acceptance. Many social workers
engage in a process described as the "interview." An interview
is a "view" between two people, each of whom may view the
world differently and come to understand the other's views.
Although the social worker may be a supervisor, the notion
that one always has "super" vision can be misleading. It can
mislead those with whom one works into thinking that one
knows everything about everything. While supervisors do know
more about the tasks of the social worker than those whom
they teach, it is very important to set and to share common
goals of achievement in working with others.

People with whom social workers share goals may not find it easy to relate to the social worker as a significant reference other. They may need others, like themselves, in groups which can satisfy needs for belonging, to experience themselves as worthwhile, to express their ideas about the world in order to allow others to influence those ideas that are destructive to their self-actualization. Social workers may find it difficult to share the goals of the groups they serve. They may catch themselves feeling impatient to change goals which are not reachable, or which are seen as destructive. The task of harnessing the energies of people to make changes in the conditions of their lives is a difficult one. At least some of the social worker's attention needs to be directed to understanding the contexts within which the consumers of social work service view social work. It is a matter of learning to direct one's change efforts toward that part of people that has the strength to change. If one believes that all people want to grow and to change, in some part of themselves, then one will take the time and the energy to locate that part. One will not confront people with one's own goals unless one has tried to know something about who they are, where they are going, and who has been going that way with them.

Social workers serve ongoing membership groups in a variety of ways. Work with families, for example, is one of them. Families have very intricate systems of communication, based on shared goals about which the social worker cannot make arbitrary decisions. Every family has a repertoire of behaviors which distinguishes that family from another. All families are organized in some way; frequently, what we perceive as disorganization has a great deal of internal consistency. Much of the normative enforcement in family groups is implicit, not consciously thought out by the members. The signals and cues which indicate the values and beliefs of family members cannot be readily inferred: they deserve considerable study.

Other membership groups may be more important to individuals than their families. Looking to the family as the sole source of the frames of reference from which the members view their lives may block out other critical reference points.

At times, social workers find themselves creating new

reference groups for people. Such groups are designed by social workers to provide new human experiences for people. Social workers may work directly with such groups in order to facilitate growth experiences for the members. To function well in this work, social workers need to understand a great deal about the dynamics of such groups in terms of the reference function they serve. The currency of exchange between and among people in these groups is based on the notion of a jury of peers who judge each other's behavior; validate or confirm each other's worth; reject or accept each other's ideas about the "oughts" and "shoulds;" make up their own ground rules for liking and disliking, loving and hating; give each other overt or covert signals and cues about the ways of perceiving themselves and others. The function of social workers in groups like this is very critical with regard to what they choose to influence.

Social workers accept the values underlying human liberation. This acceptance is critical to the code of ethics which guide the profession of social work. Social workers are people, socialized by the society in terms of their own significant groups of reference. It is not likely that social workers are free of bias in relation to their own needs for belonging and how their needs have been met by significant groups of which they have been a part in the society. It is very important for social workers to become aware of their own past conditioning, to take on new reference groups and new perspectives of human liberation. This is frequently associated with some doubts about one's self-worth or with a need to compensate for inner feelings of inadequacy. The social worker's own yearning to grow and to change, to broaden the frame of reference in order to support the liberation of human beings from restraints on their self-actualization, is self-fulfilling and well worth the cost of some struggle.

Chapter 3

Social Reality

Social reality is an elusive concept. It is difficult to conceive of a reality in terms other than those which describe what actually exists as fact or as "truth." Physical reality is fact and has high predictability. A tree is perceived as a tree, a hill as a hill, and the individual can, by referring to general experience, estimate the height of the tree or the hill without considering what mediates between these physical objects and the self. In this sense, we often call such perceptions "objective."

Perceptions of the social environment are not similarly "objective." Unlike the tree or the hill, the physical objects, social events take place in a number of different contexts, and the mediating circumstances between the social event and the self of the observer may distort the event.[1] We attribute the "event" of physical objects to causal factors in the physical environment; we can explain how they occur and their significance to ourselves. The interpretation of a social happening may locate causal factors in oneself, in the physical environment, in personal idiosyncrasies, in requirements of a situation.[2] An individual may respond positively to a task because it is one which assures success; the response may be positive because the sun is shining and the individual feels warmed and has a sense of general well-being, or because the individual is highly task-oriented and does not deal well with interpersonal situations that are not task-centered; or the response may be positive because something in the situation in which the response is elicited makes the task enjoyable. Attributing causal sources of behavior to the self, to others, or to the situations in which one finds oneself often calls for social comparisons. One will frequently find it necessary to compare one's beliefs or opinions with those of others. To decide whether the inability to do well is due to something in oneself or to something in others' definitions of doing well, people need information about how others who try to do well in the same situation manage it. To evaluate whether or not an emotional response to a situation is appropriate, people often need some social comparison with others' responses.[3]

In general, people do not perceive social reality as fact or as truth; although they may learn to take on certain views of the world which correspond to the views of others, there are many different ways of perceiving the world of social events according to the others with whom one views them. While past experience allows us to identify a physical object without difficulty, past experience may or may not help us to identify the meaning of social happenings. The future is not necessarily like the past, although it may have elements of similarity. For example, although people have internalized many audiences and have struggled to integrate, or to bring together, a fairly clear set of values and beliefs about themselves and others, they may still experience some subjective bewilderment and disorientation in new situations which require new relationship negotiations with unknown others. The discussion of reference groups has shown that people are very much influenced by others in their views of what to value and what to believe about human events, and social reality often tends to be what those who are most important to the individual think and say and do about what they believe and value. The forces in group life that restrain people from behaving in some ways or that propel them to behave in other ways are critical to the definition of social reality. And social reality may be quite different for different people.

The ways in which people view themselves as actors in their social life is developed out of reality testing. The extent to which the individual can think well or ill of himself or herself and of others may be a result of active searching for the social reality the individual shares with others. The individual may also distort reality for the sake of some inner harmony, to protect the self from painful feelings. A person may simply go along with everyone else's opinions in order to maintain a sense of belonging with others.

Social reality is not a constant, factual entity. It may be what members of face-to-face groups agree that it is, or it may be defined by larger social systems of which the individual is a part. People's views of social reality influence their aspirations to belong to one group or another. The ways in which people define social problems reflect their belief in a social reality. Social workers need this concept in order to understand a critical aspect of human behavior, and to guide their own intentions as individuals influencing and being influenced by others.

Ambiguities Associated with Social Reality Testing

In any situation in which there is no other standard for comparison, the person will evaluate behavior by comparison with the opinions and abilities of others.[4] Since nonsocial, objective means are frequently unavailable as standards for comparison, social reality tends to be what most other people who are important to the person think, say, and do about what they believe to be real. Locating what social reality is involves dependence on others; in an attempt to appraise social reality, we rely on other human beings' experiences. The less sure people are, the more dependent they are on what others see. People generally tend to refer to others' opinions of the nature of reality. It may be quite threatening to perceive things differently from the way that anyone else perceives them. Frequently, we experience a "lost" feeling when others do not give us assurance that they, too, see things in much the same way as we do. One's reality sense may be in danger when there is conflict between the evidence of one's own senses and what others see as true.[5]

Reference Groups and Reality Testing
As we have seen, reference groups function as standards of comparison for self-appraisal and as a source of the individual's value preferences, norms, and attitudes.[6] Reference groups, then, serve individuals as a way of finding out how

similar or different they are in relation to others. Groups serve individuals as a basis for reality testing, but the activity of reality testing is quite complicated. For example, groups frequently depend for the perpetuation of their life together on pluralistic ignorance. This describes a situation in which everybody in the group thinks everybody else in the group thinks so, but no one checks to find out if everyone does think so! The sway in face-to-face groups is toward uniformity of opinion, but in the instance of pluralistic ignorance, there is no clear answer as to what it is people agree to. It is as though the members cannot afford to be clear on whatever it is to which they are conforming. Checking to find out how close or far away one's own views of the world are from those held by others one cares about is a part of reality testing. In an immediate membership group, one can air ideas that do not correspond to others' ideas and have them checked by other members.

Consensual Validation
Consensual validation, that is, airing one's ideas by checking with others, is the process of getting one's ideas validated by consensus from groups. Consensual validation implies an active process of checking out one's views. Group members, however, frequently do not engage in active reality testing. In this sense, social reality may include certain behavior which people do not wish to know about. In groups, people have a general psychological tendency to experience things in relation to some frame of reference they all share. Many people aim to please themselves and others in terms of images that are shared in the group. People like other people who see things in the same way they see them, and tend to aspire to acceptance in groups that will fit the particular mixture of pleasure and pain to which they have become accustomed. To hold an opinion, then, which is different from the opinions of most others is to be alone with one's opinion.

Risks in Active Reality Testing
The extent of an individual's tolerance for the kind of "aloneness" described depends on a number of things. It may depend, in part, on whether the individual is motivated most

by basic needs or by growth needs. Usually, both kinds of needs motivate people, and these motivations may conflict with each other. In part, also, toleration of aloneness may depend on the group's importance to the individual. The more important the group is to the person, the greater is the likelihood of conflict of motivations. Actively seeking consensual validation entails taking some risk, and many people prefer not to take it.

Pressures toward Uniformity

The term *group norm*, or standard for expected behavior in a group, is used to describe findings that members of the same face-to-face group exhibit relative uniformity with respect to specified opinions and modes of behavior. Use of this term has generally carried the meaning that the observed uniformity derives in some manner from influences that the group is able to exert over its members. Similar choices in mode of dress, in recreational activities, in political affiliation, and in views of social issues are all evidences of group influences. A series of studies has shown that people's aspirations and their goal-setting behavior are strongly influenced by their information about how others behave, and by their relationships to these others. All these influences produce changes in the individual's behavior that result in more similarity to the behavior of groups to which the individual belongs.

Strength of Attraction and Relevance of Issues
Festinger found that "the stronger the attraction to the group, the stronger will be the pressure toward uniformity concerning abilities and opinions within that group."[7] The more importance the group has for one, then, the more pressure there will be for one to reduce discrepancies between oneself and the group. Festinger *et al*, found that "in highly cohesive groups, members changed their opinions more than in low cohesive groups."[8] This finding means that the greater the group cohesiveness, the more likely people are to arrive at uniform opinions. People do not want to be rejected by those who count for holding opinions that deviate from theirs. The need

for closeness and acceptance pushes one to locate reality for one's opinions in the opinions of others with whom one wishes to be associated. In turn, the group has some power over the individual, and the psychological yearning to belong and the social needs of the group to establish uniformity create reality for opinions and suppress evidence that does not fit with that reality.

The force of the pressure toward uniformity decreases as the importance, to the group, of the issue decreases. Stanley Schachter studied pressures toward uniformity with regard to the relevance the issue had for the group. He found that members whose views deviated from those of other group members were more likely to be rejected from the group in high-relevance than in low-relevance conditions.[9] This finding has implications for those who would observe and influence changes in groups. The finding can help to explain discrepancies between public and private behavior. For example, the issue of exclusion of minority members from groups is frequently not considered to be relevant until it is brought to others' attention and becomes a public concern. An illustration may clarify the point. In the instance of Congressional approval for the position of Attorney General of an appointee who was a member of such an exclusionary group, the issue became relevant for the member and for the group. In this instance, the Attorney General, in a public hearing, expressed the opinion that he had not wished to exclude minority members from his club and that there was no stated policy to the effect that minority individuals were excluded. One is left with the impression that the issue had not previously been seen as relevant, and that it was a source of embarrassment to him only at the point of obtaining Congressional approval for his new appointment. The charge brought against him was that his club was typical of many others, that no black members were admitted, and that he went along with the unstated policy. We could speculate that his behavior in "going along with the unstated policy" reflected his unwillingness to risk rejection from his club. He now openly differs with the exclusionary membership and gave up his membership in that group.

Changing the Comparability of Opinions

Festinger's work shows that individuals will tend to redefine groups in order to make incomparable those whose opinions and abilities are perceived as divergent from their own.[10] Most people are familiar with the tendency of groups to split over critical issues. For example, President Carter belonged to a church in Plains, Georgia, which practiced *de facto* segregation. Although the church members had dealt with the issue (apparently in the absence of applications for membership from black people), and Carter was among those who had voted to admit black people to membership, the vote had gone against this proposition. Apparently, those who voted for admission of black people were not rejected from church membership. When, at the election of this President, the issue came to public attention and the admission of black people was imminent, the church membership was simply redefined; those who agreed that black people should be admitted formed their own congregation, and those who did not remained in the original church. The original membership of the church is still likely to practice *de facto* segregation, but they no longer have to compare their views with those who differ with them, since the split rendered those who differed incomparable.

The option to leave groups whose beliefs block freedom to act on one's own beliefs is, of course, the essence of freedom of choice in changing reference groups. One can contrast the rejection of an individual who holds divergent views and the decision of a subgroup, of the larger membership, which supports one's views and is able to reject as well as to be rejected. While in the church example such freedom of choice was not denied to individuals, it was probably easier for individuals to leave that group because their views were shared by at least some other members.

The implications of this discussion thus far can be seen as suggesting that frequently individuals do not exercise their own freedom of choice to leave groups whose opinions they do not share. The point to be made is that pressures toward uniformity account for what many individuals do believe and value, and that testing social reality is often so complicated that individuals are likely to go along with the group without checking to what they are conforming. Individuals frequently need active support from others to test social reality in groups.

Forcing Comparability
Individuals remain in groups despite continued discomfort in two kinds of situations in which divergent opinions and abilities exist: freedom to leave the group is curtailed, or comparability is forced. We can see some of the consequences of forcing comparability in the following illustrations.
According to Festinger:

One such situation occurs when the attraction of the group is so strong that the person wishes to remain in the group. . . . Under these circumstances . . . the group has the power to influence the member effectively and . . . to be effective enough to eliminate the differences of opinion . . . in the case of an ability . . . while the group will probably succeed in motivating the member concerning this ability it is quite likely that the ability itself may not be changeable. . . . We would expect . . . deep experiences of failure and feelings of inadequacy with respect to this ability.[11]

In this situation, it is assumed that the abilities, as well as the opinions, of the individual differ from those of the other members. For example, some groups of people believe in and value hard, physical work and devalue aesthetic pursuits; some groups hold physical labor to be worthless and expect their members to be engaged only in intellectual pursuits. Many groups in this society draw the boundaries of their membership around social class lines, assuming that socioeconomic orientation defines human abilities in discrete ways. In such groups, people who value self-actualization and equality of opportunity may be viewed as unable to comprehend what others hold as worthwhile, and this bias reflects on the person's essential abilities; the person would be expected to demonstate the bias in performance and may fail to do so. If people stay in the group under these circumstances, it is possible that they may simply experience feelings of inadequacy in relation to the majority. We do not always consider this possibility. We tend to think that individuals know their minds and hearts so well that they will choose to be nonconformists, and that they will set themselves free from the groups with which they differ but which seem to have so much power over them. This is the resolution found by the subjects of human tragedies in great plays and novels. It is the stuff of which the courage referred to by the existential writers is composed. In the affairs of many people, such courage may take a lifetime to express, and in some people it may never be realized. There are situations in which people never seem to get quite enough support to test their own abilities in comparison with people like themselves, to seek new social realities, or to change the social reality in groups to which they belong. Without such support from caring others, many people tend to expect of themselves what most others expect of them.

The second situation in which comparability to others is forced and in which people are not free to leave groups is illustrated by imprisonment.[12] In this situation, the group frequently has no attraction to the individual at all, but the individual in prison cannot leave the group. Most societies single out groups of people who are adjudged to be criminals and isolate them in prisons. The organizational problems of prisons hardly need documentation; they include overcrowding, poor facilities, and lack of service personnel who are oriented to the impact of this situation on the inmates. Of critical concern to those who work with people at the interface of the individual and the social institution is the forced comparability aspect of their group life.

In this situation, freedom to leave the group becomes a reward for "good" behavior. The reference, in purely social terms, for what is "good" lies in the behavior of those who are responsible for the prisoners, but who are not the prisoners. This group of others appears to be the group that is presumed to offer alternative comparability with regard to group norms. Such a situation creates considerable difficulty for individuals in prison groups who do not share their lives with those who are not prisoners, as well as for those who comprise the staffs of prisons. If we add to this the general expectations of most people that prisoners are likely to "create trouble" for those in charge and will not engage in creative self-realization, we can hardly expect that a situation like this will result in growth experiences for prisoners.

In many situations, of course, the social reality created by groups does not counter the needs of group members for growth and change. These groups are characterized by freedom of the members to differ with the views of others, to engage in group conflict, to resolve differences or to sustain differences. Interaction is based on both agreement and disagreement. Otherwise there is little, if any, potential for people to grow and to change. Some groups appear to have such a low level of tension that nothing happens which inspires anyone to accomplish anything or which motivates members to achieve anything together.

Groups tend to strive for equilibrium; the fact that there was a balance achieved by groups can be seen when it is upset. Group members work rather hard to stabilize their expectations of each other, to achieve a balance and to keep it. Group norms serve as ground rules for the members, and in this way they serve an important function with regard to the need people have for structuring their energies. The question is not whether groups should be organized or balanced. The reason to question pressures toward uniformity lies in the nature of group expectations and the freedom with which the members can bear to change their expectations of each other. Many balances are upset in groups; this is the basis for social change.

Self-Consistency

The point that pressures toward uniformity restrain individuals from exercising freedom of choice has implications for one's own tendency to maintain balance in the ways in which one views the world. Uniformity has something in common with consistency and orderliness. When balances in groups are upset, we can see conflict; individuals quite frequently do not wish to engage in conflict. It has been pointed out that groups have a tendency to stabilize, to achieve a balance and to keep it. In general, individuals, as individuals, seek to create an orderly and a coherent view of themselves and those around them.[13] People bring to the group a striving for orderliness and simplicity in their own perceptions of interpersonal relations. When individuals experience differences, in their opinions and abilities, they also experience incongruity and inconsistency in their expectations of behavior. Such psychological discomfort creates conflict in the individual, which runs counter to the individual's tendency to create a consistent and congruent view of the self and the interpersonal environment.

Testing the social reality is a two-way street. It is important to others that the individual agrees with them, but it is also important to the individual that others agree with him or her.

In order to understand the ways in which people experience conflict and reduce the tension associated with it, it will be helpful to examine some of the interconnections of perception, cognition, and inner harmony.

Perception, Cognition, and Inner Harmony

Experiences that run counter to the individual's tendency to create a consistent view of self and of interpersonal relations upset the way in which that individual has organized knowledge about the self, about the behavior of the self, and about the environment. To achieve orderliness and coherence, people perceive all events by relating them to categories; perception is a process of categorization. Perception is thus not simply a passive, receptive, and automatic interpretation of whatever a person is stimulated to respond to. Relating the stimulus to a category is an active process in which the person selects the appropriate category, that is, the one which allows for identifying the event and its meaning.[14] People strive to bring together or to integrate knowledge of social events. And it is not until one examines more closely, or tries to analyze, this process that one becomes aware of the categories one has been using. The general proposition "that behavior is organized, that this organization is molar and that the most important element in this organization is cognition"[15] has significance for the way people perceive human behavior.

The proposition means that the person perceives behavior according to internal sets of related categories of knowledge that give the behavior some organized meaning; such organization is "holistic"; that is, it is not broken down into discrete elements of the behavior perceived. The categories to which individuals relate their perceptions serve as an organized "subset of the given cognitive universe in terms of which the

individual identifies and discriminates a particular object or
event."[16] Cognition may be defined as that which is known, or
knowledge acquired through life experience; it includes "the
things a person knows about himself, his behavior, and his surroundings."[17] William Scott has defined the term "cognitive
structure" to mean "those structures whose elements consist of
ideas consciously held by the person or as the set of ideas
maintained by a person and relatively available to conscious
awareness."[18] The categories to which perceptions are referred
are organized "into more complex structural assemblies, and it
is these structures that give meaning to specific elements
(for example, particular beliefs, knowledges, values, expect-
ancies)."[19]

These definitions are useful to the student who would
comprehend the complex relations between perception and
psychological balance or imbalance. Notice here how they
elaborate the discussion, in the preceding chapter, of "frame of
reference." All behavior is referred to some frame of reference
which is used to predict causal expectations among related
events. If the predictions are confirmed the person experiences
cognitive harmony.

Discussing Fritz Heider's theory of balance, Morton
Deutsch and Robert Krauss summarize a large body of
technical findings.

cognitive stability requires a congruence among causal expectations
with respect to related objects. For a state of complete cognitive
harmony to exist, the various implications of a person's expectations
or judgments of any one aspect of the cognitive environment may not
contradict the implications of his expectations or judgments in
respect to any other aspect of the cognized environment.[20]

This means, for example, that if an individual judges two
others, person A and person B, to be important to his sense of
well-being, he cannot at the same time judge that A and B are
antagonistic to each other and still maintain a balanced cognitive structure. When the cognitive structure is in a state of
imbalance or is threatened by imbalance, forces will arise to
produce a tendency to change the psychological environment
or a tendency toward change in the cognition of the environment. In our example, an individual judges both A and B as

important to that individual's sense of well-being. The knowledge that A and B dislike each other intensely threatens to throw the individual's perceptions out of balance. To regain the balance, the individual may come to dislike either A or B or feel that they do not dislike each other, or to feel that she or he likes A because A is kind and sensitive and B dislikes A because A has a great deal of money, and that there is no connection between these characteristics of A—kindness and wealth. "In general, the nature of the cognitive changes resulting from an imbalance will tend to produce the most congruence and least changes in the perceptual-cognitive field."[21]

Heider's theory of balance has a great deal in common with theories of self-consistency and attitudinal congruity. All these theories predict that individuals will try to perceive or evaluate the various aspects of their environment and of the self in such a way that the behavioral implications of their perceptions will not be contradictory.[22]

Cognitive Dissonance

The theory of cognitive dissonance also emphasizes the need for consistency in judgment. Festinger developed this theory in connection with the theory of social comparison. It will be recalled that social comparison develops from the need to know how similar or different one's judgment is in relation to the judgments of others, how similar to or different one is from others in regard to a number of characteristics. Dissonance theory indicates that the need is to have consistent knowledge, that is, cognitions that are not different from each other. While this is stressed by a number of theorists, Festinger's theory places particular emphasis on the consequences of decisions, and in this way differs from other theories of consistency in perception.[23]

Earlier in this chapter, cognition was defined as including "the things a person knows about himself, his behavior and his surroundings." Festinger, who supplies this definition, uses the term "cognitive elements" or "knowledges" to represent the "things" the person knows. Rather than speaking of these "elements" or "knowledges" as consistent or inconsistent, Festinger substitutes the terms "consonance" and "dissonance"; knowledges which are related are either consonant or dissonant.[24] The question of consonance or dissonance arises only when knowledges are related. For example, one may know the time span within which ocean tides change and one may also know that it rarely snows in Phoenix, Arizona; these are unrelated cognitive elements, and knowing one implies nothing about knowing the other. However, cognitions may be related and imply something about each other; in such case, the relationship between them may be either dissonant or consonant. Two cognitions would be related, for example, if one follows from the other. It would follow that if a person is standing in the rain without a waterproof cover, the person would get wet. Cognitions of the person standing in the rain without a waterproof cover and of the person not getting wet would be dissonant; the relation between the two cognitions would be a dissonant relation.[25]

Festinger suggests that dissonance would arise from several sources:

1. *Logical inconsistency*. The obverse of one cognition may follow from another on logical grounds. The belief that water freezes at thirty-two degrees is logically inconsistent with the belief that a chunk of ice will not melt at one hundred degrees.

2. *Opinion generally*. Dissonance may arise because an opinion is included in a more general opinion. A Democrat's preference for a Republican candidate should arouse dissonance because being a Democrat implies a preference for Democratic candidates.

3. *Past experience*. If a cognition is inconsistent with knowledge based on past experience, dissonance will arise. In the example of the person standing in the rain and not getting wet, dissonance is based on the fact that in past instances a person standing in the rain has always gotten wet.[26]

When people experience dissonance between cognitions that are of critical importance to them, they are psychologically uncomfortable and motivated to reduce the discomfort by reducing the dissonance. Dissonance reduction includes avoidance of information that is likely to increase the dissonance. Festinger discussed three possible ways of reducing dissonance: the individual may change a behavioral element, change an environmental cognitive element, or add new cognitive elements.[27] Suppose, for example, a person buys a car and his friends point out that it doesn't operate as it should. The person can reduce the dissonance which the decision to buy *that* car produces by getting rid of the car, thus changing a behavioral element. However, selling a car one has just purchased may mean a loss of money. The person may try, instead, to change the friend's opinion, thus changing an environmental cognitive element. Should this not succeed, the person might seek out others who like the car and think it operates very well, thus adding new cognitive elements.

According to Festinger, dissonance is an inevitable consequence of any decision that is important to a person. People decide between alternatives in the process of making a decision. Dissonance occurs after the person has felt conflict about which choice to make. Not all choices are made between conflicting alternatives—alternatives are hardly conflicting for the person when one is all good and another is all bad.[28] People are in conflict about which alternative to choose when all alternatives have some positive and some negative aspects, or when alternatives appear to have equally positive or equally negative aspects. The choice of one alternative over others results in dissonance among the negative elements of the alternatives that have been rejected.

Most readers are familiar with decisions about which one has "second thoughts." One aspect of dissonance describes the "second thoughts," which are composed of a tendency to see attractive aspects of the rejected alternative and unattractive aspects of the chosen alternative. Festinger's theory of cognitive dissonance takes us further than this, by explaining the process of dissonance reduction when the individual has made a commitment to the decision.

An illustration of the relevance of Festinger's theory for social work practice comes from Nelida Ferrari's study of what happened to 112 aged persons who made a decision to change their residence.[29] Ferrari, a social worker, was interested in the decisions and their consequences for these aged persons, and she had an opportunity to talk with and learn from them over a nine-month period. At the beginning, each faced a decision whether to apply to move from an established living arrangement to a new, well-equipped residence offering structured living arrangements and nursing care. Some of these subjects were living alone, some with families, and some in small group residences; all needed some care. All were attracted, in one way or another, to staying where they were, but this meant being often fatigued by the demands of complete self-care, or living with and fitting into the lives of younger members of their families, or fitting into the expectations and images of illness that were equated with the situation of group home living for the aged. The new structure for residential care offered considerable freedom. They could come and go as long as they were able; rooms were large and airy; the location was within fairly close distance of their present homes.

Each of the 112 persons Ferrari followed did make application to move, and was accepted. Subsequent to the acceptance, almost two thirds of them acted on their decision. Ferrari continued to follow those who made the move, making contact with them four weeks later and again three and a half months after their entry into the new living situation. She found considerable difference in the consequences of the move among those elderly persons who had had, and those who had not actually had freedom of choice about a decision. All these aged persons had experienced dissonance by virtue of the decision; the question was whether, and how, they were able to reduce it. Those who freely chose to move actively reduced the dissonance created by the decision. Initially they discussed their lingering doubts about the attractiveness of the alternative they had rejected and the negative features of the one they had selected. Subsequently, they found a greater number of attractive features in the selected alternative (the new living situation) and reduced their contacts with those who continued to express doubts that they had made the best choice. They increasingly chose to relate to those who agreed that it was a good choice. Eventually they resolved the dissonance, becoming more and more attracted to the option they had chosen. Those who did not have freedom to choose, but had to change their life situations under duress, were observed to withdraw gradually from all social contacts and to become much weaker physically, often becoming ill quite rapidly after the change. Medical records corroborated the significantly higher incidence of acute physical decline among those whose decisions were made without freedom of choice, and the physical advances of those whose decisions were made freely.

Since Ferrari's study has not, to anyone's knowledge, been replicated, it is simply not known whether her findings can be generalized beyond the group of elderly persons with whom she worked. The study, however, illustrates the implications that knowledge of dissonance-reducing behavior may have for many critical life decisions. The variable, "freedom of choice," is also highlighted in the study as a basic ingredient of decision-making. When people are free to change their minds and engage in dissonance-reducing behavior directed to sustaining a decision, it appears to be highly likely that the decision will serve their needs; at least we know that they prefer to "live with" the decision. When there is freedom to make the decision but no freedom to change it once it is made, the person will experience dissonance, and dissonance-reducing behavior is very important for that person.

Ego Defenses and Tension Reduction

The frame of reference for this explanation of why people defend themselves and what they defend themselves against comes from ego psychology, an elaboration of traditional psychoanalytic theory. A brief review of dissonance theory may clarify those psychological mechanisms which are described as ego defenses.

Dissonance was described as psychological discomfort in the context of post-decision behavior. In that context, the source of the psychological discomfort was outside the individual, for the most part. The individual defended against disruption of inner harmony which was threatened by feelings of dissonance between negative and positive attractions of alternatives existing in the environment. Another source of psychological discomfort is explained by the ego psychologists as coming from within the individual, that is, from one's own unacceptable motives.

For example, in situations in which a person's actions cause others inconvenience or actual pain, the person is frequently called to account for such behavior. There may be a number of reasons for the behavior. The person may have been trying to protect other people from some contagious disease, and the behavior of bringing them together, administering medication, and so forth, was necessary for their greater good. The person's behavior may have been a result of an automobile accident in which the individual responsible for the accident was swerving out of the way of a reckless driver. In this instance the person usually is extremely regretful and sorry for himself or herself and for everyone else involved in the accident. Another person may deny responsibility for the inconvenience or the pain caused to others, despite the fact that responsibility rests with that individual. Another individual may justify the behavior through rationalization, which deals with motives in such a way as to suggest that the person responsible for the behavior is entirely on the side of the angels.

The last two explanations for the behavior, denial and rationalization, are examples of unconscious maneuvers designed to defend the person against knowing inner motives. Irving Sarnoff defines that configuration of perceptual and motor skills which enables the person "to maximize the reduction of the tension of his motives within the scope of the constraints of his environment"[30] as the ego. From this point of view, the ego is responsible for accurate perception of the individual's own motives and those social prescriptions for acceptable tension reduction: ego functions are viewed as including perception, cognition, and other characteristics of reality testing. Accurate perception of the individual's own motives is threatened when the individual either does not perceive, or cannot locate, acceptable tension-reducing channels in the environment. The individual, then, defends the ego by removing from consciousness those motives associated with the threat in an effort to maintain the perceptual functioning of the ego. Ego defenses are defined as protective responses, in this sense. One protects the self from knowing one's own motives because such knowledge would create considerable anxiety.

Although all ego defenses function to obliterate consciously unacceptable motives, two of them, denial and identification with the aggressor, perform this function by distorting the perception of the objects in the external environment. Thus, one way to avoid the threatening aspects of the environment is to fail to acknowledge their presence.

Some ego defenses function to eliminate the perception of the internal stimulus of the threatening internal impulses (motives) from the individual's conscious perception. When the individual cannot fully remove an internal motive from conscious perception through repression, he might then acknowledge the existence of the motive, but instead of attributing it to himself, he projects it on to others.[31]

The prototype of all ego defenses is repression, which differs from suppression. "In suppression we are making a deliberate effort to rid our minds, and certainly our communication, of a thought that has come to consciousness. In repression . . . the whole procedure is unconscious."[32] The person may be aware of the behavior which makes up the defense, but unaware of the purpose of the behavior.

The study of ego defenses is frequently associated with abnormal psychology; many people assume that all defensive maneuvers are presumed to represent deviations from natural or "normal" social functioning. The notion that protective defenses distort reality is sometimes taken to mean that people suffer some inner weakness, some lack of integrity. But most defensive maneuvers are "normal"; most are used to protect one's integrity. We can see this in examples of the two defenses first mentioned in the quotation, denial and identification with the aggressor.

People may block threatening events from consciousness temporarily through the use of denial and thereby gain time to deal with overwhelming crises in their lives. Those readers who have dealt with grief reactions will recognize the need people have to deny the loss of a loved one when first confronted with this truth. People need a little time to accept such an awesome event, which they feel as a serious threat to their inner wholeness. It is in the protest that frequently accompanies the denial that one senses the inner motivation to hurt as one has been hurt, to defend by attacking those who confront a person with this knowledge, and to blame the loved one for dying. In this situation, denial is not weakness nor is it "abnormal." Social workers learn to expect this first stage of grief and to give people time to engage in their denial.

Identification with the aggressor is a common maneuver used by children in play. Margaret Yeakel studied children's reactions to surgery through play situations in which children had the opportunity to repeat their versions of surgery on dolls

and toy animals; to do to these toys what they thought had
been done to them; to identify with the doctors and other hospital personnel, whose treatment of them was often perceived
by the children as a kind of assault on their physical integrity.
They had the opportunity to play out what many children might take years to work through in dreams, called
"nightmares."[33]

The third defense mentioned in the quotation is projection. The common human defense associated with projection is
called displacement. Most people are familiar with the
example of the individual who, at work, has been hurt by
others through verbal attack on work performance but has
been prohibited from fighting back, and who verbally attacks
the first member of the family encountered on returning home.
Such behavior illustrates displacement. Again, one can speculate that displacement is illustrated in the story of the man
who ran out of gas five miles from the nearest house, walked
this distance becoming increasingly angry, arrived at the
house, knocked on the door, and said to the person who
answered, "Keep your . . . damned gasoline!" What is displaced is the anger at himself. The assumption that he would
be met by an angry response displaces the anger and allows
him to place the blame for not having any gas on the unknown
person answering the door.

In both these examples, those who displaced their anger
were often able to reverse the behavior and to accept responsibility for it. In this event, the person returning home from an
unpleasant and trying day at work would get angry without
provocation, might elicit anger, a fight, but would still have
the ability to recover a sense of responsibility for initiating the
fight. This person could recognize the precipitating event as
the abuse suffered at work. The traveler who ran out of gas
would be faced with the reaction of the stranger he met at the
door and would try to extricate himself from an embarrassing
situation. This is to say that the common, human defensive
maneuvers are temporary and reflect the need to reduce tension felt as a threat to internal harmony.

We begin to see, in examples of displacement associated
with projection, why people's defensive behavior is often seen
as "deviant." The point is that it is as natural to defend

oneself from emotional pain as it is to defend oneself from physical pain. Indeed, many people describe emotional pain in physical terms. For example, "heartbreak" conveys the meaning of being hurt at the center of one's life, and leads people to suggest a number of actions that might ease the heartbreak. These include forgetting, turning the cause of the misery around and considering it a blessing in disguise, considering it not to be one's own fault, and so forth. There are common human defenses which are normal and which are characteristic of the social functioning of all people, from this point of view.

Implications for Self-Actualization and Growth Motivations

Psychoanalytic theory developed to explain behavior called mental illness; evaluations of mental illness often describe defensive behavior of long duration and great intensity. Such behavior defines symptoms, which are viewed as imposing their own demands on the person's relations with others; symptoms are seen as

leading to "as if" assumptions in the areas of distorted relationships. For example, the person acts "as if" others were criticizing him, or devaluating him, or depriving him of what is emotionally rightfully his, and so on, but also often assumes that this is the way it is, and there can be no other way. . . . finally the symptom is a form of communication to others, having as its special purpose to invite responses appropriate to the person's symptom pattern.[34]

The "as if" assumptions are the consequences of avoidance of painful knowledge about the self and about the outside world. Maslow clarifies this:

Inner problems and outer problems tend to be deeply similar and to be related to each other. Therefore we speak simply of fear of knowledge in general, without discriminating too sharply fear-of-the-inner from fear-of-the-outer. . . . this kind of fear is defensive, in the sense that it is a protection of our self-esteem, of our love and respect for ourselves. We tend to be afraid of any knowledge that could cause us to despise ourselves or to make us feel inferior, weak, worthless, evil, shameful. We protect ourselves and our ideal image of ourselves by repression and similar defenses, which are essentially techniques by which we avoid becoming conscious of unpleasant or dangerous truths.[35]

People may also defend against their human potential, their drive toward self-actualization. Perhaps people defend against knowledge of their essential goodness and creativity because this contains another kind of danger. Recognizing the drive to fulfillment of one's human potential may also create feelings of vulnerability; accepting one's difference, one's tendency to create something new, or to behave according to one's difference, makes one feel daring, "putting oneself on the line."

Everyone of our . . . creators . . . has testified to the element of courage that is needed in the lonely moment of creation, affirming something new (contradictory to the old). This is a kind of daring, a going out in front all alone, a defiance, a challenge.[36]

Because behavior which differs from normative expectations has often been equated with deviance, and deviance is often associated with mental illness, many people tend to think of behavior that differs from normative expectations in any way as motivated by some sort of destructive instinct. This notion suggests that since the causes of mental illness are associated with the unconscious into which unacceptable motives are repressed, people tend to define the unconscious as a mass of destructive energies ready to explode at any moment and to expel the contents of all that is evil. The unconscious is "also the source of creativeness, of art, of love, of humor and play,"[37] and of impulses to seek for knowledge on the basis of which to experience growth.

In this sense, then, psychoanalytic interpretations of ego defenses are sometimes misleading. Freud was concerned with curing aberrations in mental and emotional life which caused great pain to those whose behavior expressed them, or which blocked their growth. Looking for the motivation of this kind of behavior, he found dangerous impulses and motivations in the experiences of people who were struggling with unmet basic needs and unable to struggle with growth needs. "It is no wonder that such people should fear and even loathe their impulses which have made so much trouble for them and which they handle so badly, and that a usual way of handling them is repression."[38] All people are not engaged in pathology.

Defenses do not necessarily lead to symptom formation.

Allport emphasizes the openness of the individual human system to growth:

Deficit motives do, in fact, call for reduction of tension and restoration of equilibrium. Growth motives, on the other hand, maintain tension in the interest of distant and often unattainable goals. As such they distinguish human from animal becoming, and adult from infant becoming."[39]

Many people tend to confuse irrational responses to rational circumstances with rational responses to irrational circumstances. What is to be feared and defended against in the environment is the irrational tendency to place the responsibility for those conditions of life that block people's ability to reach their human potential on the individuals whose human potential is blocked. This tendency is what William Ryan describes as "blaming the victim."[40] The behavior of people who experience economic exploitation, have low incomes, live in overcrowded, inadequate housing, have inadequate education and poor health care, is frequently explained as deficit personality functioning. The cause is seen in the person, in the person's inability to control or to regulate motives, but the deficit exists in irrational social conditions. A person may behave in ways that are assessed as highly symptomatic of mental illness when no such symptoms are present. The behavior necessary to realize authentic, self-actualizing, productive maturity may, under irrational social conditions, look the same. Such behavior may be a response to growth drives, to maintain tension rather than to seek tension reduction of these drives.

The definition of the ego previously noted as "maximizing the reduction of the tension of . . . motives within the scope of the constraints of . . . environment"[41] identifies ego functioning with coping, adjusting, and adapting. Such definition narrows the explanation of defensive behavior to reduction of tension created by drives whose unacceptability to the individual is in response to the individual's inability to locate acceptable channels for their expression. The theory of ego defenses sensitizes us to the need to defend against inner or outer events which threaten to overwhelm the individual, and increases understanding of some common human defenses. The theory does not allow for much understanding of the unconscious motivations for growth since it is designed to explain irrational behavior derived from inner-motivated destructive impulses.

Allport and Maslow take exception to psychoanalytic explanations of the unconscious, pointing out that while "deficit motives" do require reduction of tension, growth needs are not necessarily adaptive or shaped by social reality, by what Sarnoff calls "social prescriptions." Further, it has been pointed out that the social reality for individuals may include expectations that they take the blame for adverse social conditions; this fact further complicates the usefulness of the psychoanalytic explanation of the unconscious. If conditions in the environment prohibit growth toward self-actualization of one's human potential, why should one be expected to adapt to such reality? If one does not adapt or adjust one's behavior to the expectations of such an environment, why should one be viewed as functioning from the standpoint of some internal deficit? Our understanding of human behavior must include the need to react to irrational circumstances by changing them in the service of growth needs. People who are upset by change may defend against it by perceiving the conditions in the environment as rational and the behavior to change conditions as irrational. They may see those who are trying to change adverse conditions as irrational people whose behavior stems from internal deficits.

Implications for the Social Worker

Freud and his followers were concerned with human misery at the level of individual perception. Psychoanalytic theory is preoccupied with "sickness" and those miseries attendant upon it. It is as though the environment is the same for all individuals and all problems stem from within the individual, who must consequently be changed to fit whatever social reality exists, to come to terms with reality. At the same time, the theory suggests that people adjust their perceptions of reality in order to change what they see in order to bring it into harmony with what the ego can tolerate.

The social worker who accepts the concept of social reality despite its elusive quality will understand that there may be few objective bases for deciding what reality is. Social reality is not constant; it is subject to interpretation according to the needs of many individuals and the ways in which they have organized their transactions. The environment is not constant; it is not the same for all people. People do not have equal opportunity to cope with, or to adapt their behavior to, the same environment for maximum growth satisfaction. Both the individual and the environment are subject to change. When environmental change is threatened, group forces operate to reduce tension and to place the blame for the tension on the individual. We have shown the implications of group pressures toward conformity and the difficulties they pose for individuals whose natural tendencies, or growth needs, push them to test reality.

This also raises the question of overgeneralizing from one or another theoretical premise, of categorizing all human events by one or another explanation, of seeing in all behavior which deviates from social norms (the expectable "shoulds" and "oughts," the "normal") an expression of some basic personality problem. The following section deals with a systemic view of social organization, which helps to clarify the causes of the tendency toward such overgeneralization.

Social Reality and a Systems View of Large Social Organizations

William Gordon suggests that social workers should direct their interventions to the interface between the individual and the environment.

The best transactions are those that promote natural growth and development of the organism and also are ameliorative to the environment. Ameliorative here means making the environment more conducive to the growth and development of other members of the human species.[42]

Up to this point we have emphasized the individual and those groups to which the individual belongs or aspires to belong, or to which the person belongs by reason of location in the social structure. Discussion of the individual's environment has

focused attention primarily upon that environment which is
experienced in immediate transactions with others and has
illustrated problems at the level of their impact on the individual. Another important way to view human transactions in
the larger organized society is defined by a social systems
framework, or by explanations of social systems. This view is
critical to understanding those transactions that ameliorate
problems in social organization. The term "system" is so much
a part of many people's vocabulary that its application to
human affairs is often taken for granted, without attempts to
explicate its meanings. Let us begin, then, by calling attention
to some of the implications of the notion of a social system.

When one calls something a system, one is referring to the
interdependence and mutual interaction of a number of elements. The elements in a system complement each other and
make it possible for the system to achieve its goal. Most terms
used to describe systems are taken from physical systems, such
as electrical or heating systems. Each part of the system is
part of the whole, and if something goes wrong in one part, the
whole system will be affected; that is, a short circuit in one
part of an electrical system will shut down lighting, and the
lighting shutdown is a result, or product, of the intricate mesh-
ing of many components that work interdependently. An
electrical system cannot be understood by examining one
component in isolation from the system of which it is a part.
The complex components of an electrical system—generators,
transformers, and so forth—are subsystems of the electrical
system in its entirety. In themselves, they are units of other
interdependent and interconnected components. If one is
thinking solely about the generator, one may think of it as a
system which is contained in the larger electrical system. Such
a system contained within a larger system is referred to as a
subsystem when the focus is on the whole system.

Human interaction systems are also made up of complex
components that are mutually dependent and therefore complementary to each other. These systems have boundaries; for
example, we can distinguish among the family system, the
educational system, the welfare system. All identifiable human
relationship arrangements are organized for some purpose, but
their boundaries are not always rigidly defined. That is, most
human relationship systems are open to influence, to evalua-

tion, and to change in organization terms. For example, in their work with individuals, social workers often recognize that they have access only to a very small part of a subsystem and need access to other parts, such as an individual's family, the school, the court, and other subsystems in the community. Social workers also work with some systems that appear to be completely closed to outside influences. Closed systems are totally dependent on forces already present within them. They do not allow for feedback into the system. Open systems are open to evaluation and to change, but a major problem in bringing about change is the need of systems to maintain balance among their components. In this sense, the individual's striving for consistency can be used as an example of the ways in which the larger social system can distort reality in order to maintain the complementary transactions among those groups which compose it. Much of this striving is carried on through transactions in identifiable groups of individuals whose own life together is characterized by pressures to maintain interconsistency, which we characterize as "shared images" of reality.

Social systems frequently depend on institutionalized behaviors in order to perpetuate their functioning. Institutionalized behaviors are those which have happened again and again until they are below the level of people's awareness. People often do not question the "oughts" and the "shoulds" of their behavior within the system because they are taken for granted; they are normative and therefore they are viewed as "normal." Indeed, people often cannot even conceive of the possibility of questioning what is taken for granted; they cannot think of questions that might be asked. When individuals or groups, components of a social system, change their behavior, they are often viewed as deviant and subject to reprisal. Frequently, in order to maintain itself, the system needs people to behave in ways that are not conducive to growth. Let us look at an example that illustrates these aspects of system dynamics.

Information Dependence and the Right to Know

The notion that knowledge is available, on the basis of which to make accurate judgments about the nature of social reality, is often misleading. There are instances in which the information needed in order to take action is simply not available.

The way in which individuals view themselves and others is dependent on information they have about themselves and about other people. Efforts to test social reality are, in large measure, efforts to get information on the basis of which one can feel confident of one's assessments of what reality is. People make judgments and take assertive action on the basis of the information they have, and they will be uncertain and hesitant to act when information is not clear or not available. The ways in which people behave can be seen as an index of the information they have about themselves, about others, and about situations within which behavior takes place. The reader will recall the discussion of the need people have for clear information in order to be free to make choices.

Harold Kelley, a social psychologist, presents the general view that

a person (A) is informationally dependent on another person (B) if B can raise A's level of information to a higher level than A can attain from other sources. . . . In general, an individual may be expected to seek information when his information drops below the level that he expects to be able to attain. These information-seeking activities lead to increased interaction with other persons upon whom the individual is informationally dependent.[43]

People are subject to considerable social influence from those on whom they depend for information. The more uncertain one is, the more dependent one will be on what others know, and the more easily one will be influenced by others' knowledge. Dependence on consensus in groups is associated with persuasion, and people who lack knowledge on which they can depend are more likely to be persuaded to see things as others see them, whether or not what others see is based on accurate perceptions of what actually exists. The impact of access to information on system change is evident in the following example of the operation of the public welfare system in regard to information sharing.

Welfare clients have considerable difficulty finding out what rights they have to obtain assistance under federal and state legal requirements. This fact led to the development of the welfare rights movement. The welfare rights movement was designed to inform the clients of welfare agencies about what their rights were, to provide information on the basis of which they could obtain needed assistance, and to promote the organization of self-help groups of welfare clients who could engage in action to obtain these rights. The movement developed from observations that welfare clients were unable to obtain accurate knowledge from those who had access to it and who were responsible for applying it in their administration of services to welfare agency clients. Blocked from obtaining it from those in charge of granting assistance, welfare clients compared what they had learned with other welfare clients and reinforced partial, and misleading, information in this dependence on each other. Social workers, who were largely responsible for the welfare rights movement, intervened in this consensual activity, providing accurate data to large groups of welfare clients. They also directed the energies of welfare clients toward organized demands to obtain their rights.

This example points to a number of levels on which information dependence operates. First, the difficulty in getting information suggests that those who had it withheld it. This idea describes a situation in which those who have information maintain control over those who need it. The transactions in this situation take place within a hierarchical relationship arrangement; the closer one is to the top of this hierarchy, the more information one has, and the closer one is to the bottom, the less one has. In order from top to bottom, then, those with the least amount will be most uncertain, most hesitant to act, and most vulnerable to social control by those in higher positions to whose information they do not have access. Those at the bottom of the hierarchy will seek knowledge from others like themselves to whom they do have access, with the consequence that their problem-solving energies, based on inaccuracies about themselves, are ineffectual.

We need to look beyond the interactions between the welfare clients to understand the larger system dynamics of this example. Those who determine the rights of people to public assistance and those who apply these determinations in

their work with welfare clients are presumed to have the
needed information. They have the power to determine who
gets assistance. They are in control, and they defend their
right to control through a process of rationalization. The institutionalized rationalization for this social control is based on
the belief that welfare clients are somehow inadequate and
incompetent people who understand very little about how legal
procedures are implemented, and who need protection from
information which would confuse them or which they might
misuse. This belief is reinforced by the responses of many
clients whose knowledge of requirements of the welfare system
is so limited that they cannot formulate the kinds of questions
that might alert those at the top of their real ability to participate in a reasonable discussion of their rights. The distortion is also reinforced by a great many people in the society
who persist in comparing their own economic welfare with that
of welfare clients who are not faring well. The nonwelfare
clients, then, enhance their own sense of well-being. The
process is reminiscent of the concept of relative deprivation
which underlies comparative reference group theory. It is as
though people feel better about themselves when they can
compare themselves with people who are in greater trouble.

The problem thus goes beyond the welfare clients and the
workers who see them in welfare offices. The behavior takes
place in a larger organizational and institutional context. In
this context, behaviors are so highly institutionalized that they
cannot be understood by analyzing the responses of welfare
clients and workers in isolation from the social system in which
they occur.

Comprehending the shift in context, from the individual
and the group of individuals who share the same images and
sense of vulnerability, to the needs of the system of which individuals and groups are components, calls on us to look at different levels of transaction. An individual welfare client and an
individual welfare worker in the larger welfare system may
engage in behavior which is not characteristic of the outcomes
of information channeling we have described. A welfare worker
who does not wish to withhold information from a client, or
who is sympathetic to the latter's need for information, may be
accessible to the client, may give as much information as that

worker has to give, and may set out to defend the client's rights with those at each successive level of the hierarchy, with only relative success.

Very likely most people have heard of welfare workers, usually social workers, who find loopholes in the requirements, or ways of getting around the system by reinterpreting the client's responses to questions about need so that the client will receive more aid. Such activity is a way of coping with the requirements of the system, of seeing the system as a problem *to* the worker and the client, rather than seeing the system *with* its problems and confronting those problems. Such behavior does not change the rules and regulations that affect all welfare clients. On the other hand, the organizing of all, or the majority, of welfare clients for the purpose of confronting the problems in the system has brought about some changes in the welfare system.

How shall we understand such changes? When we look at the system in its entirety, we have in mind that welfare clients are one component of the welfare system, and that all of the system components are interdependent and complementary. Thus when welfare clients change their expected behavior, other behaviors in the system are also subject to change. Other components of the system which are complemented by the expected behavior of welfare clients, and which depend upon the perpetuation of that behavior, are thrown out of balance. Of course, those rationalizations which justify treating welfare clients as inadequate people whose behavior has to be controlled will become more obvious as the other components of the system, including most people who are not on welfare, whose nonwelfare boundary is dependent on having people on welfare, struggle to maintain the system as it is. As people get more upset, they attribute more and more negative characteristics to welfare clients who are "getting out of control." Confrontation in some local welfare offices is pictured as violent threats to the physical integrity of welfare workers, and so forth.

The forces in group life that restrain people from behaving in some ways and that propel them to behave in other ways are critical to the definition of social reality. The ways in which people view themselves as actors in organized social life is

developed out of reality testing, which is an active searching
for knowledge about what reality is. All components of human
systems have a limited number of possible actions open to
them, but they also have some choices within these limitations. Welfare clients were alerted to their choices through the
welfare rights movement. From this perspective, we can
examine the effect of the choice, made by many welfare clients
in large cities, to confront the system.

In some cities, welfare rights groups patterned their
organized responses after those of the controlling system
components. They joined together to demand their rights on
legal grounds. They used information as a way of controlling
the behavior of those in power. They took the adversary position, brought legal suits against the officially sanctioned
agents of the welfare system, and in many instances they
changed the nature of the communication between these
agents and welfare clients. Such activities helped to bring
to public awareness institutionalized behaviors that had
systematically denied rights to welfare clients. In these cities,
well-organized groups of welfare clients were able to obtain
public funds through state auspices for purposes of disseminat-
ing information about welfare rights to welfare clients. Some
welfare clients, acting as representatives of the welfare rights
organization, also obtained space within welfare offices, where
they functioned as resource persons to other welfare clients,
using their knowledge of legal provisions to assure that other
clients obtained their rights.

This example illustrates human transactions, within a
social system, which depend on expected behavior that
expresses complementarity between and among its components. The example shows how the expected behaviors of
welfare clients in the welfare system are complementary to the
controlling components of the system, and how a change in the
expected behavior of that component challenges the balance of
the system. At the point at which welfare clients confronted
those who controlled their right to knowledge, those defensive
rationalizations on the basis of which knowledge was withheld
were challenged. In this instance, we saw some change, for
some groups of welfare clients, in the behavior of those in control of the system. However, the pressures toward conformity

of welfare clients to the role behaviors expected of them still exist in the welfare system, for the most part. The next chapter will discuss in more depth the dynamics of systems in terms of expected role behavior, and those social-organizational factors that determine the roles people are expected to play.

Social Role

The term "role" describes an actor's responses to other actors. The word has its root in the Latin word for the roller about which a parchment was rolled and from which an actor read.[1] The root meaning of the word "actor" can be traced to the Greek word *persona*, which described the masks people wore in order to identify the characters they portrayed in the early Greek theater. The reader may recognize the term *dramatis personae*, which is still used to designate the characters in a play by denoting the role a person enacts in the drama.[2] Anyone who has tried out for a role in a play will know how it is to audition, or to read for the role from the script.

In a metaphorical sense, there is a kind of script for all the roles we play in our lives. Perhaps it is not by accident that we refer to different phases of human development as life stages. The questions of whether we read the scripts we want to read, whether we get the parts we want to play on these life stages, whether we have any chance to try out for the roles we play in our lives, are rarely raised. In fact, there is very little time to audition. If tryouts are scheduled, they are not available to everyone, and it is difficult for many people to gain access to the places where such tryouts are held. The freedom with which we choose the roles we play, and the freedom we experience to imbue them with our own style of acting, is often quite limited. How much freedom we have depends, in large measure, on our location in the social structure, on the availability of roles we want, and on the need people have for someone to play them.

By definition, social roles are not played in isolation. It is the relationship of one's own perception of a role one is performing to its perception by others that largely determines the nature of one's social functioning. In this human drama in which we are all engaged, there are not very many stars, and most of us play supporting parts of one kind or another. The social psychological premise is that there are internal determinants that push people to take on certain roles reflected in their aspirations and real abilities. But society tends to assign roles to individuals according to its needs.

The term "status" is often used interchangeably with "role." Although both role and status are always linked together, they have somewhat different meanings. Status indicates "the individual's location in a given framework of a hierarchy of positions"; role indicates "how the individual is expected to behave in that status."[3] It is possible for us to hold in mind at the same time a whole series of images which denote very intricate patterns of interaction between roles without individualizing the people who are playing them. If one simply says to oneself the word "hospital," for example, one can envision doctors, nurses, aides of all kinds, patients, and so forth. An interesting mental exercise is involved in this. One usually begins at the top of the hierarchy and adds role images from the most to the least important role performances defined by the authority structure of a hospital. And one does not have to put actual persons in the roles; one does not have to recall a particular doctor or nurse or patient in order to conceptualize the whole system. A hospital is a formal organization which may be viewed structurally as an interlocking complex of positions. As in any formal organization, these positions "represent the functional divisions of labor deemed useful to achievement of the system's goals and are populated by a collection of particular individuals each of whom occupies at least one . . . of them."[4]

The content of the position has behavioral implications for those who occupy the position. Each person in the organization has a role which is defined by the roles of other actors and which is dependent upon the roles of related others in the social context. The survival of the organization depends upon the links between the roles of the various actors. The doctor in a hospital needs patients, patients need doctors, and so forth. Position-role differentiation refers to complementarity. This can be seen in a family system in which actors perceive themselves and all the other actors in the family in more or less complementary terms. For example, the role of father presumes complementary roles, such as child and mother. Keeping in mind that the role indicates how the father is expected to behave, then, the role of father is expected to fit, or to be complementary to, the child's or the mother's expectations of the role. The family system in which the actors are cast in these roles is a highly traditional one. Some parental roles follow a child-mother, or child-father, script which can lead to a severely limited resolution of conflict in the family drama when children change their roles to those of adults, and parents continue to play the roles of mother and father as though adults were still children. Husband-wife and mother-father scripts are presumed to express reciprocity described by mutually contingent exchange of satisfactions. But there are some conditions under which one partner may be expected to provide gratification to the other despite a lack of reciprocity. The family system is perceived in traditional terms as containing compensatory arrangements that provide means of controlling tensions arising from lack of reciprocity. For example, some parents believe they should stay together because of their duty to the children. Some parents appear to ban the examination of certain interactions among family members from the viewpoint of reciprocity and continue unequal exchanges with each other which are dysfunctional for all family members.

New family life styles which are receiving increasing acceptance in society attest to the fact that the boundaries of the family system are relatively open to change in role expectations. This suggests that the family system can survive a number of role changes which are complementary and which involve new forms of reciprocity, such as more freedom of choice in role behavior for women. However, families are components of the larger society, and when new family roles emerge, other role behavior which is linked to the roles of family members is thrown out of balance. In the example of the welfare system we showed that when individuals or groups which are components of formal social organizations change the behavior which is expected of them according to their position in the social organization, other components of the organization must also change.

The individual plays many roles. The person's role set combines many individual roles. At any one time, individuals usually occupy age, sex, and family roles of one sort or another in addition to a number of other roles—occupational roles, for example. The roles occupied by any one individual may be clearly defined, or they may be unclear and difficult for the individual to comprehend. They may be complementary or conflicting; they may be more or less reciprocal. Social roles may change abruptly without preparation, and they may involve sudden redirection of one's understanding of what is expected by others. The roles one plays in one's life may also change gradually and smoothly through the course of life's ages and stages. Individuals might be well-prepared to play a role and never have the opportunity to play it for reasons quite outside their own choice. They may choose to play roles which they do not wish to play because of pressures to conform. Certain life stages give the players clear-cut cues and signals as to when to make their contribution, and at these stages players are often assured of high praise if they read "the script" well. At other stages there are few clear-cut roles. For example, few, if any, significant role expectations exist for aged persons in our society.

Role Continuity and Discontinuity

Earlier, in discussion of the self-concept, we saw that Erikson's views of identity included a striving for continuity in order somehow to synthesize the self that one was, and is, and wants to be. The roles one plays are symbolic indicators of one's social identity. This does not mean that one *is* what one is defined to be by nature of one's social roles, but our perceptions of who we are and where we belong are very much involved in the roles by which we are most often identified by others. Many mothers, for example, have longed to say to devoted children and husbands, "There is more to me than you see—I am not just a mother and a wife—even without all that, there's a person here."

The problem of continuity, of integrating past and present, is concerned, in part, with learning enough about what to expect so that the transitions from one role to another can be experienced as part of oneself. Operationally, continuity in role expectations means that "the child is taught nothing it must unlearn later."[5] That is, the child is taught enough about what will be expected of it later so that those expectations will not be perceived by the child as discontinuous. Discontinuity involves both contradictions in expectations and the absence of preparation for future roles.

Discontinuity is the basis of many human problems. There are a number of ambiguities in the social learning we expect people to accomplish, especially during childhood. Most children are prepared by religious teachings, or by significant caretakers, not to cheat or to hate or to kill others, for example. These behaviors are then encouraged in a highly industrialized military complex which approves of killing enemies in war and of undercutting one's competitor in business dealings. Love and hate may be on the same continuum and can be interchanged. We frequently tend to expect people to behave in ways for which they are ill-prepared. Later discussion of stages of human development will develop this theme, especially with regard to attitudes built up in early life toward sexuality and sex roles.

"Who am I" strivings are also involved with a sense of knowing where one is going as well as where one is. Of course, this depends on having somewhere to go, on a supportive social situation, on the availability of roles which one wants and which one can play. Role continuity and the struggle to find a place to belong in society depend on the provision of rites of passage. This society provides few such transitional transactions. For example, common American rites of passage are sadly lacking for the majority of young people, who are not quite children and not quite adults. Those that do exist are not available to everyone. The most clearly helpful transitional rites are marked by religious ceremonies, such as bar mitzvah and confirmation, and by graduation ceremonies which mark

educational achievements. In the wisdom of society, graduation ceremonies are called "commencements," presuming new
beginnings. But many people are not welcomed into adult
roles. Even those who are, sometimes have great difficulty
fulfilling the expectation that they will take on some meaningful occupational role, because of the sheer unavailability of
such roles. This depends, in large measure, on where people
are located in the social structure. Certain groups are located
at lower, and other groups are regularly located at higher, positions in the structure. The general consensus in the society is
that those who occupy middle- or upper-income positions work
harder and better, are more competent than those in the lower
income groups and therefore maintain these positions. This
differentiation is complementary to the goals of the society; it
is not a function of individual or group superiority. Inaccessibility of roles which have high valuation in the society
accounts for the unemployed status of a majority of young
black people.

Role discontinuity is a major cause of the inability of
many aged persons to continue social functioning at the level
of their previous work roles. The collective wisdom of this
society, and of most Western societies, has little to bring to
bear on the problem. Social roles are ascribed to most other
stages, at least in terms of expectations. Childhood is
presumed to be ended after high school begins. High school is
generally perceived as leading to work or to college, and college
is perceived as leading to more specialized occupational roles
for most people. Adults are generally expected to marry and
play caretaker roles in families. Some adults may have careers
without family responsibilities. All these transitions are
fraught with problems, but none of these stages is lacking in
role expectations. The middle years are less clearly defined in
role terms by the society than are preceding stages, but the
last stage in life is the least clearly defined of all the stages of
life. All other stages are on a more gradual succession. They
tend to call up images of expectations, at least, and suggest
which constraints one may have to fight against. Few people
are prepared for the last stage of life, and role discontinuity is
a result of this.

Acquiring Roles through Social Learning

The reasons it is difficult to have direct influence on role expectations are implied in the ways in which roles are acquired through social learning. Some roles—for example, roles of social worker, doctor, lawyer—are learned in formal structures such as schools, hospitals, and courts. In such structures, roles are learned verbally and by abstractions. They are often taught by others in the roles, by field instructors, directors of interns, judges in whose law offices beginning lawyers serve. Roles are also learned in informal structures, such as families, in which role relationships are much more general. In families, in subsequent peer groups, and other groups of significant others, knowledge is transferred at a preconscious level. Roles tend to be learned as total gestalts rather than with respect to parts. Without breaking roles down and building them back up in verbal and abstract terms, these groups are highly influential in role learning.

Roles are also learned by near approximations in apprentice fashion, through imitation. In stabilized social systems, groups with which a role is actively to be played usually participate in the educational process. Field instruction in social work education, or internship in medical education, for example, illustrate the participation of members of professional organizations in the induction of students into the roles for which they are preparing. All these forms of role learning can overlap and usually do.

Certain components of roles reinforce the behavior expected as people play them, and these aspects of role learning also underlie the difficulties involved in influencing people to distance themselves from the roles they play and to change them. A role has aspects of the proscribed. It is interesting in this connection to consider what is proscribed that one cannot do, what the social situation forbids. While it is hoped that students will learn by attending school, they cannot maintain the role of student if they miss too many of their classes. A role has within it values which range in intensity of value judgments, and this underlies an important dichotomy in role definition, namely, roles that are achieved and roles that are ascribed.

Theodore Sarbin analyzed the implications which ascribed and achieved roles have for social identity.[6]

Ascribed Roles

According to Sarbin, very little positive value is assigned to individuals for the enactment of ascribed or granted roles. For example, an individual is not praised for participating in society as an adult. Persons are expected to enact the role without public acclaim. This is true of a number of roles considered to be stage-specific and which are generally taken for granted and enacted without expectations of financial reward or special recognition. Nevertheless, the nonperformance of such roles elicits a great deal of negative valuation.

Consider the valuations made when a male fails to perform according to the expectations for masculine sexuality; consider the sanctions imposed when a mother fails to be interested in the care and welfare of her children; consider the value-judgments rendered upon people who fail to act according to age standards; consider the value assigned to a man who publicly insults his father; and so on. . . . role requirements are perceived as being violated, the individual holding the minimal granted position is negatively valued and marked with a pejorative label. There are many forms of the label, and they all denote the social identity of a non-person. That is to say, if the pejorative label is applied, then the society goes to work to treat the individual as if he were not a person.[7]

Sarbin suggests some of the labels which barely disguise negative valuations: "slum-dwellers, low-class, schizophrenic, charity cases, welfare recipients."[8] Such labels identify persons by categories of expectations which are negatively valued. They tend to identify people by a degraded social identity. One could challenge this claim on the premise that it all depends on one's own perspective of the meaning of such labels; that is, one might not use them to degrade anyone. The point is that they classify people according to a generalized, negative consensus.

Achieved Roles

A great deal of positive value is assigned to individuals for the enactment of achieved roles. These are roles, such as professional roles of all kinds, that afford a great deal of free movement and choice.

In general, negative valuations are not applied to people who fail in their attempts at validating statuses heavily weighted with choice, such as occupational and recreational statuses. Being fired from a job, dropped from a team or dismissed from college does not enrage or perturb a community. The responses to such outcomes of nonperformance may be formalized as failure, underachievement, poor judgment, or misfortune, and noted with verbal expressions of sadness, disappointment, sympathy, regret, and so on. On the other hand, the proper performance of role behaviors at the choice end earns tokens of high positive value, such as Nobel prizes, public recognition, monetary rewards, and other indications of esteem.[9]

Achieved roles are associated with highly valued social identity. They can be differentiated from ascribed roles by the freedom with which they are chosen and by the high esteem in which people who play them are held. They can also be identified by the extent to which the actors are involved in role enactment. Ascribed roles are associated with behavior which is highly involving and leaves little freedom to enact additional roles. To be cast in the role of a prisoner, or a mental patient in a state hospital, or an unemployed worker means being in the role nearly all the time. At the achieved or choice end of role enactment one may be involved in the role at some times and not at other times.[10] The extent to which people have freedom to choose the roles they can play and want to play is rarely considered as a determinant of role behavior.

Freedom of Choice in Role Behavior

Roles which carry expectations of highest involvement are those with least freedom of choice. Freedom of choice is closely tied to the availability and accessibility of roles which people want and which they are able to play. Large groups of people in the society are assigned to play roles which fit the organizational plan by which the society is designed but which do not fit the growth needs of people. There are factors within individuals—their aspirations and abilities, their inner drive for self-actualization—that propel them to take on certain roles. And there are factors in the social structure that determine the roles which society needs to have played in order to achieve its goals. For example, reports of discussions among economic advisers to the President regarding the percentage of unemployment needed to contain inflation attest to this point. It appears that a certain percentage of the population is needed to be unemployed in the over-all economic plan.

Unemployment is therefore institutionalized in this society; some people are always cast in the role of unemployed persons. The role is given negative valuation. It is assumed that the majority of people in this role have freedom of choice in the matter. The purpose of the campaign to decrease the number of people who receive direct grants-in-aid as welfare recipients is to get people who are assumed not to want to work to take employment. The fact that the majority of people on welfare rolls are elderly persons, persons who are physically disabled, and children, does not seem to make any difference to those who support the campaign.

But not all victims of unemployment are blamed for their plight. Ryan discusses the implications of victim blaming in this connection.[11] Many attitudes toward the poor, those who are relatively powerless to change their life conditions, are firmly held beliefs that people somehow deserve the misery that goes along with these conditions. These are attitudes, anchored in feelings about morality issues, which are acquired through social learning. It is those people who have the least freedom of choice and the fewest opportunities to work who are most likely to be blamed for being unemployed. People at the achieved end of the role continuum who do not work are not likely to be negatively valuated. This is the sense in which social reality defines what most people believe. It is an instance of pluralistic ignorance in which almost everybody applies negative valuations to welfare clients, but few people test the reality of the belief that leads to negative valuation.

Social Roles and the Maintenance of Social Systems

The definition of a social system was introduced in the last chapter. We have seen that all behavior takes place in an organizational and institutional context and that the system over all contains some unique characteristics not found among its individual components. These interdependent system components have a common boundary which identifies the system of which they are a part. The elements of a system have their own internal network of communication and are linked in such a way that a change in one affects the entire system. Each component in a system has a limited number of possible interactions open to it but also has some choice within this limitation. We have noted that welfare clients were free to organize to obtain their right to information. This was the space of free movement they had as components of the larger welfare system. They engaged in behavior which provided some feedback into the system in an effort to spark it to change its internal structure and to adapt to new conditions. The behavior in which they engaged was a change from their expected role behavior.

The role performances of individuals are determined by the social system which defines the formal organization, and social role performances are also the means by which the social system is defined. At each level of organization in the society, it is possible to evaluate the extent to which individuals are enacting roles according to expectations which fit the needs of that level of organization. For example, we can identify the differences in role expectations of parents in families, teachers in the educational system, and legislators in the political system. The roles of parents complement the family system but would not complement the expectations of the educational or political system. Role behavior which deviates from what is expected helps to define the boundaries of social systems that depend upon complementary role behavior.

The Role of the Deviant in the Social System

Deviance is defined in both psychological and social terms; it has many labels. All these labels categorize behavior which differs from behavior that is routinely expected and which therefore is seen as "normal." Although most people conduct their human relationships as though what is "normal" and what is "abnormal" are clearly defined, many ambiguities are associated with the definition process. This process is carried on through numerous transactions between those who do the defining and those whose behavior is defined.

At the level of the microsystem such evaluative transactions occur within the boundaries of individuals and small groups. At the mezzosystem level such evaluative transactions occur within the boundaries of larger groups identified by common characteristics, such as neighborhoods, wider geographical communities, or more formally constituted organizations which link individuals and small groups to the whole society, to the macrosystem. The macrosystem level is the broadest level of formal social organization; it extends beyond individuals, groups, and intermediary organizations. At this level, criteria for the assessment of deviance are associated with the rules and regulations which define and order the social relationship arrangements within the society. At each level, the process of defining expected role behavior is complicated by both a tolerance and an intolerance for behavior which deviates from normative expectations and by the social needs deviants serve.

The labeling process. We have seen that people are socialized into expecting their behavior and the behavior of others to complement social norms within some generally accepted space of free movement. This space for free choice may be limited by life conditions over which the person has little control. In general, most people tend to expect of themselves what others expect of them, and for some people in the society,

a realization occurs, whether suddenly or gradually, that they are less or will be treated as less than they have learned to expect of and for themselves, and that the frustration of these ingrained expectations is due to the possession of an attribute that functions as a social stigma. Defining themselves as persons who will run a particular race, they come to find that they have been partly disqualified and involuntarily reidentified in terms of their disqualification. The new category to which they find they belong separates them from those whom they thought they were like, and brings them together with those from whom they previously differed.[12]

This describes the process of assigning individuals to the role of the deviant. These individuals find they belong to the deviant category through comparative evaluation of what is expected of their behavior with the expected behavior of others who are nondeviants. This process usually begins at the microsystem level.

At the microsystem level any individual evaluator may understand the behavior of the deviant actor through efforts to take this actor's perspective. A person may try, for example, to assume the role of the other, to "get into the other's shoes." In this instance, the evaluator tries to become empathic, sensitized to the motivation of the other's behavior. To the extent that the individual evaluator's frame of reference includes life experiences which make it possible to put the self in the place of the other, these efforts may succeed. When such efforts fail, the person is likely to categorize or label the behavior. David Mechanic observes:

It is primarily in those cases where the evaluator feels at a loss in adequately empathizing with the actor and where he finds it difficult to understand what attributed to the response that the behavior is more likely to be labeled "queer," "strange," "odd," or "sick."[13]

The label may have more or less impact on the person's social identity. For example, labeling individuals as "sick" may identify them as physically ill or as mentally ill. Physical illness is likely to receive positive responses from others in the form of sympathy, encouragement to get well, and general acceptance of the cause as being outside the person's control. Mental illness elicits different responses and is generally negatively evaluated. The popular conception of mental illness is not the same as the conception of physical illness.

A great many people continue to invest mental illness, for example, with stereotypical responses which do not suggest any real human suffering. People who are evaluated as mental patients are frequently seen simply as mentally inadequate and dangerous to other people. Responses of those related to the mental patient often reflect embarrassment and fear of association. These responses locate the sick role of the mentally ill person within a social context.

In earlier discussion of defensive behavior we indicated that mental illness was diagnosed on the basis of evaluation of symptoms which describe defensive behavior of long duration and intensity viewed as destructive to the person and to others in the person's life. This is the basis on which those specialized in evaluating psychological pathology usually make such diagnoses. If we look closely at the behavioral implications of many physical illnesses we can see that they are also destructive to the person and may be destructive to others. For example, some illnesses may be contagious and some may be terminal. If mental illness is indeed "illness," we should see a fairly close correspondence between responses to physical and to mental illness.

The tendency of many lay people to evaluate behavior as "sick" suggests that the behavior they perceive presents a threat to their own self-consistency, which depends upon the ability to predict behavior of others. Role behavior has high predictability, and is assessed as deviant when it does not conform to what is expected. It is expected that a psychiatrist, specialized in diagnosis and treatment of mental illness, would be free of similar threats to self-consistency by reason of training and experience, and that the final evaluation of mental illness would be made by this specialist whose frame of reference is presumed to include different criteria for explaining deviant behavior as illness. But in many instances, especially during screening for admissions to large state mental hospitals, psychiatrists are heavily influenced by assessments made by those responsible for getting the deviant individual to the hospital.

In a study of the process of admitting patients to a number of large state mental hospitals, Mechanic found that

The layman usually assumes that his conception of "mental illness" is not the important definition, since the psychiatrist is the expert and presumably makes the final decision. On the contrary, community persons are brought to the hospital on the basis of lay definitions and once they arrive, their appearance alone is usually regarded as sufficient evidence of "illness."[14]

The person evaluated as mentally ill by community persons, then, frequently becomes a mental patient and is expected to play that role.

At the mezzosystem level, the role is associated with a subordinate minority whose status determines the expected role behavior. According to Scheff:

In order to understand the situation of the mentally ill . . . one could profit by comparing their position with that of other subordinate minorities. Psychological processes such as stereotyping, projections, and stigmatization, and social processes such as rejection, segregation, and isolation characterize, to some degree, the orientation of the in-group toward the out-group, regardless of the basis of distinction. The recurring cycle of exposé, reform and apathy in mental hospitals, the failure of mental health campaigns, and many other large-scale phenomena in the area of mental illness can be understood within the framework of the social processes connected with the formation of status distinctions.[15]

The status distinctions to which Scheff refers are those which often reidentify mental patients in overcrowded state hospitals as nonpersons. The role of mental patient in this situation is negatively valued, has very little space for free movement within it, and restrains the person from playing other roles. The rights of mental patients to knowledge of their diagnosis, of the treatment prescribed, and of the length of time they will be required to spend in hospitals are frequently denied. Recent developments in the area of patients' rights are based on a movement designed to organize patients to obtain rights to information about their illness. Legal suits have resulted in clear statements of patients' legal rights, but mental patients are extremely vulnerable and are much less likely to claim their rights than are people adjudged to be physically ill. In this connection, it is of critical importance to note that people who are most likely to be regarded as nonpersons are those whose life conditions are characterized by relative powerlessness associated with low income, inadequate housing, poor education, and racial discrimination. These are the people who are most likely to receive poor health care and whose human rights are most often violated.

Deviance as a function of system maintenance. At the level of the macrosystem, deviance has been traditionally described as system breakdown. It has been explained as

a vagrant form of human activity, moving outside the more orderly currents of social life. And since this type of abberation could only occur (in theory) if something were wrong within the social organization itself, deviant behavior is described almost as if it were leakage from machinery in poor condition: it is an accidental result of disorder and anomie, a symptom of internal breakdown.[16]

Kai Erikson takes issue with this traditional view. He observes that "the study of deviant behavior is as much a study of social organization as it is a study of disorganization."[17] Deviant behavior is not a result of disorder and breakdown. According to Erikson there is evidence that deviant activities can be absorbed into the system and that extreme deviant activities are needed by the system to maintain its boundaries. With regard to absorption of deviant activities into the system, Erikson observes that

deviant activities can generate a good deal of momentum once they are set into motion: they develop forms of organization, persist over time, and sometimes remain intact long after the strains which originally produced them have disappeared. In this respect, deviant activities are often absorbed into the main tissue of society and derive support from the same forces which stabilize other forms of social life. There are persons in society, for example, who make career commitments to deviant styles of conduct, impelled by some inner need for continuity rather than by any urgencies in the immediate social setting. There are groups in society which actively encourage new deviant trends, often prolonging them beyond the point where they represent an adaptation to strain. These sources of support for deviant behavior are difficult to visualize when we use terms like "strain," "anomie" or "breakdown" in discussion of the problem.[18]

There are groups within the system that resist the expectations of behavior of those who are relegated to subordinate minorities; these are the sources of support for deviance. We have shown that people are impelled by inner needs for continuity and for self-actualization. The pressures to conform to the expectations associated with the status of a nonperson may be so powerful as to make it impossible for individuals who have been relegated to this status to deviate from these expectations without supportive others. But the drive for self-continuity and the offer of support from groups are normal processes which can be absorbed within the system. The system is subject to continuing influence from social movements. We have seen the beginnings of system change illustrated by increasing tolerance for new family life styles, for increasing liberation of women, and indirectly of men, for recognition of the rights of welfare clients and of mental patients. The extent to which deviance from expected behavior can be tolerated depends on the permeability of system boundaries.

Actions which continue to represent adaptation to strain, which are supported by the existing expectations within the system and represent extreme differences from expected role behavior of the society, serve to define the boundaries of the social system. For example, enormous pressures brought to bear on the mental patient to take on the status of a nonperson may result in conformity on the part of the patient. Being regarded as a nonperson, the patient may come to regard himself or herself as less than human, thereby making those who are not mental patients appear more human by comparison. In this sense, the behavior defines the boundaries of the patient group and the nonpatient group.

All systems define their boundaries by the behavior of those people around whose interactions they are organized. For all its apparent abstractness, a social system is organized around the movements of persons joined together in

regular social relations. The only material found in a system for marking boundaries, then, is the behavior of its participants; and the form of behavior which best performs this function would seem to be deviant almost by definition, since it is the most extreme variety of conduct to be found within the experience of the group. In this respect, transactions taking place between deviant persons on the one side and agencies of control on the other are boundary maintaining mechanisms. They mark the outside limits of the area in which the norm has jurisdiction, and in this way assert how much diversity and variability can be contained within the system.[19]

The traditional view of deviance as a symptom of internal breakdown is disproved by evidences of the functions which deviance serves in the system. The system that is threatened by breakdown can only be rebalanced if deviance is eliminated. The system needs deviance to maintain its balance of forces. We have seen that deviance may be absorbed into the system and supported by the organizational forces within it. Deviance also serves to keep the system intact by defining its social behavioral boundaries. While boundary maintenance is necessary for survival of the system as it is at any particular moment, survival over the course of time is also dependent upon the support that deviant activities can derive from forces within the system, the nature of these activities, and their absorption into the system. Those who support system change work to open further the boundaries of the system. The time this takes depends upon the willingness of the majority in the society to change that role behavior which supports the system as it exists. Roles that support system boundaries are institutionalized. They are simply taken for granted; they are below the awareness of most of the people who play them. It is in the deinstitutionalization of social roles which are dysfunctional for all members of the society that the hope for macrosystem change lies. For purposes of illustration we have chosen to discuss in detail those social roles which have been used to perpetuate institutionalized racism in this society. This is an example of why racism has been perpetuated and the potential for change in the role behaviors which have perpetuated it in this society.

Institutionalization and Deinstitutionalization of Racism

Institutionalized racism is destructive to self-actualization of all people in society. The playing out of social roles which are needed to maintain it has developed through the socialization of the majority of the people. The frame of reference within which most members of the majority group regard the members of the minority reflects learned behaviors which operate as restraints on self-actualization. The attitudes of the majority toward the minority are firmly held beliefs rooted in feelings which are shared by significant groups of reference. These attitudes are supported by forces in the society associated with the need to maintain an underclass to take up the slack of unemployment, to maintain a mood of adaptation among low- and middle-income workers who see themselves as faring well in comparison with the underclass, and to function as an identifiable group onto whom members of the majority can displace their own unresolved social and psychological problems. A high degree of consensus among the majority group in the society reinforces these attitudes, which are expressed as opinions of the majority group about the minority group. This leads to considerable pressure toward uniformity of opinion. As a result, there is little space of free movement to test the social reality which represents what most people think and say and do.

The response of white people to the human relationships within which they live and work are defined, in part, by institutional racism. Both white and black people are locked into this system of relationships. White people are often viewed by black people as oppressors and as symbols of white power. As members of the dominant group in this society, many white persons remain relatively unaware of their contribution to the perpetuation of racism. Institutionalized behaviors which express it have happened again and again until they are below the awareness of many whites. These behaviors are a response to pressures to conform to the attitudes of the white society into which people have been born and in which they have been socialized. As a result, many whites tend to be willing to play roles which maintain the racist system that locks in everyone.

Most whites tend to go along with the myth of white power despite the fact that real power is held only by a few people, institutions, and corporations.[20] Other myths are deeply embedded in white history. Whites suffer from a confusion of heroism. Columbus Day, for instance, is celebrated despite the fact that there were people here to meet the boat of that early explorer, people to whom the country belonged. Of black history, white people learn very little. Until very recently, many white people did not consider the significance of the fact that the entry of blacks into this society was forced, that they were enslaved, and that they did not come here for a better life as did whites. They were systematically stripped of their names and their culture in the course of slavery. This was in contrast to the ancestors of white people who brought their cultural traditions along and were relatively free to feel, and to encourage their progeny to feel, ethnic pride.

Many whites are only vaguely aware that problems labeled "bussing" are problems associated with housing patterns and that low income, poor health care, inadequate housing, and poor education are combined in poverty for a majority of black people. These social conditions were caused and continue to be maintained by white people, and a large number of whites blame the victims of these conditions for their plight. The deficit model of personality functioning, used this way, is an institutionalized way of explaining many rational responses of black people, in this country, to the irrational institutions of racism.

Traditionally, white people have taken on two social roles in support of racism. Whites tend to be either pawns or patrons in the process of maintaining it.[21] Both roles are institutionalized. White persons have been confronted with these role expectations in two ways in recent years. The first is related to the participation of some of those whites who were activists in the civil rights movement of the 1960s. Some of these people experienced good feelings as liberals and then became disenchanted and resentful when black people organized their own liberation movements. The responses of these white people reflect the playing out of the patron role. Their subsequent sense of loss of role behavior which is highly valued and rewarded by our society attests to the importance of the role. Many white people have been pawns in perpetuating the myth of the white majority, and are now confronted with the truth of white minority status among world populations. This is being experienced in some quarters of white society as an assault on white social identity.

The foregoing is an illustration of the institutionalized roles which many white people are conditioned to play by nature of social learning. There is a supportive environment within which such roles are perpetuated. The social system supports these roles, but the expected behavior of the white majority is dysfunctional for both the majority and the minority. This is not apparent if we see role behaviors solely from the point of view of system dynamics. The psychological component of social role explains the need people have for freedom of choice to play roles which move their humanness ahead and the drive for actualization of the self in terms of human potential. Most readers are aware of the tragic implications racism has had for the lives of people who are black. The implications it has had for white people are less well-known.

Whites who have become conscious of their racial identity problems have recognized that racism is in the responses of white people to black people. The conversion experience of many blacks from "Negro to Black"[22] has played an important part in this. The black liberation movement has worked to liberate black people from the acceptance of those role behaviors which complement the pawn and patron roles. Black people have less need to refer their behavior to that of white groups for judgment and appraisal. Black reference groups are used for comparative appraisal of the behavior of black people. White persons can no longer be conflict-free since part of their own human integrity has been lost through the playing out of institutionalized roles associated with racism. The cost to whites of regaining it is not simply a material one. White social work students, for example, are not dedicated to the perpetuation of the superwealthy. When people are no longer willing to be pawns or patrons, they acknowledge the fixed roles they have been playing. Since they are not responsible for their history or for their socialization into a system that gave them little choice, they can bear to raise questions as to whether their whiteness can stand for anything positive and constructive.

The change from stereotypical whites to white people who are moving their own humanness ahead involves a kind of grief work for many white people. The loss of human dignity is implicated in the bad faith with which many whites have dealt with themselves and others. The grief process begins with denial and protest that anything of human integrity has been lost. The second phase is characterized by guilt and despair, and the third by integration of the loss into the continuity of self-actualization, in laying claim to the right to choose which roles to play.[23]

Implications for Social Work

The discussion of institutionalized racism suggests that those who work to change behavior associated with the perpetuation of racism learn to accept the fact that racism is institutionalized in the society. It is embedded in the way in which the society is organized; it is part of the social structure. It has both social and psychological implications.

Social workers, in large measure, direct their energies to changing the ways in which people behave. They frequently occupy positions at the boundaries of the social system, and they endeavor to keep these boundaries open. In the social agencies in which most social workers are employed, they serve to maintain open boundaries so that agency systems can be responsive to the social psychological needs of those who are served. Some social agencies are responsive to the needs of the consumers of their services. There is much to be learned from these agencies. Quite a different kind of learning is involved in social work with highly traditional agencies. In some of these agencies, the role of the social worker may involve the introduction of services which require that people change institutionalized role behaviors, especially those associated with the perpetuation of the role behavior of minority groups who have been relegated to a subordinate status. Many social workers are already at work in this area, but there is much more work to be done.

Those who introduce new role behavior into already established and highly traditional social agencies accustomed to viewing services in institutionalized ways have great difficulty changing role behavior which is dysfunctional. Introduction of new orientations to the delivery of social services requires a break with traditions which reflect the firmly held beliefs of people, rooted in feelings. Energies that are so organized and directed are not easily disengaged. The social worker responsible for part of the admission process to the state hospital or to the local detention center, for example, is frequently not in a role which has much space for free movement within it. The need for support from others is critical, if one is to survive within a system which appears to be closed to new procedures. If one refuses to conform to existing expectations of one's role performance, one may be seen as a deviant, and pressures toward uniformity will probably be applied. Social reality testing can then be quite difficult unless one has support from enough like-minded others to maintain self-consistency without distorting the situation. The person who can withstand pressures toward uniformity may test the social reality and decide to separate from it. In this instance, the person does not change or compromise integrity, but the situation does not change either.

If one stays in the situation, and uses even the small space for free movement within an existing role to promote change in the behavior of others in the service system, the effect of change may be quite disorganizing to these other actors. The conflict which is created is at the level of the social structural organization of services, but people may react to organizational conflict in psychological terms. In a sense, structure is human energy regarded in terms of the ways in which it is directed socially. People expect to have their energies structured by procedures which operate to institutionalize established rules and regulations. Structure binds anxiety; it protects self-consistency. People see others in relation to themselves and expect to complement the roles of others in the social organization of which they are a part. At the level of established and traditional institutions, one may find high reciprocity in role behavior. In this sense social role represents the structure on which people depend.

We have seen how dependent people are on signals and cues which they can understand, which can be interpreted within the frame of reference built from past experience. When a situation is changed, then, it is frequently reacted to as a new situation. People cannot then make thoughtful choices as to how to behave, and they may defend against change of any kind. If they are involved in changing the role structures to which they have become accustomed, however, they will understand the new situation because they have participated in creating it. But people often resist social change and will not participate in it unless the social forces which support traditional behaviors no longer support those behaviors. Thus, we see more change in behavior which discriminates against selected minority groups of people when social legislation requires such change than we see at the level of work with individuals or small groups to change social attitudes. Social workers who promote change in role behavior which is dysfunctional for the consumers of social services need to have knowledge of the forces in the society which propel and the forces which restrain those in traditional roles from changing them; only then are they likely to succeed in mobilizing to support changes in dysfunctional role behavior.

The concept of social role is the last link in the chain of concepts on which we have built a frame of reference within which the practice of social work can be guided. Throughout the presentation of the four concepts, the self, reference groups, social reality, and social role, we have indicated some of the ways in which each may be used to guide social work practice. Within the scope of this presentation, we did not attempt to cover the full range of implications these concepts may have for practice. In this section, the illustration of introducing new behavior into the existing role expectations of social agencies suggests the linking propensities of the concepts which we shall examine further.

Chapter 5

Linking the Concepts

The preceding chapters have developed, in some depth, four major concepts. Each of the four major concepts—self-concept, reference group, social reality and social role—has been selected as a focal construct because each provides a way of organizing the social worker's awareness of the diversity of forces that shape the behavior both of individuals and of groups. Each concept helps to explain a facet of the human experience of individuals that is significant for social workers. The social worker can understand the complexity of human experience only to the extent that the concepts that are linked in the worker's mind reflect that complexity. Linking the concepts for use requires a grasp of their capacity for explaining human behavior in terms both of the effects of the individual on the group, or on the social situation, and of the effects of groups or social situations on individuals. The connections between these concepts are made at the level of complexity at which both the individual and the social situation, or the environment, are assumed to be variable.

This level of complexity contrasts with the levels at which traditional sociologies and psychologies operate. For example, depth psychology assumes an average, expectable environment as constant. From this point of view, variations between and within individuals are conceived to be primarily the operation of individual dynamics and factors within the individual. Most social workers view with concern the systematic neglect of environmental forces which some of these psychologies assume.

In our view, total disregard for environmental forces is found more often in theory than in practice. As Maslow points out:

Certainly no psychologist in his right mind would dream of denying a degree of personal helplessness before these forces. But after all, his prime professional obligation is the study of the individual person rather than of extrapsychic social determinants.[1]

Some depth psychologies appear to imply that victims of institutionalized social conditions, such as, poverty, racism, sexism, ageism, are responsible for their plight. It is as though all individuals make themselves by their own choices all the time, without consideration for those social forces which often render individuals helpless to change their social reality.

If psychology tends to neglect environmental forces, traditional sociologists tend to neglect individual determinants of behavior. They concentrate on variations in the environment as causes of human problems. This presumes an average, expectable individual as constant. It implies a neglect for individual differences. The underlying assumption is that people are products of their social conditions. Individuals are average and expectable, and determined solely by their environment. In the same way that psychologists appear to neglect social forces, the sociologists

stress social forces too exclusively and forget about the autonomy of the personality, of will, of responsibility. . . . It would be better to think of both groups as specialists rather than as blind or foolish.[2]

It is not necessary for social workers to make a choice among a set of premises developed from one or another of these disciplines, nor is it necessary to take each of these points of view. That would be like trying to dance at two weddings at the same time. Social workers need to learn to bridge their understanding of the individual and the environment and to accept the relative importance of both. Such acceptance makes it possible to deepen knowledge in one or another area according to what is needed relevant to the kind of social work in which one is engaged. We have tended sometimes to identify knowledge with method of work, as though people who worked with individuals needed only to know the psychological side and those who worked with the community needed to know only the social side.

This can be misleading for those who are entering the social work profession. At times, it is a matter of which level is most critical and immediate. For example, individual and small group work with those who are terminally ill requires a good deal of knowledge of psychological processes. Accepting the needs of such persons to deny and to go through anticipatory stages of grief demands thoughtful handling of many psychological matters. But the psychological aspects of an individual's behavior are influenced by variations in individual environments, and in the reference groups within which the individual has learned to handle stress. The ways in which the community regards terminal illness and death may have great influence on the person's attitude toward the illness. The implications the illness has for others with whom the individual plays reciprocal roles are also important to understand, as is knowledge of the major effects and progress of the physiological disease which is leading to the end of life.

Social workers whose immediate attention is directed to community planning or organization need to know a great deal about the social forces and conditions that determine the ways in which people in the target community are able to function. Their efforts are directed to harnessing the human efforts of many others in a community in order that they may take some action to change or forestall destructive social conditions. These social workers need to appreciate the psychological implications that such social conditions have for people in the community. Frequently, the ability to relate to their feelings of powerlessness as well as to their fear of social change is the ingredient that makes such change possible.

The concepts we have presented provide a scaffolding on which a bridge can be built between the individual and the social reality. Social workers need a framework to which to refer that allows them to select concepts that do not lead them to only one set of explanations. The need is for concepts that link up enough social and psychological experiences so that psychological problems can be defined in psychological terms and social problems in social terms. It is difficult to locate that point at which the society ends and the individual begins; the individual and the society are interdependent. The social worker begins to locate people in their social situation through becoming familiar with the ways in which they conceive of themselves. It is very important to understand the conceptions people have of themselves. The social worker learns to know how free individuals have been to define their relationships to others and how much they have been defined by these relationships. This knowledge is reflected in the number and nature of the significant reference groups in people's lives, in understanding which groups have been internalized and are still a part of the internalized audience of individuals. Such knowledge is obtained from learning how much the present is like the past for those with whom one works, from learning how much people depend upon social definitions to define themselves. Social definitions are critical to what most people expect of others throughout the stages of life.

In the following chapters we have chosen to apply the framework we have developed to some concentrated discussion of the life stages of human development. These chapters are designed to present some of the major social psychological implications of the life stages from infancy to aging. Prior to beginning that discussion, we will remind the reader of what has gone before by developing further that material related to social and psychological definitions which has specific relevance to the life stages we will be discussing.

Social Definition Revisited

We have seen that the "Who am I?" question is not completely answered by those social categories to which one belongs. For example, one's self is not necessarily defined by one's social class, race, age, or sex. Differences exist within each of these categories, and assuming that all people in any category are the same leads to stereotypical notions which separate and stigmatize people. Our discussion of social reality has shown some of the implications of labeling. It is also true that people depend upon social definitions of behavior, on learning the "do's" and "don'ts" defined by normative reference groups. We have shown that normative reference groups enforce conformity to average, expectable behavior. In this sense, social definitions operate as a determinant of an individual's self-concept. Social theorists discuss the extent to which social definition becomes a forceful determinant. According to George McCall and J. L. Simmons:

This force is exerted not only upon the behavior of the person; it also tremendously affects the very shape and fabric of the individual by selectively supporting and, at least by default, discouraging various of his identities. . . . These pressures tend to conventualize career, marriage, education, creativity, the very self of the person.[3]

It is as though one has to "live up to" one's social identity. People frequently require that others "act their age," for example. In fact, each age and stage of life is associated with role behavior bounded by social definitions, and in some measure, such boundaries give meaning to life. While it is somehow ennobling to think of ourselves as questioning commonly expected and accepted meanings and as searching for a final truth, we are all guided to some extent by generally accepted meanings which make life ultimately comprehensible. The extent to which society defines us as "good" and worthy of positive regard is critical to our willing acceptance of social definition. Society offers very little unconditional, positive regard, and there are times when the conditions require alienation from one's self. This is the point at which some people encounter social definition and begin to question what they have taken for granted.

From the point of view of the social theorists, the perpetuation of conceptions of what life stages are expected to mean depends upon the willingness of people to take such conceptions for granted.

In every society and epoch there is a model trajectory of successive life phases. These notions that the members of the culture learn are often taken so for granted that they are considered self-evident, and their arbitrariness is never glimpsed. Indeed, as the individual grows up in that social grouping, he internalizes and acts in terms of these conceptions of what each life phase is, so that he makes the conceptions "come true" by dutifully fulfilling them.[4]

We have said that social reality may be defined by large social systems of which the individual is a part. We have seen that people frequently go along with everyone else's opinions in order to maintain a sense of belonging with everyone else. In this sense, the "taken for granted" aspect of what the life stages are is illustrative of pluralistic ignorance.

Social work requires of its practitioners a willingness to learn what people's social reality is, which pressures to conform have shaped people's attitudes, the extent to which they demand conformity from others, and the degree of difference between themselves and others which they can accept. It is important for social workers to understand which roles people play and which ones they want to play, how continuous or discontinuous their life roles have been, and the extent to which they are engaged in reciprocal role behavior. In order to pick up the signals and cues in human behavior which these factors disclose, social workers need an unusual respect for differences and an awareness of the normative behavior expected by the society. Social workers also need to understand their own expectations of people and the extent to which these expectations reflect their own life conditioning. For example, the ideas one has learned of what an adolescent is, or the meanings attributed to being a small child, are socially defined and simply taken for granted. Behavior tends to be viewed from an "as if" stance—"as if" all the members of a social grouping would define their behavior the same way as everyone outside that grouping would define it. One would expect all entities such as race, social class, sexuality, maturity, to be viewed similarly; and, without describing what this view is, it would somehow be taken for granted that all knew what they were expected to view.

The social worker is more concerned with what the consumers of their services make of the everyday world than whether it exists as they view it. We do not prejudge the social reality of the existence of life stages, and we regard them as entities to the exent that they structure the lives of people in the society. Jaber Gubrium and David Buckholdt observe that

the important question is how do members of the world of everyday life collectively negotiate, come to accept, and settle on such "entities" as real, independent of themselves, and somehow subject to their fate? To negotiate is to tacitly and collectively entertain, interpret, and evaluate any number of practical "theories" of entities in order to deal with them as things. . . . On some occasions, it is particularly visible, as in plea bargaining, psychotherapeutic engagement, and scientific criticism; on other occasions, it is fleeting and subtle, as in casual banter about the alleged decline in the morality of today's youth. The reality of entities is a product of people's treatments of their existence. Of central concern are the social processes by which people come to have a sense of maturity, social class, public opinion, social order, normality, and the like.[5]

In the following we will discuss some theory which emphasizes psychological definitions of behavior associated with life stages, and evaluate the implications it has for the ways in which a large number of people appear to treat their existence.

Psychological Definition

From the psychological point of view, people negotiate and come to obtain consensual validation on what is real outside themselves in order to meet inner needs to grow. In this view, people do not simply internalize social definitions of themselves; they participate in the process of defining themselves. In general, most psychological theorists assume that people make themselves by their own choices according to the extent to which they are able to meet basic needs for love, safety, belonging, and freedom to realize self-potentials. We have suggested that the extent to which individuals can participate in the definition of their social identity depends on how much space for free movement they have in the social roles which are open to them. Social theorists have suggested that the meaning of life stages is so set by normative expectations as to require that individuals fulfill only prescribed role behaviors. We have discussed some of the problems which face individuals who do not conform to these expectations. Psychological theorists have explained conformity and nonconformity in a number of ways depending on their conceptions of the motivation and the goals of individual behavior.

According to Maslow and Rogers, there is an inner force, a drive toward self-actualization which propels the individual's behavior. If this inner motivation toward growth is encouraged by complementary experiences in the environment the individual can realize human potential without excessive stress. If the environment blocks the drive, the individual may get out of touch with his or her self temporarily or may become alienated from the self. But the force behind the drive is never entirely lost to the individual whose ultimate goal is self-actualization. Such actualization also includes a striving for realization of human values which go beyond the self.

Freud advanced quite a different conception. He originally posited a theory of instincts, among which sexual energy or libido was a major force. According to Freud's early psychoanalytic theory, the aim of the instincts is reduction of tension through a maturational sequence of discharge which becomes a model of stages of development. Freud viewed the environment as determining the fate of the instincts, which are subject to social regulation.

For purposes of contrast, the differences in these two views can be seen in the goals of behavior. The drive toward self-actualization is growth-oriented; people take pleasure in environmental mastery, in creativity, in exposing the self to new stimulation. As they were described, instincts provide uncomfortable somatic stimuli. The individual is driven to relate to others and to deal with the social world, simply to relieve the unpleasantness of the organically derived discomfort. From the point of view of the instinct theory, pleasurable activity was always linked to tension reduction. The need to find appropriate channels for tension reduction was presumed to lead to adjustment and adaptation to the social reality. In contrast, the drive for self-actualization often leads away from adjustment and adaptation, toward more independence from those social pressures to conform. Those premises associated with self-actualization theory, or with theories which posit an intrinsic motivation toward growth in general, are drawn from observations of people who have been able to realize their human potential in their relationships or who are striving to do so. Since this is the kind of behavior which might best be expected to move the society forward, it would seem likely that some consensus would evolve around successive expectations of growth toward such fulfillment.

This does not appear to be the case. If we look at the taboos associated with sexuality, at the secrecy and embarrassment which are widely associated with body functions in this society, we find the origin of such taboos and embarrassment in at least some general consensus that behavior is instinctually determined according to the early psychosexual stages originally described by Freud. To understand this idea more clearly it will be helpful to see the background against which the theory was developed and review it briefly.

Freud's original observations were made in his work as a physician committed to cure sick people who had had very destructive experiences in their lives and who regarded their instincts as dangerous. Freud was led to the premise that all behavior has the ulterior goal of simply reducing tension rising from instinctual needs—hunger, sex, or, in general, pain avoidance. His original conception emphasized libido or sexual energy. Robert White has provided a summary of the critical points in Freud's original theory.

Conceiving sexuality broadly to include the obtaining of pleasure from various zones of the body, he postulated a maturational sequence whereby first the mouth, then the anal zone, finally the genitals become the dominant source of libidinal gratification.[6]

The theory provided a model or prototype of behavior which included

the infant at the breast, the child on the toilet, the phallic child concerned about genital impulses toward family members, the physically mature adult in the heterosexual relation. It tells us, moreover, that these prototypes are truly basic, that events in these situations are really the most important things that happen, so that if we know just these aspects of a person's history, we know all that counts.[7]

In his own criticism of this highly deterministic view of life stages, White protested the emphasis placed upon the supremacy of libido or sexual energy as the singular driving force for behavior, and the sexual model as adequate to do justice to the individual's emotional development. Cognizant of research findings on motivation of behavior subsequent to Freud's early work, he observed the wide range of mastery required of infants and children and their continued curiosity, exploration, manipulation, and delight in social responses beyond the meeting of basic needs. His work followed the tradition of the Neo-Freudians, Karen Horney,[8] Harry Stack Sullivan,[9] Erich Fromm,[10] and the theory development of Erik Erikson.[11]White viewed the individual as initiating "transactions with the environment which result in its maintaining itself, growing and flourishing."[12] Many contemporary theorists agree with him. Motivations which are independent of tension reduction are widely accepted. The drive toward "health" is recognized as a critical factor in psychotherapeutic engagement.

Efforts to define "mental health" have revealed some consensus among major psychological theorists. Mental health is no longer simply defined as an absence of disease. It includes a sense of identity that is arrived at independently of environmental pressures to conform, self-observing ability, commitment to values beyond the self, integration of life experiences, ability to function in accord with one's own choices, and perception of others without distortion by one's own needs.[13] If mental health is defined in these terms, then they describe the goals of behavior which might be expected to be accepted by the society. Models of successive life stages are built on some generally accepted notions of what is "good" or ideal for each stage, and some optimal human functioning criteria toward which all stages ultimately lead. Nevertheless, the society does not appear to project a model of life stages which emphasizes the forwarding of individuals' human possibilities. A great many people in this society appear to be preoccupied with sexual taboos and body function. The prototypes set down by psychosexual theory still seem to influence people's expectations of life stages. The children of the society appear to continue to be acculturated according to behavior expected by such prototypes. Apparently, these are the psychological definitions of behavior which most heavily influence the ways in which people view human behavior.

Infancy and Early Childhood

Those human relationship arrangements within which birth is expected to take place are socially defined. The society into which the baby is born precedes the newborn, and the pattern of beliefs and values most characteristic of the society determines the ways in which the birth experience is interpreted. Social expectations are explicated by legal and religious rules and regulations; they are implied in the role definitions of mother, father, baby, and other family members. They are reflected in a wide range of responses to the event of birth, including the sex of the child, the age of the parents, and the composition of the family.

Those years immediately following the child's first year—roughly speaking, the second through the fourth—are also associated with role behaviors bounded by social definition. In these early years, children are most impressionable and dependent, and their self-concept is heavily influenced by individual caretakers and beginning play groups. Child-rearing practices include expections of control of body functions and initial learning of sexual behavior. This early learning has implications for stereotyping and labeling and is associated with the beginning of some common defenses against painful human experience.

The developing sense of self is impelled by the drive for growth and motivated by competence. The young child is encouraged to move forward, or restrained, in transactions with significant reference groups. On the part of the care-givers, these transactions include the giving of love, warmth, and positive regard, and the maintenance of flexibility in their demands on the infant and young child. The child's ability to develop basic trust in them, to begin to experience self-autonomy and to become self-initiating, is influenced by the outcome of these transactions.

Social reality pressures people to conform to many social structures which often make personal growth for parents and their young children difficult. The heavy responsibility which the society places upon the mother, who is frequently assumed to "make" the child's personality, creates many problems for "mothering" persons and for young children. Social reality influences the relatively high degree of concern expressed by many segments of the society over the incidence of abortions and the relatively low degree of concern expressed over the high mortality rate of infants in the black community as compared to the white community, over the systematic discrepancy between mortality rates for white and nonwhite infants throughout the society. In a society in which deviance is often associated with pathology concern is expressed by many people that the baby and young child be "normal," and this leads to a greater sense of ease with little children who look, think, and behave according to average, expectable standards.[1] There is not much understanding of the unusual child, especially if the child is slow to grow in expected directions.

In the following sections, we shall look at these issues in more depth. We begin by bringing back into focus the question of the self and its boundaries.

Developing Self-Boundaries

The development of self-boundaries involves learning where other selves end and one's self begins. The self is energized from inner drives and by stimuli from the environment. The developing self-sense is vulnerable to loss of its own boundaries. Changes in the feelings associated with the self-image may enhance or threaten the sense of self. Becoming social, as a human being, carries with it the implication of continuous vulnerability and experiencing of differences in states of being as well as of uncertainty as to where self-boundaries are located.

Most students of behavior agree that the infant has potential for growth, that it will be forward-moving, and that physical, emotional, and social changes can be identified in successive stages from almost total dependency to increasing independence, or autonomy. Personality theorists disagree on the nature of the dependency in infancy, the length of time it takes for a boundary sense to begin, and the extent to which such dependency in early life experience is critical to ongoing social relationships. Earlier we noted Mead's view that the self is not present at birth but evolves through social experience. We have discussed Freud's views on the matter, which include the idea that the mother's ability to separate from the infant and the growing child is critical to the development of the self. We have seen that Rank emphasized the physical separation from the mother at infancy and viewed the development of the child's self as a process of differentiation, through succeeding separations from the mother and significant others.

The reader will recall Rogers's view that the infant is inherently driven to grow toward productivity and creativity, but may be restrained by environmental conditions, especially by interactions with significant others. Rogers believes that if people are not forced to conform to rigidly constructed, socially institutionalized behavior, and are accepted for what they are, they will live their lives to enhance themselves and society.

The preceding chapter reviewed the question of the extent to which people are products of social expectations, the extent to which they are determined by biological predispositions to reduce tension derived from instincts, and the extent to which they are propelled by a drive toward self-actualization. The paradigm we have presented has emphasized the self-concept and how it develops, and the influences of reference individuals and reference groups in its development. The social reality, which corresponds in a general way to what the social theorists call social definition, gives to the newborn the shape, the content, and the expectations of its growth. How this growth will be shaped socially as well as certain social identities become givens for the baby at birth because it is born into a particular part of a particular society. These givens include a particular language, the one the child will first speak, a sex role, a religious identity for the majority of children, a racial identity, an ethnic history, and, as we have noted, a model trajectory of successive life phases.

These givens are postulated for newborns by the society into which they come, as the boundaries of their self-conceptions. The idea of successive life phases implies a succession of potential self-definitions and redefinitions through the individual's encounters with these parameters, and efforts to move beyond or to change them. Such encounters have been recognized by many theorists in terms of life crises, suggesting as their outcomes the potential for certain more or less radical shifts in the individual's perspective, regardless of what these crises are called.

Psychosocial Crises of Infancy and Early Childhood

Psychoanalytic theory directs attention primarily to pathology. The model or prototype of behavior emphasizing libido or sexual energy as the singular driving force for behavior excludes a great deal of knowledge, including those transactions with the environment that are initiated by the infant and young child in the service of its own growth. Such transactions provide a great deal of understanding of infant and early childhood behavior, and those theorists whose work came after the original psychoanalytic explanations became increasingly aware of their significance to the understanding of human behavior.

Erik Erikson is a major contemporary theorist whose work illustrates this gradual shift in emphasis. He describes eight stages of human life which encompass the life span from infancy to old age. The first three stages parallel those described by Freud, but go considerably beyond preoccupation with psychosexual development to more general psychosocial aspects of growth. Erikson takes the unconscious for granted and places his emphasis "on the ego's synthesizing function in developing stable conceptions—meaning, images, themes—of self, significant other, individual and symbolic entities."[2] Erikson tends to assume an average, predictable environment with which growth is coordinated, especially in infancy and childhood. Despite this, his compassionate discussion of the search for identity and an integration of life experiences provides insight into those processes through which people come to experience themselves as worthwhile human beings.

Critical to Erikson's scheme is a time sequence for accomplishment of psychological and social tasks.

Anything that grows has a ground plan, and . . . out of this plan the parts arise, each part having its time of special ascendancy, until all parts have arisen to form a functioning whole. At birth the baby leaves the chemical exchange of the womb for the social exchange system of his society, where his gradually increasing capacities meet the opportunities and limitations of his culture. . . . Personality can be said to develop according to steps predetermined in the human organism's readiness to be driven toward, or be aware of, and to interact with, a widening social radius, beginning with the dim image of a mother and ending with mankind, or at any rate that segment of mankind that "counts" in the particular individual's life.[3]

Erikson's interest in bridging the psychological and social implications of human growth are clear. The best known parts of his work are his descriptions of psychosocial crises which have specific relevance to each of the stages of development. We shall be presenting those crises which he sees as needing resolution in sequence from infancy, through the second and third, and the fourth and fifth, years of life.

In order to place emphasis on the child's readiness to be driven forward and to initiate and be influenced by increasing social interaction, we shall discuss, in tandem with Erikson's views, Robert White's insights on the relationship of competence to the child's readiness to move ahead.

The psychosocial crises identified by Erikson for early life are shown in the following table.

Life Stage	Approximate Age	Psychosocial Crisis
Infancy	First year	Basic trust *vs.* mistrust
Early childhood	Second/third years	Autonomy *vs.* shame, doubt
Play age	Fourth/fifth years	Initiative *vs.* guilt

Erikson emphasizes the relationship between children's developing capacities and their encounters with the social environment. He views development in early life as a process of mutual regulation between the child and the parents. The unfolding capacities of the child and the changing demands of the parents result in a series of critical encounters, and it is the outcomes of these encounters which are predictive of future development and growth. These encounters progressively involve more and more of the social environment as the child continues to grow.[4]

Learning to Develop Basic Trust

Erikson discusses the development of basic trust within the model of the feeding child. The mother is the central reference person on whom the infant is completely dependent for this critical learning.

The amount of trust derived from earliest infantile experience does not seem to depend on absolute quantities of food or demonstrations of love, but rather on the quality of the maternal relationship. Mothers create a sense of trust in their children by that kind of administration which in its quality combines sensitive care of the baby's individual needs and a firm sense of personal trustworthiness within the trusted framework of their community's life style.[5]

The early development of trust, according to this theory, leads to a basic hopefulness about life. It acts as an "inner, untouchable cache of warmth and richness; a personal, unlosable, unspendable treasure; an emotional insulation against psychological chill or shock."[6] The baby develops an attitude toward the self and the world in this first year of life. It appears to be up to the mother to convince the infant that she or he can begin to trust the sense of beginning separateness from her. The baby discovers what it takes to get food, affection, physical fondling. There is a back and forth fitting together by both the baby and the major caretaker. If all goes well, there is a mutuality. If the getting and giving are mutually satisfying, they are regulated by the baby's great dependency, limited abilities for communicating, and by the mother's ability to complement the baby's needs. Mutuality presumes that the baby will settle the trust versus mistrust question in the direction of trust, not once and for all, but to establish the foundations, resolving the first crisis of life.

Let us look at this first phase from the point of view of Robert White's theory of competence. Erikson's emphasis on the maternal relationship appears to be appropriate to the earliest infantile experience, but it is as though nothing else happens during the first year of life, although interactions between the baby and its environment during the first stage described by Erikson continue through the first year. Without changing the central position of the mother with regard to emotional development, White suggests that the child also engages in exploratory play. He considers

the whole range of what a child must learn in order to deal effectively with its surroundings. . . . He has much to learn about . . . coordination of hand and eye . . . must work out the difficult problem of the constancy of objects.[7]

In this sense, White takes issue with the notion that "the infant's cognitive outlook, his knowledge of reality, and his discrimination between self and outer world are all . . . taking place almost exclusively in relation to the food-providing mother."[8] The infant initiates explorations, concomitant with interactions with the mother, that contribute importantly to the developing self-sense in this first year.

Gaining a Sense of Autonomy and Resolving Shame and Doubt

Both White and Erikson agree that during the child's second year the significant crisis for the child is in autonomy. Erikson focuses on the experience of toilet training as the prototype for the development of autonomy. White focuses on children's testing of their own sense of competence.

In Erikson's view, the baby learns first to trust that the world will be kind and relatively dependable, and then faces the crisis of autonomy versus shame and doubt. The general significance of this stage is in the maturation of the muscle system. According to Erikson, the crisis is almost always associated with toilet training.

The anal zone lends itself more than any other to the expression of stubborn insistence on conflicting impulses because, for one thing, it is the model zone for two contradictory modes which must become alternating; namely, retention and elimination. . . . This whole stage, then, becomes a battle for autonomy. For as he gets ready to stand on his feet more firmly, the infant delineates his world as "I" and "you," "me" and "mine."[9]

This stage is viewed by Erikson as critical to the development of self-control.

The stage, therefore, becomes decisive for the ratio between love and hate, for that between cooperation and willfulness, and for that between the freedom of self-expression and its suppression. From a sense of self-control without loss of self-esteem comes a lasting sense of autonomy and pride; from a sense of muscular and anal impotence, of loss of self-control, and of parental overcontrol comes a lasting sense of doubt and shame.[10]

Erikson recognizes that the existing society into which the infant is born will determine the extent to which, for the majority of people, maturation of the neuromuscular system is emphasized by toilet training. Thus, he observes that, in most societies,

People seem convinced that to make the right (meaning *their*) kind of human being, one must consistently introduce the sense of shame, doubt, guilt and fear into a child's life. . . . Some cultures begin to restrict early in life, some late, some abruptly, others more gradually. Until enough comparative observations are available, we are apt to add further superstitions. . . . For no matter what we do in detail, the child will feel primarily what we live by, what makes us loving, cooperative, and firm beings, and what makes us hateful, anxious and divided in ourselves.[11]

Both Erikson and White discuss the emerging wish on the part of the two- and three-year-old to resist influences from important people in the environment. White disagrees that the major stimulus for this surge toward autonomy is derived from anal libido—from heightened conscious preoccupation with the processes and sensations of elimination and retention of body wastes. He does not agree that the major struggle is expressed through bowel control; rather, he describes a much broader range of muscular development leading to a great deal of mastery of the physical world with concomitant outcomes of self-confidence and esteem. While this is going on, there is an increase in the child's capacity to anticipate both the sense of efficacy associated with completing a self-initiated activity and the frustrations of interference with such pursuit. Concomitantly, increasing facility in language use encourages children to test the consequences of their ability verbally to influence others and to refuse influences that interrupt movement toward a goal. These developments, which impel children's explorations of the symbolic world in the same fashion that motor developments impel them in the physical world, lead them to initiate tests of their social competence, reflecting a conscious affirmation of a self-sense. It is as though young children testing their capacities to distinguish that point at which others end and they begin, sense that there would be no way to develop self-control if controls from others were always accepted and affirmed.[12]

Developing a Sense of Initiative
and Resolving a Sense of Guilt

The next developmental task described by Erikson requires the child to acquire a sense of initiative and overcome a sense of guilt. If the child has accomplished basic trust in infancy and won out over shame and doubt by establishing a measure of autonomy in the second and third years, its chances of resolving this next crisis are enhanced. There is no disagreement in the views of Erikson and White that the child is brought to this crisis by growth in physical strength and coordination. The child can dress itself, walk, run, jump, throw, climb, use tools and other implements, is able to employ more elaborate speech, and has developed a great deal of imagination. Through increased language children can also widen their understanding of the world, and increase social exchange. During the years from three to five, learning and socialization are accelerated by beginning separation from home, association with other children, little and big, and usually some form of preschool.

With the emergence of many adult-like patterns of behavior, children compare themselves with adults. According to Erikson, the major comparison is made between the child's and the adult's genitals. From this view, physical sensitivity has shifted from the anal to the genital area, and children become preoccupied with the nature of sexual relationships between their parents. Here the society's definition of sexuality influences the child's perception of adult relationships. For Erikson, as for Freud, genital inferiority takes precedence over other comparative differences, and he describes a fairly classical oedipal conflict which is ultimately fraught with guilt. He believes that

pride in being big now and almost as good as father and mother receives its severest setback in the clear fact that in the genital sphere one is vastly inferior; furthermore, it receives an additional setback in the fact that not even in the distant future is one ever going to be father in sexual relationship to mother, or mother in sexual relationship to father.[13]

Children's fantasies, then, are encouraged by feelings of rivalry toward the parent of the opposite sex, and they have difficulty differentiating between the content of their thoughts and their intentions. The child who has succeeded in the experience of autonomy, who is able to differentiate the self from others, and who has parents who can sensitively communicate their understanding of all this, can give up the oedipal feelings. In this instance, initiative wins out over guilt.

White, in contrast, does not view the oedipal prototype as a general model for this stage.

Freud selected as his central image a hopeless situation, one where defeat for the child is inevitable. The child must learn to renounce the whole oedipal wish, just as he must learn to renounce any thought of not being bowel trained. . . . If these were the true and determinate models, it would be quite a problem to explain the survival of any sense of initiative.[14]

White's views suggest that while the model explains shame and guilt, it raises questions as to how the young child emerges with autonomy and initiative. According to the competence model, the child's mastery of the world continues during this stage. The growth of competence in itself leads to crises in interpersonal relationships. The child is curious about differences of all kinds and is interested in becoming like adults in a number of ways. A great deal of learning is going on in a wide range of areas. The young child is beginning to want to learn about sexuality and is increasing its understanding of other family members. Questions of sex relations of the parents are very likely; the child may be subject to rebuffs to questions of any kind, may at times feel humiliated and be frightened of fantasies and bad dreams. The child may also experience a great deal of progress and success. This stage accentuates learning of the social self.[15]

We have chosen to discuss these crises because, as we have said, the problem is not in what the crises are called. Erikson has captured a good deal of the social reality, and his effort to include the social side has resulted in many explanations that hold up in the face of the social-psychological thrust of our own concepts.

We do not want to convey the idea that we believe that the most critical issues around which autonomy and initiative are developed are management of body wastes and oedipal strivings. We go along with White's thoughts on these stages. This is why we presented them, because he points out that the child's forward thrust is of neural as well as visceral origins and that either of these energizing centers would propel the young child toward critical encounters with caretakers. Without disclaiming the sexual awareness of the young child, we would, in the light of current findings, reject the oedipal pattern as the necessary and sufficient model of affective and perceptual growth in these years.

Cognitive Growth

We have called attention to Robert White's conception of competence as a primary motivating force that underlies the individual's propensity for knowledge seeking. White's introduction of a competence motive reflects his response to explanations of children's behavior in theories which deal with cognitive growth. Many people tend to think of the early years of the child's life as "precognitive" (prior to the accumulation of knowledge),[16] perhaps because of the tendency to associate knowledge with what can be communicated through speech. As we shall see, the social context within which the child's thought and speech develop has important implications. At this point, however, we are concerned to round out the discussion by referring to some of the insights on children's development that are available to us through the work of cognitive theorists. The reader should be aware, in what follows here, that we are temporarily narrowing and shifting our perspective in order to highlight the cognitive component of attitude development.

Cognitive theorists emphasize the means through which children represent their experience of the world and organize experiences for use in the future. They concentrate on the ways in which human beings increase and use knowledge, on mental development and its relation to social transactions; they deal with perception and cognition, with imaging and thinking and their relationships to action. Perceptual and cognitive processes usually mean mental processes. Ulric Neisser presents the view that the young child's perception and cognition are not just mental operations separate from transactions with the world. The child is both informed and transformed by such transactions. Neisser suggests that "images are essentially perceptual anticipations, preparations for picking up certain kinds of information."[17] They are organized through a set of cognitive processes to form a cognitive map which can guide further expectations and explorations.

We have previously discussed some of the implications of perception, cognition, and inner harmony for self-consistency. The reader may recall that all behavior is referred to some frame of reference which is used to predict causal expectations among related events. The child at birth enters both a social and a physical world. The child's sense of competence in the physical world depends upon actions that are guided by more or less accurate ideas about the characteristics of nonpersonal objects, their effects on each other, and the effects of the child's actions on these relationships. In the sphere of social relationships, children's sense of knowing how the world works tends to be confirmed by responses of others to their efforts to evoke responses that complement their expectations of what those others are like and what moves them. Close observation of children's behavior has suggested that the child comes to recognize during the first year of life that other persons act under their own power.[18] As we have seen, during the second year the child first evidences an awareness of his or her self as a source of power, independent of what others do. This implies that actions have become known to the child as "proceeding from a self that exists apart from what it does."[19]

Jean Piaget suggests that the infant does not initially distinguish among self, objects, actions, and causes.[20] A repertoire of actions implies a repertoire of knowledge, but action and knowledge are not, for the infant, initially distinguishable from each other. Even the sense of what is part and what is not part of one's own body is not at all precise or firm for the baby; it becomes clearer during the first two years, as the child tests out what sources of sensation can be changed or avoided by muscular movement. According to Piaget, knowledge exists first at a sensori-motor level;[21] through the muscular movement that characterizes the earliest transactions with the world, the physical boundaries between body and not-body come to be known, and the child's own body is one aspect of what will be conceived of as self.[22] This is a point to which we shall refer again in the next chapter.

In a similar fashion, thinking, feeling, and intending are not distinguishable from each other for the infant and very young child. Children's first reality testing is through action, and this involves their discoveries of the consequences of their own actions on the "not self" part of their universe. Appraisals of reality appear to begin quite early,[23] but the physical and the psychosocial worlds only gradually become distinguishable.

White's formulations about the motives of competence and efficacy propose that it is the child's discovery of its ability to create differences in its environment that urge it on toward further reality testing and consequent learning. This is in some contrast to Piaget's conceptions. His work suggests that growth of intellect is motivated by disequilibrium, by an imbalance between the child's model of the environment and newly learned complexities in the environment. When children's expectations, anticipations, and predictions do not serve them in relating to complex features of the environment, it is necessary for them to overcome the problem, to seek competence.[24] It is as though it is the child's experience of cognitive dissonance, rather than the child's discovery of its own activity as the source of the dissonance, that motivates the child's continuing knowledge-seeking. Overcoming "trouble" because of the bad fit with the nature of one's models or representations is certainly one aspect of seeking competence. But there are many cognitive conflicts of this kind that do not lead a child to grow.

Through interactions with both the physical and the social worlds, the small child is accumulating a store of impressions and images, to which the acquisition and mastering of language bring a new means of putting knowledge in order. According to Jerome Bruner:

at first the child's world is known to him principally by the habitual actions he uses for coping with it. In time there is added a technique of representation through imagery that is relatively free of action. Gradually there is added a new and powerful method of translating action and image into language, providing still a third system of representation. . . . Each of the three modes of representation . . . places a powerful impress on the mental life of human beings of different ages, and their interplay persists as one of the major features of adult intellectual life.[25]

Conceptual ability introduces the child into the linguistic community of its culture, and opens the possibility of exploring the social reality more extensively. Bruner refers to this as the child's "becoming linked with culturally transmitted 'amplifiers.'"[26] While it provides the child with a more powerful means of learning, it also narrows the child's sights, depending on what its particular culture chooses to "amplify." We shall elaborate on this more fully in the following section.

The young child's growing repertoire of impressions, images, and words by which to represent its first explanations of its own and others' behavior might be thought of as the history of the child's own thought. Similarly, the child accumulates a history of action and its consequences. In White's view, this history is one of the sources of the child's self-esteem; the other source is the esteem in which the child is held by others.[27]

Speech and Learning

Earlier, we have noted that acquiring speech provides the child with a new mode of experience and interaction with its environment. The baby's organization of its knowledge of the world might be thought of as a plan for action and for orienting itself in the world through locomotion and sensory cues. With accumulating experience, babies' thinking changes; they take in a great many impressions and sensations but begin to be able to orient themselves not only in space but also in time, and can wait for things, although as yet they do not give meaning to the words "time" or "space." With speech, children can begin to orient themselves in the environment through verbal as well as action and other sensory cues, and the world looks different to them.

Speech makes it possible for children to pick up a great deal of information about the world in a symbolized form, and to apprehend the existence of, and relationships between, things that are beyond their reach. They transform experiences into symbols, including verbal symbols, which at first are regarded as if they are part of the people and objects they represent. Later, children comprehend words and verbal expressions as referring to another order of reality. This order is related to, but distinct from, the things to which they were originally attached. It means that the child's thinking about things gradually becomes detached from the necessity of being directly in contact with them. Children can thus learn, verbally, about things never observed, and in their thinking can take account of them and give meaning to them. This abstract world takes on a reality of its own; the way words are put together begins to be taken as the way events themselves are related.

The verbal formulations, or themes, by which growing children increasingly organize their experiences are crude, but such themes include the experience both of the pattern of interrelationships among things, and of the regularities with which they occur. Knowledge of regularities in the environment permits prediction. As children grow, they seek to widen the scope of their awareness of what can be predicted and this brings more and more of the environment under control.

Increasing social experience of children facilitates this learning, as language takes on the function of mobilizing the child to attend to what is new, or novel, in its experience. What is strange invites exploration and this complements the child's inherent knowledge-seeking attitude. Children increasingly search out formulations that can represent what is strange and formulations that fit those they have already learned to use.

Earlier we have illustrated, by way of Erikson's and White's formulations, the notion that the child's earliest frame of reference is heavily influenced by the responses of the significant caretakers. A frame of reference, it will be recalled, is critical to people's needs to find a way to make sense out of continuing experience. The frame of reference includes perceptions and standards of judgment reflected in attitudes, in firmly held beliefs anchored in feelings. The first set of self-attitudes is formed out of what the child knows about the world; what the infant and young child know about the world is bounded by the responses of the first significant others; and the child's first set of attitudes toward the self reflects what they transmit to it of the society's priorities.

Developing Attitudes toward the Self and Others

During the first years of life, expectations of the society are taken in gradually, before self-boundaries have been drawn and before the child has enough knowledge and understanding of the world to engage in conscious evaluation. The expectations of infant and early childhood behavior are the norms and taboos, the "do's and don'ts" by which the baby and young child are judged as good or bad. These are initially transmitted through early significant others, when children are quite dependent, vulnerable, and more impressionable than they are likely to be when their own self-boundaries are drawn. In early years, then, the child is more likely to perceive the self as others perceive it, that is, from the perspective of early significant people. This has to do with the internalized audience, which is composed first of the most significant caretakers, and subsequently broadened to include the community of elders and early play groups.

Young children are largely unselfconscious of their acts as self-representations. They are also unaware of the extensive ramifications of the "do's and don'ts" they encounter.

Although the child does not realize it, the perspective of the internalized audience of early significant others implies a conception of infancy and childhood, and an explanation of child development and childhood socialization, even though these may not have been verbalized or consciously examined by the caretakers. Interest in articulating child development theories began in the society during the second half of the nineteenth century. Discussing the history of these interests during the late 1800s, a time of heavy immigration and threatened change to the existing social order, Norman Denzin says:

Social workers, philanthropists, social thinkers, and reformers defined children as vehicles for the transmission of social values. . . . If children could be lifted out of their barbarism, society as a whole could hope for redemption. The innocence and purity of "properly trained" children represented the hope of succeeding generations. Although there were certainly exceptions, most of the related theories of children were implicitly sexist; others were ethnocentric at best and explicitly racist at worst. From the viewpoint of symbolic interactionism, the majority of childhood socialization theories were "adultist," in that they viewed children as passive or resistant participants in the socialization process.[28]

It will be important to keep in mind that we are going to consider some of the implications of early learning that reflects the "isms" that Denzin refers to. We think that some early social workers were among those groups who shared this view. Earlier, we have noted that social workers frequently occupy positions at the boundaries of social systems, functioning to keep them open. We have noted the kinds of changes that make it possible for people to experience more space for free movement, and the kinds of service orientations that enhance the rights of people to work for such changes. We have suggested that such orientations frequently require of people that they break with traditional views and role behaviors. It seems to us to be very important that social workers demand of themselves, at least, respect for differences, and that they help those with whom they work to respect the rights of groups of people to difference.

So, we shall discuss the social implications of attitudes toward babies and young children; we shall put some emphasis on some of the wider implications of such attitudes, for other age groups and for the general society, especially with reference to attitudes toward body function and sexuality.

It may be helpful at this juncture to review briefly the earlier definition of attitude as a predisposition to evaluate some symbol or object or aspect of the world in a favorable or unfavorable manner. Attitudes may function as adjustment in the service of reward, as defense, as value expression, as knowledge-seeking. Attitudes have both a cognitive and an emotional aspect.

The first attitudes the child takes toward itself and toward others reflect the influences of environmental forces toward knowledge-seeking or toward the avoidance of knowledge. We have assumed that there is an innate drive in the individual toward self-development. This drive is subject to both propelling and restraining forces in the social environment. Behaviors that lead to basic trust, autonomy, and initiative encourage self-development; such attitudes toward the self and the world function as knowledge-seeking. Behaviors that lead to mistrust or doubt restrain self-development; such attitudes imply self-compromise and function as adjustment, or as avoidance of knowing. If the content of transactions between significant others and the child accentuates shame and doubt and implies guilt, the child is likely to perceive the self from that frame of reference; this will become the context that influences the child's standards of judgment for his or her own behavior. The child will feel self-doubt, self-reproach, guilt, and shame. It is important to note that somewhat like Franz Kafka's dreamer, young children may not understand what they were guilty of and be unable to defend themselves. As children encounter new contexts within which the same behavior may be judged differently, they may change the frame of reference within which their thinking has been organized.

This is why the child needs the opportunity to search for knowledge beyond the limits of the old frame of reference. This is the point at which the striving for self-development is emphasized. Most children seek more and more understanding of behavior as they grow beyond the earliest caretakers, and experience behavior in new contexts. We know that in continuing contact with the community of elders, early play groups, and all subsequent significant reference groups, the child will seek more and more understanding beyond the boundaries of its first frame of reference, moving from one context to another in the search for more and more knowledge.

But there are some areas of those early learnings associated with shame, doubt, and guilt about which a majority of people appear to have a consensus about normative behavior. The child may not have the opportunity to view body function and sexuality in different contexts. It is not that the child necessarily views the world as the parents viewed it and thereby blocks out all knowledge-seeking in these areas because of identification with parents' attitudes. Rather, subsequent reference groups in any society are highly likely to continue to associate shame, doubt, and guilt with discharge of body wastes and with sexual functioning. These human and natural functions are socially defined; the society's values are still embedded in the nineteenth-century view of people as somehow impulse-ridden and in need of restraint in attitudes toward body wastes and sexuality. Value-laden behaviors associated with discharge of body wastes, with cleanliness, and with the expression of sexuality are embedded in the society's belief system. A majority of people, especially those in the middle socioeconomic class, still tend to endow body wastes and sexuality with negative meaning. For many people, there is a high degree of secrecy associated with how the body functions. Embarrassment and discomfort are evidenced in attitudes toward body parts, in the verbal expressions some caretakers use in toilet training their young, in four-letter words associated with body wastes and sexual intercourse which are used to express anger in the language of older children and adults, in name-calling, in graffiti, and in scapegoating.

Graffiti, for example, include drawings and inscriptions frequently found on walls of buildings, subways, and bus stations in inner cities, and walls of rest rooms in public places. A great many of these inscriptions and drawings refer to elimination of body wastes and to sexual functioning. They are intended in part to embarrass viewers; they function to express anger, a kind of flaunting of society's taboos. They pick up the theme of shame and doubt and make accusations. Some of these inscriptions suggest both a fascination with, and a fear of, body function, a certain sense of powerlessness which is compensated for in this handwriting on the walls. It is as though these walls symbolize those the society builds around knowledge of the naturalness of body function and acceptance of sexual pleasure, around knowledge and understanding of the body as an expression of the self and its integrity.

Another important area of behavior which expresses the values of a large segment of society is stereotyping. The terms used to denigrate minority groups are taken directly from society's expectations of the behavior of infants and young children conceived as passive, unreliable, impulse-ridden beings. Stereotypes applied to groups identified primarily by racial difference from the majority, and by religious and ethnic differences, suggest that members of these groups are dependent and untrustworthy, or unclean, messy, greedy, bad-smelling, or sexually uninhibited or precocious. Such beliefs are less pervasive than they once were, but they persist in many quarters.

People who stereotype other people do not engage in active reality testing. They have a psychological tendency to experience members of minorities in relation to a frame of reference they share with others like themselves. It is as though the risk in active reality testing is that some frightening truth will be uncovered, and they must protect against acknowledging what they suspect about themselves. The function of the attitude underlying stereotyping behavior is closely associated with avoidance, denial, and projection of shame and guilt.

The most likely and the most damaging defense is projection. Let us look again at the content of such projection. The stereotypes take up, or project, the negative outcomes of psychosocial crises in infancy and early childhood. Stereotyping is oversimplified opinion, judgment rendered uncritically, about a comparative reference group. The behavior of stereotyping suggests that those who use it simply cannot bear the thought that they are projecting characteristics they suspect they themselves have. At the risk of oversimplifying, the view is suggested that many people may suffer from fear that they are somehow "uncivilized," likely to be overpowered by dreadful instincts, and thus they project in the service of avoiding a discovery of a truth which is too painful to be borne.

Child-rearing practices, as we have noted, communicate to young children what others value and devalue about them, how those others perceive them, and what meanings it is desired that they will come to hold toward their own feelings of delight and fear in discovering their own capacities to elicit one or another response in themselves and in those around them. Young children's impact on their environment is visible in the extent to which they become a reference for others around them.

At the beginning of this chapter, we observed that social reality pressures people to conform to many social structures which often make personal growth for parents, as well as for young children, difficult. We turn now to some consideration of expectations associated with the roles of caretakers, who are expected to make the bridge between the developing self of the child and the social reality, and examine some of the consequences for caretaking adults of the ways in which these roles are defined.

Social Implications of Parent Roles

There are a number of social implications with regard to parent roles and the human relationship arrangements within which birth is expected to fit. Although all babies are not the same, it is expected that they will behave similarly and that the baby will be born into a nuclear family in which a father and a mother behave in a standard way. A few other children may have already arrived and be growing in the family, and the parents' focus is expected to be on the family.

For a time, the newborn child is seen as an extension of the mother. The role of all mothers is defined similarly by the society. Actually, there are many different kinds of mothers, and there are many different kinds of children, but to be defined as a mother is to be endowed with all the meanings of the average and the expectable. The mother role has little space for free movement within it, for many women.

In the American nuclear family, the responsibility placed on the mother is often so extensive as to suggest that the child is simply a product of her ministrations. According to Annaliese Korner,

often when parent-child interaction is discussed, reference is really being made to what a mother does *with* or *to* a child. Unwittingly, the interaction is seen as a one-way street rather than as a true reciprocal exchange.[29]

The mother is frequently judged by the extent to which the baby follows normative expectations of growth and behavior. She is expected to anticipate, elicit, and respond to phase-specific behavior of the child, and to do this intuitively. Louis Sander discusses the phase-specific needs of the infant to which the mother is generally expected to respond in the first eighteen months of the baby's life. During the first few months, she is expected to be the object of the symbiotic relationship, to shield the baby, mediating between it and excessive stimulation, to provide stimuli and to reciprocate the child's first efforts at play and initiative. After the sixth month, she is expected to accept both the assertiveness of the baby and its demands that she alone meet its needs.[30] Korner has also suggested that there is no one correct way to deal with children or to be a parent.

The hidden assumption underlying the expectations for the mother's role is that mothering is a natural function for women. It is assumed that women already have all the art, talent, continuing support, and resources they need to fill these highly idealized role expectations. The role is essentially learned and conceived as a gestalt, and there appears to be resistance among many people to breaking it down into its parts. While there are exceptions, the notion of a dormant "maternal instinct" still has wide acceptance. It is as though this "instinct" were triggered by giving birth to a child, and from that point on it serves as a kind of automatic pilot for any mother who is not too perverse or unintelligent to be guided by it. Resistance to education for the role of mother attests to these assumptions. The role of mother is ascribed, and generally taken for granted. It is enacted without expectations of financial reward, and for many mothers it carries little special recognition. But the nonperformance of the role may elicit severe negative evaluation, and the mother who may be inept in her mothering is not infrequently regarded and treated as somehow "unnatural" or "uncaring."

Women have a wide range of responses to the role. Many find it self-actualizing; others do not. In order to play the role comfortably, to continue to experience self-actualization in it, one has to be able to differentiate one's selfhood from one's motherhood. The greater the freedom of choice in taking on the role, and the greater the space for free movement within it, the more likely such differentiation will be possible.

Historically, the role has its background in the social organization of the larger society and the expected division of labor in the nuclear family. Later, we will discuss some of the problems associated with the ideal of the American family. At this point, it seems important to suggest that findings of earlier studies, of the destructive consequences of separation of infants and young children from their mothers, might be interpreted as a form of self-fulfilling prophecy. The assumption already existed that separations of mothers and their children had extremely untoward results. In the last decade, studies of short-term separations and of some long-term separations have tended to reverse findings that the continued presence of the biological mother is the critical factor to healthy development. More critical than the mother's presence, per se, is the nature of stimulating interactions in infant and early childhood development, the presence of caring adults, and the conscious and continued efforts to meet the social and psychological needs of children. This is not to say that children should be separated from their mothers. It is simply to suggest that the woman's need to mother is not all-pervasive and may demand too high a cost in the idealized American family.

Therese Benedek makes the point that the child has an absolute need for mothering but that the woman's need to mother is relative.[31] Alice Rossi observes that

from a concern for the child, this discrepancy in need leads to an analysis of the impact on the child of separation from the mother or inadequacy of mothering. Family systems that provide numerous adults to care for the young child can make up for this discrepancy in need between mother and child, which may be why ethnographic accounts give little evidence of postpartum depression following childbirth in simpler societies. Yet our family system of isolated households, increasingly distant from kinswomen to assist in mothering, requires that new mothers shoulder total responsibility for the infant precisely for that stage of the child's life when his need for mothering is far in excess of the mother's need for the child.[32]

A new recognition, complementary to Rossi's observation, has been occurring with regard to the real capacity of the father for tenderness and caring, directly associated with an interest of many fathers in further involvement with infants and young children. Traditionally, the father has been left out of the process. Those maternal transactions between babies and young children and their mothers have historically not included the father, whose responsibility lay outside the nurturing and rearing of young children. The father role is also a product of social definition. Recent liberation of fathers from traditional expectations has resulted in supportive participation in the birth process and more direct involvement of numbers of fathers in infant and child rearing, but many pressures continue to make this difficult for men.

Many babies and young children within highly traditional families can develop basic trust, autonomy, and initiative, and experience joy and growth toward self-fulfillment. There are numbers of children born into nuclear families whose chances to live creatively and to grow are enhanced by the composition of their family. There are also numbers of families that are not composed in the traditional way, in which babies can similarly experience behaviors that accentuate trust, autonomy, and initiative. We may think, for example, of families whose composition includes only one biological parent, or one parent only, families composed by adoption rather than by biological parentage, families whose boundaries are not defined solely in terms of parents and biological children. Such families need to be valued positively; they need to be seen as worthwhile family forms whose outcomes for children can be positive and supportive of children's self-development.

There are many women who freely choose to become mothers, and for whom this life choice is a true self-option; it leads to satisfying and fulfilling life relationships which result in growth and integration of human experience, to self-actualization, and to the actualization of others. There are also women who do not have freedom of choice to play or not to play this life role. It is not only that in many families the role is so highly valued that the pressure to choose the role is very strong; in addition, in many other groups, such negative valuation is associated with the woman who is not a mother, that for some women playing the role is not a self-option. The current controversy over the right to choose abortion, which is generally couched in terms of whether human life exists or does not exist *in utero*, tends to obscure the extent to which the right to commit the self to the role with a sense of sovereignty about the choice is denied to many women.

The Problem of Being Called Illegitimate

Positive and negative valuation of human life expresses itself socially in a variety of ways. Earlier we have discussed what we see as some of the negative implications of self-development in an interpersonal context of behaviors that accentuate the learning of self-doubt, self-reproach, guilt and shame. At this point we are going to raise for consideration some implications of self-development in a context of societal behavior that defines the roles of infant and young child from legal and economic perspectives. We shall discuss this first in the aspect of the problem created by calling children illegitimate.

In recent years, most states have given up the designation of "illegitimate" for babies whose parents have not had legally sanctioned marriages. In the recent past, when a child's parents had not made a legal marriage contract before its birth, the society, through its legal machinery, could declare that that child's existence was not a legitimate existence.

Society's declaration was heavily influenced by the economic order and by negative attitudes toward sexuality, entrenched in a conventional morality that assumed a "moral order of rights and duties"[33] from which the value of a human life was derived according to its presumed place within that scheme. Based on this social reality, the society defined a boundary between some human lives as legal and others as illegal, depending on their parents' commitment to maintain the social order, as evidenced in a legal marriage contract. Evidence for the arbitrary nature of this assumption comes from our knowledge that although the equivalent of our word "baby" exists in all languages in all societies, some societies have no language equivalent for the concept of "illegitimate baby."[34] This is to say that in such societies the possibility of a conception of a new human life as illegal does not exist. In the wisdom of such societies, the "human value of respect for the individual as an object of moral principle"[35] appears to extend to all infants, regardless of the circumstances of their birth.

That infants and children have rights as persons, and a conception of their selfhood or personhood, is becoming an accepted concept in this society, but the implementation of human rights has advanced very slowly. The difficult questions posed by the challenge to the notion that a baby's life can be illegal are yet to be answered by the majority of people in the society, who perceive birth without a legally sanctioned marriage between parents as deviance from the society's expectations regarding the form and function of the family. From this perspective, the mere existence of children so born is viewed as weakening family life.[36] Harry Krause reviewed a wide range of legal arguments supporting legislation that sanctions discrimination between "legitimate" and "illegitimate" children. Writing in 1969, he concluded that the view that the family is endangered if legal distinctions between "legitimate" and "illegitimate" children are not maintained is not rational.

No rational reason supports the wholesale discrimination imposed by our present legal order. . . . It seems clear that a great advancement in the legal position of the illegitimate will be realized . . . without harm to existing institutions. The family will not cease to exist. This is a tired concern.[37]

Along with the close association between the law and social attitudes which are expressed in legislation that attempts to define the rights of human beings, the economic order has also historically influenced heavily the society's institutionalized attitudes and behavior toward children's births. This same society, which until very recently defined as illegal any birth outside a legally sanctioned family unit, has in its history the deliberate breaking up of black families to serve economic interests, and denial to black parents of the

right to engage legally in a marriage.[38] Some of the assumptions underlying these acts have their echoes in the more
recent economic history of the society's response toward people
who are poor. Many people with readier access to the economic
goods and resources of the society assume that people who are
poor are characterized by sexual promiscuity, low moral
values, and low commitment to enduring human relationship
patterns which are believed to complement most adequately
the social and psychological needs of young children. Ryan has
analyzed the relationship between poverty, illegitimacy, and
the society's dominant attitudes toward social and economic
provision of support for poor families. He concludes that

illegitimacy is functionally useful to society. . . . Society encourages
illegitimacy . . . by discouraging responsible parenthood through
making it impossible for the black and the poor to make responsible
choices about parenthood.[39]

Social workers, we believe, need to be very clear about the
implications, for the young child's self-development, of the
society's boundary drawing between "good" and "bad,"
"legitimate" and "illegitimate" roles. Application of "legitimate" and "illegitimate" to infants, toddlers, and young
children is a form of labeling that seems to share many of the
characteristics we have discussed earlier with regard to
stereotyping.

Wanted and Unwanted Children
The economic order of the society influences other social
definitions of babies and young children as highly or not highly
valued. One of the ways in which a society expresses its positive valuation of children's lives is through seeing to it that
their nutritional and health needs are adequately met. Our
society has thus far failed to solve the problem of universal,
expectable, and equitable distribution of food and health care
to all its component groups. It has been documented that
"nutritional deprivations or imbalances occurring early in life
(prenatal or postnatal) will interfere with the normal development of the brain and of learning ability."[40] We have referred
earlier to the fact that the mortality rate for nonwhite infants
has always been higher in the United States than it has for

white infants. A 1967 study, by the U.S. Children's Bureau, of deaths of infants before their first birthday showed that although mortality rates of both nonwhite and white infants had decreased between 1950 and 1964, the gap between the survival chances for nonwhite and white infants had drastically widened between those years. Additionally, there is reason to believe that if services were improved, between 20 percent and 50 percent of infant deaths would be preventable. The nutritional and health state of pregnant women also affects their babies' chances of being born healthy, and of surviving the first year of life.[41]

Given the long-term effects of nutritional deficiency or imbalance in early life, and inequalities in the accessibility of pre- and postnatal health care to infants and their mothers, caretaking behaviors that accentuate the learning of trust, autonomy, and initiative may be difficult to sustain when caretakers are powerless to meet their own and their children's nutritional and health needs.

This raises question of whether all babies are approved and wanted, or whether economics is recognized as the major force that determines which babies survive. For a number of reasons people may not want to have children, and economic means is one of them. The infant's life chances often depend on the parents' ability to pay for special care. Lack of adequate medical care accounts for many of these deaths; inadequate nutrition, medical care, and the circumstances of life for their mothers account for complications in pregnancy that have serious consequences for growth *in utero* and for the physical integrity and survival of the newborn. We have referred earlier to the implications for some women of lack of freedom to choose the role of mother. Freedom to choose the role, and to meet the expectations that it is the right of every child to be wanted, may be seriously curtailed when inaccessibility of food, of health care, and of education for the role make responsible choices difficult for parents.

Childhood

No absolute point marks a time or place at which childhood begins and earlier life stages end. Human growth is cumulative, and is not marked by discrete sequences. Phases of development overlap, not smoothly but marked by occasional growth spurts and plateaus.

Childhood tends to be defined by the society's response to the need of its young to seek knowledge; society also defines the condition of childhood by its own need to educate children according to the value it places on what they should know. The school is the social institution responsible for continuing the acculturation of children who become identified as preschool or school-age children. Children identify themselves, as well, according to their position in the graded hierarchy of the school, and by the interim rites of passage within and from preschool to elementary to high school.

Perspectives on Childhood

Frequently, adults idealize childhood as a time of freedom from responsibility, worry, and anxiety, a time of blissful and carefree play in a land of toys and make-believe. Adults also identify children as a comparative reference group, seeing the child as having a mind inferior to that of the adult, or as weaker and less competent. When people fail to fulfill the expectations of adulthood, they are sometimes referred to as "childish," or as behaving like a child. Children also compare themselves with those who are older and more powerful, and they see themselves as less adequate and less well-off.

Underlying the transactions which children initiate with others is a yearning to gain knowledge and skills and to become more adequate in the eyes of others.

Psychologically, a great deal of attention is paid to the needs of children to explore and to learn about the world in the service of the drive to grow and to exercise competence. While children are propelled by inner forces to realize their human potential, they are also restrained by social definitions of childhood and by certain normative expectations of their behavior. Significant reference individuals and groups do not entirely determine their self-esteem, but they are still quite impressionable and strongly influenced by approval and disapproval from those who exercise authority over them as well as by the expectations of their peers. Negative responses associated with discrimination against minority groups hurt the children in these groups; sex role socialization limits the realization of self-potential of girls and to a much lesser extent of boys, and developmentally disabled children are also subject to multiple forces that restrain self-realization.

Getting the Child's Perspective on Childhood

Very few theories of child development are based on exhaustive investigation of children's behavior; this fact qualifies their predictive value. Those "average, expectable" children and adults on whose transactions most child development theories are based may not always be the majority of children and adults. Moreover, there are relatively few studies of child-adult transactions in periods of active social change; we have a great deal still to learn about how the changing conditions of children's lives affect them.

One of the reasons that such learning is difficult is that those of us who presume to study children have frequently found it difficult to learn directly from them. Sometimes they tell us about their lives, and we do not understand what it is they are saying. Our own adult socialization has changed our perspective on childhood and our observations of children tend to confirm our preconceived beliefs, which in turn have influenced what we have chosen to observe. Social workers need to consider dominant social and psychological theories of childhood from this point of view.

Having learned the language of adults, children can engage in complex and often quite subtle communication from which adult observers can make many inferences. For example, children enjoy puns and words with double meanings, but frequently they cannot find the words to express their feelings. Many children keep their thoughts to themselves in the presence of adults. Often adults do not take children's ideas about things seriously except when they have violated some moral regulation. In such a situation it is difficult for children to translate their thoughts into words; it can be quite risky to do so, if those thoughts are about feelings which may violate the standards of morality held by significant adults in their lives. In their own world of thought, children may dream of unreality; they may endow people and objects in their surroundings with meanings which have no actual relationship to these people or objects, and they may create imaginary others with whom private thoughts can be shared.

Self-Regard and Body Image

Body image is an important part of the self-image, and the image one has of one's self ultimately determines self-regard. To take on the child's perspective may, for example, mean understanding how interested children are in their bodies. Young children are fascinated by what they can do with their bodies—for example, wiggling their ears, touching their noses with their fingers, crossing their eyes, starting and stopping urination with studied intent, turning cartwheels.

Most adults want children to be comfortable in their bodies, but adults, pressed to make children conform to normative behavior, may be quite inflexible in their demands for conformity in children's responses to their own bodies. We have discussed some of the problems associated with restricting those responses, of suggesting that certain body parts are "bad" or "wrong." There is reason to believe that the less sure adults are of the value of conformity in this area, the more inflexible they become. Sometimes adults' own prior socialization has left a need to deny their own childhood experiences because those experiences were painful for them.

It is very important, then, to allow children to be their own people and not to make them miniatures of ourselves. Children solve many problems in new ways; adults are not always the experts in solving children's problems. In fact, as adults we need to see children with their problems rather than as problems to ourselves. If we get this perspective, we will not impose our solutions on them so much.

Some Social and Psychological Theories of Childhood

Bearing these ideas in mind as some ways of looking at the social reality of children, we turn now to several lines of theory which explain some of the sources of the expectations that make up that social reality.

The Sources of Positive Self-Regard
According to Robert White

The reader will recall Robert White's view of the dual sources out of which the child synthesizes both an awareness of a self that is independent of its actions, and a history of actions in and on its environment, and their potential for providing a sense of efficacy. In his discussion of the bases of self-esteem, White observes that esteem for the self "has its deepest roots in the experience of efficacy. It is not constructed out of what others do or what the environment gratuitously provides."[1] White's views emphasize the child's motivation to master the environment. To him, the source of self-esteem is the child's sense of competence that results from those transactions in which what the child is able to accomplish and encouragement from those that count are complementary.[2] Children acquire competence through eliciting positive response from others, and they are encouraged by the recognition they receive. The point is that children can and do initiate action which fulfills the need for real accomplishment for which they can be respected. Self-respect is critical to self-esteem, and self-esteem reflects positive self-regard. Children are not likely to respect themselves unless they can do things they can be proud of doing.

At a time when self-regard depends so much on the actual

accomplishment of mastery, children are frequently seen by adults as incompetent. The things that children make and do are then not taken seriously because children's productions are assumed to be inferior to what adults can produce. Highly motivated to initiate action which fulfills the need for competence, the child is nevertheless influenced by what the society expects and defines as competence.

Inner Speech and Self-Reference

Earlier, we have noted that acquiring speech provides the child with a new model of experience and interaction with its environment. This new mode implies a change in perspective in that the child now acquires a verbal self, can begin to attend to that self, and also begins to decipher and order the world, to classify things, and to make generalizations. Increasing mastery of speech allows children not only to communicate more accurately and deliberately with others, but also enables them to begin to detach themselves from the immediate situation, as well as to communicate with themselves. Children work very hard to master the language with which their society provides them, and one of the outcomes of increasing language facility is the achievement of a capacity for "inner speech." Through speech, children acquire an instrument for discovering their own thoughts, and for beginning to distinguish between thoughts and intentions, not only of others but, equally important, their own. Although the inner speech of young children may take the form more of a monologue than a dialogue, the capacity to put experience into verbal form allows the child to become, eventually, both speaker and audience. With speech, the child begins to develop self-awareness, to take a perspective on the self as an actor, and to "experience the self as experiencing."[3] In the development of this dual perspective, whereby the child not only perceives the world, but is aware of the self as perceiving, acquiring language plays an important role, and mastery of language propels the child toward a more "relativistic" stance, from which the child can eventually experience a sense of freedom from being locked into his or her own point of view.[4]

Children, then, experience themselves in a new way, as the authors of their own ideas and utterances, and self-respect comes to be linked with the way in which their verbal, as well as motor, behavior is received.

Erikson's Formulation: Industry versus Inferiority

Erikson equates a sense of industry with a sense of usefulness, of being able to make things well.[5] In this view, a critical component of the individual's transactions is the struggle to maintain a sense of industry in the face of pressures to feel inferior. Erikson sees the danger that the child can develop a lasting sense of inadequacy and inferiority. He discusses the need of children for encouragement and support from parents and positive responses from those adults who function as their teachers. Erikson deals with interpersonal bases for the child's continued growth and development. He sees the child's neighborhood, community of others, and the school as the radius of significant relations. Their significance lies in the fact that they can accentuate for the child an expectation that its ability to have an effect on its environment will be recognized and welcomed. When, instead, others demonstrate to the child that such an expectation is unwarranted, their response will accentuate a sense of inferiority.

The Myth of Latency

Traditional psychoanalytic theory referred to childhood as "latency." It was assumed that the superego became established, although not highly developed, as a result of the resolution of the oedipal conflict. The child had internalized the prohibitions of the parents and could subsequently control instinctual urges. Erotic impulses, then, were repressed, but remained "latent" until the onset of puberty, when they would be stirred up again.[6] From this perspective, childhood was generally viewed as a peaceful and innocent time in which conflicts were held in abeyance and in which the child was motivated to learn and to master the environment.

This view suggests that sexuality is not part of the environment of children and that what a child wants to learn, or fears to learn, is determined by repression and has nothing to do with the expectations of those who are closest to it. Most observers of human behavior have learned much more about childhood and recognize the sampling errors in Freud's early work,[7] but a large number of people continue to reflect expectations associated with the "latency" view. For example, a pervasive attitude is that sexuality is bad and wrong, and should be hidden from children.

In contrast to this view, childhood is a time of learning how to resolve many conflicts. Those children for whom it is relatively peaceful do not appear to be in the majority. Those things which the child wants to learn, and the attitudes of adults toward the child's right to learn, may create dread and emotional crises for children. Childhood is a time of forwarding mastery of the environment, of shifting reference groups, of dealing with many pressures to conform to what the majority of people believe about childhood. The secrecy surrounding sexuality may be a source of conflict for many children. This behavior is a product of transactions which do not complement the child's ability to understand and to grow.

The "Juvenile Era"
Harry Stack Sullivan has discussed the years from six to twelve as the "juvenile era."[8] Sullivan is responsible for a revision in child development theory which emphasizes interpersonal relationships and life crises in terms of social transactions. He described those social transactions most critical to childhood as occurring with other children. For Sullivan, the major problems of childhood were compromise and competition in peer relationships. These relationships do not initially offer gratification of needs for love. Children do not necessarily nurture each other; they put each other to a variety of tests of physical and mental strength and quickness. In their relationships with other children, they learn new ways of relating, of giving and taking, and of protecting themselves and each other. Sullivan stressed progressively complex development of competence through learning new role behaviors.

Sullivan introduced the notion of the critical reference group of other children and viewed the development of peer transactions as having new relationship elements which challenge the child's abilities. His view stresses the shift from preoccupation with adult caretakers to the world of school. In preschool, children begin to orient themselves to other children. In the present day, many children are beginning school much earlier than kindergarten, and by the time they have reached the first grade of formal school, they are oriented to others like themselves with whom they learn to play and to work at social organization. The social organization created by children through their transactions with each other is the society of children, and the child's self-boundaries are related to this society.

Children soon learn to measure themselves by standards set by the school; for most of them, these standards are a carry-over from those set by adults at home. The important new group of peers will serve the growing child in many ways. Peers will offer acceptance when adults do not accept; they will most often recognize accomplishments and accept or reject in complementary fashion. They are not likely to keep secrets from each other; they share the world of school and play, and offer, for most children, somewhat more equal comparative reference groups than adults do. If children learn how to compromise and to compete, at least they can be matched with others like themselves more often than with adults.

Taking the Role of the Other
In earlier discussion we presented George Herbert Mead's conceptions of self-development. His conceptions were based on observations of children at play. It was through play, he proposed, that the child learns to take the role of another person and, eventually, of many others. Through taking the roles of others, the child can explore others' attitudes toward the self, respond to the self from the perspective of these attitudes, and become an object to herself or himself. Mead viewed the child as an active explorer at an early age; he viewed play as the first stage of self-consciousness, and organized games as the second stage of self-development.

Unlike play, which may be solitary, games are organized social activities which include rules and clear-cut expectations of each player. Mead used team games as illustrations of that level of social organization at which the child must be aware of the attitudes of all other players. From learning to generalize—that is, holding a number of factors in mind at the same time and generalizing from them—the child, he thought, becomes aware of the complexity of social relationships. The child generalizes from many constellations of others, of rules and regulations and expectations of behavior which elicit positive or negative response from others beyond the family. The child thus learns about the self in increasingly complex role relationships.[9]

Mead has provided a view of self-development which emphasizes learning and competence, and which explains how, though not why, competence develops. He believed that children come to be aware of themselves as they play and use their own creativity. The child learns most, that is, in situations which challenge old ways of behaving. In Mead's eyes, the child is open to new experiences and capable of making things happen in new ways.

Traditional theories of learning define the child as a passive recipient of preplanned offerings of teachers, of adult approval and disapproval. Self-learning requires freedom to explore, to follow through on activities which may not always make sense to teachers, and which may not fit preplanned curricula. From Mead's point of view, learning is a social process through which the child, as participant, becomes aware of the self and can understand many self-motivated behaviors. The self becomes more and more independent of others, although always related to other selves, as the child takes on and organizes more and more knowledge of the complexity of organized human relationships.

The School as a Socializing Institution

When we discussed infancy and early childhood, we noted that environmental influences operate as both propelling and restraining forces on the individual's intrinsic motivation toward self-management. Our discussion of the significance of the child's social environment has highlighted self-development in terms of the development of attitudes toward the self and others. Since the school is a major institution for continuing children's acculturation, its influence on the attitudes they develop is significant.

It will be recalled that one of the major functions of attitudes is knowledge-seeking. Attitudes are developed according to the need people have to give meaning to relationships with others; they function so that situations which are otherwise ambiguous can be organized in such a way as to help individuals to make sense out of what is happening in their lives. Children's attitudes toward learning are primarily characterized by knowledge-seeking, and this attitude is frequently changed in the formal school situation. In many schools children are still expected to be inactive, to accept passively what they are offered by the school, and to give up their own knowledge-seeking initiative.

Children spend a good part of their lives in school, where the expectations of children which are sanctioned by the society are taught primarily through formal instruction. Formal instruction frequently precludes spontaneity in knowledge-seeking and self-learning. Children may take on the role of a first grader with some pride and find themselves facing many contradictory definitions of what it is to be a school-age child. Sometimes they are viewed as deficient adults, small and incompetent replicas. As a comparative reference group, adults offer little children very little reason to believe that they are important. Much of the behavior of children is seen as irrelevant except as it reflects assumptions of ideal values of behavior which are not usually reflected in adult behavior. Children are often viewed in the school situation according to the scores they achieve on certain general tests of intelligence. They are also defined by the instructior's past experience with children of their race, sex, age, and socioeconomic level, and they are frequently endowed with characeristics they do not have. In general, the more children are like their teachers, the greater are the chances that they will be liked by these teachers.

The extent to which children are able to determine the nature of their relationship to the world of the school may depend upon the prejudgments existing in the society into which they were born and in which they will develop their conception of self. To a large extent, the pattern of expectations, the values and the options available to children are determined by the ways in which the society responds to them as human resources.

As a socializing agent of the society, the school is not an entirely free agent. The educational arrangements which are characteristic of most schools have recurred again and again until they are below the psychological sights of people. They are simply taken for granted, and it is very difficult for schools to change their programs. Most people do not want change, and they see the schools of the present and the future in terms of those of the past. There appears to be much less concern in the community about providing a stimulating learning experience for children than about maintaining discipline and good conduct.

Many teachers continue to follow theories of learning which support the notion that children are passive learners and thus disregard the autonomy and initiative underlying the child's knowledge-seeking. According to Denzin:

These theories of learning, which view the child in passive terms, have been systematically translated into theories of education. Teachers, not children, are seen as experts on all matters. Children are thought to be unreliable objects, who must be actively controlled, tested repeatedly, never given a say in what they are taught, and rewarded for passive acceptance of the teacher's and the school's point of view. These theories of learning, then, complement and support the broader position that children are incompetent social beings.[10]

If we see this in the light of the young child's need for self-esteem based on encouragement which complements an inner force toward realization of potential for competence, we can understand some of the reasons many children wall themselves off from their teachers or give conventional responses in the classroom. From the point of view of the child, we can begin to appreciate the sense of powerlessness in the role. It is no wonder that the relationship between teacher and child often becomes a power struggle under such conditions.

The Child's Right to Self-Actualization
The child has a human right to grow toward self-actualization, but few attempts have been made to clarify this right and its implementation. Albert E. Wilkerson discusses the rights of children as emergent concepts in the society. He observes that

The capacity of a society to value human rights and the determination to give them substance . . . is related to its long process of social maturation. This maturation has to do with increasing faith in human potentialities and a decreasing fear of wider human freedoms, and to a value orientation that places the individual at the center of the human drama—even above economic systems and political ideologies.

Within this kind of social maturation, the child is discovered, too, as a person. In long historical perspective, this involves moving from a view of the child's worth primarily for his future potential as a carrier of the culture, to perceiving him as an adult in miniature, to seeing him as having a right to the status of childhood with its own needs and peculiarities, to a perception of the child as a person with his full range of rights with societal mechanisms for their enhancement.[11]

Social workers have worked to protect the rights of children, and they have a history of work with schools, in which they have variously been employed as trouble shooters, counselors, advisers on children's problems, consultants to teachers, parents, and community groups. In recent years, they have been in the forefront of advocacy for children's right to a learning environment conducive to the realization of their human potential. A number of schools and innovative programs do take account of the rights of children. In observing these schools and the outcomes for those children who attend them, one is tempted to believe that the society has achieved the maturation to which Wilkerson refers. But such schools appear to be the exception. The current conflict over desegregation in the schools and the extent to which the victims of poor education are blamed for their failure to learn attest to the scarcity of such programs. We can only hope that the present turmoil is a response to the transition from the past and that the society will implement its capacity to value the human rights of children.

The School and Standards of Measurement
Social workers are especially concerned with traditional stereotypic assumptions about differences between white children and nonwhite and other minority children. Such assumptions are reflected in the standards of measurement used to assess children's learning ability and their progress in the school system. Application of these standards of measure-

ment has been closely linked to a conception of intelligence level as a genetic or biological given. Recent developments strongly indicate that intelligence cannot be accurately measured through testing. Nevertheless, intelligence testing has been used as a basis for labeling children, many of whom have subsequently been denied educational opportunities. Many young children have been classified as intellectually inferior, without regard for their potential for intellectual functioning.

Relatively recent research by Arthur Jensen, directed to proving racial genetic inequality in intelligence, provides reinforcement for a major assumption of limited learning capacity of black people. In pursuit of the genetic hypothesis, Jensen and his associates tested matched groups of white and black elementary school children and found conceptual ability differences between the groups. Black children performed significantly less well than white children on those tasks that required conceptual ability.[12] Jensen used his findings to support his contention that genetic difference rather than environmental influences account for poorer performance of black children on scholastic aptitude and achievement tests.

Following Jensen's work, Philip Scrofani, Antanas Suziedelis, and Milton Shore submitted the theory of inherent conceptual ability differences between black and white children to further inquiry. They used Jensen's tests and procedures to locate matched samples of children of high and low intelligence. They provided half the children in their samples with pretraining in concept formation. Results of their study revealed that pretrained, low IQ children demonstrated higher conceptual problem-solving abilities than did their untrained counterparts. There was no evidence to indicate that black children were different from white children in their conceptual functioning. If Jensen's theory had been correct, the effect of training would have been to widen the gap between performance levels of black and white children, since training would not be able to influence a genetically determined level of conceptual problem-solving ability.[13]

Many investigators have found an educational gap between black and white students, comparing black students in ghetto schools and white students in schools situated outside the inner cities. Ryan has observed that the differences in achievement between black and nonblack students in these school environments describe surface aspects of the deeper problem. He advances several linked hypotheses which are supported by investigations of the underlying problem:

... first, that the *effect* of poverty, race, and family background can be observed to a small extent in the minds of the children but to a much greater extent in the interactions in the classroom, which ultimately produces a falling off of academic performance; second, that the primary effect of poverty, race and family background is not on the children, but on the teacher, who is led to *expect* poorer performance from black and poor children . . . and finally, that the expectations of the teacher are a major determinant of the children's performances. [14]

The consequences of teachers' expectations were illustrated in an investigation undertaken by Robert Rosenthal and Lenore Jacobson. In this experiment, teachers were told that some of their students could be expected to improve their academic performance during the school year. The teachers were persuaded that these children would show spurts in achievement, indicated by new tests of intelligence which were designed to predict academic gains. The children whom Rosenthal and his fellow experimenters designated as "spurters" were simply chosen at random. They were not different from other students in the class; they did not show higher scores than did other students. Nevertheless, the children for whom the teachers were led to expect higher achievement did show marked improvement in comparison with the other students. They also showed gains in IQ scores which were especially marked in the first and second grades, in which the average gains in IQ were 27 and 16 points, respectively. Teachers expressed many more positive attitudes toward these children and responded to "nonspurters" (control group children) more negatively. [15]

Findings like this indicate that the solution does not lie in changing underachievers but in changing the interpersonal environment, changing the nature of their transactions with those who control, assess, or judge them. The educational environment within which minority children are expected to learn is quite frequently characterized by expectations that they will fail. Such expectations define the role of a failing person; they define the kinds of expectations that children who fill the role are to hold of themselves. Since failing, or "low achievement," implies performance that by definition is not congruent with the range of desired or acceptable behaviors, the child can only succeed in, and maintain, such a role by fulfilling expectations of inadequacy or incompetence.

The findings of studies such as those of Rosenthal and Scrofani and their associates reveal that it is not that low-achieving children lack conceptual ability, but that denying educational opportunity to children labeled on the basis of intelligence tests as lacking, or deficient, in such ability means that they are denied the opportunity to learn what they are capable of and to know that this capability is useful.

Expectations of failure are frequently associated with the labels "disadvantaged" and "culturally deprived." Although many poverty-oriented children live in conditions which disadvantage them—hunger, poor health care, inadequate housing, no play space—it is not clear just what culture they are deprived of. In addition to this, there are many black and other minority children who do not live in poverty; within minority communities there are differences in economic and educational status of parents and families. If the label "disadvantaged" refers to conditions of poverty outside the school, then equating disadvantaged with culturally deprived strongly suggests that the idea of "culture" is being defined in terms of possession of, or access to, economic goods and resources. But if culture is understood to refer to beliefs and values that characterize an identified community, then people who constitute that community are not deprived of a culture because they have differential access to economic resources. Minority communities have cultures, and cultural histories, which most members of the majority community know very little about, and which many do not very much care to know about. This situation helps to explain why the designation of culturally deprived is not so commonly assigned, in our society and in its schools, to nonminority children; the term culturally deprived child calls up, for most people, the image of a black or other minority child. There is, in addition, cultural variation within minority as within majority communities.

Studies of racially homogeneous groups of minority children have been conducted from the point of view that race does not define a condition of being culturally deprived, but that this characterization of children confuses race and economic conditions of life. In these studies, children defined as culturally deprived on the basis not of race, but of great poverty and its concomitants, showed no differences in academic achievement in early grades, first through fourth. It could be that the effects of what the child brings with him to the school would be most evident in these eary years. In the fifth and subsequent grades, however, those children originally seen as culturally deprived, that is, economically much poorer children, began to do less well. This occurred when the cumulative influence of the school might be expected to be greater; the observed differences have been attributed to the child's experiences in the school environment.[16]

Most teachers want children to do well in school; it is not that they are deliberately unkind or neglectful. We have noted that schools are not entirely free agents; teachers similarly are not completely free, but are bound by the institutionalized expectations and beliefs that have informed their own acculturation and their own preparation for their roles, as well as by the pressures to conform to judgments and attitudes of the wider society outside the school. As we have noted, many teachers continue to follow, and many schools continue to reflect in what they offer to children, theories of learning that disregard children's problem-solving initiative.

The education of Puerto Rican children, for example, has been evaluated in regard to language and learning. According to Joseph Fitzpatrick, the failure of the school system to respond to Puerto Rican children's style of communication has resulted in an inability on the part of many Puerto Rican children to learn. He describes the school as

too inflexible to adapt itself to the capacity of Puerto Rican children to learn if their creativity and style of expression do not fit into its standardized curriculum and methods. It has failed to win the support of Puerto Rican parents because they feel largely excluded from it.[17]

The institutionalized behaviors and expectations of most schools have largely ignored the reference groups, the community of elders, and the institutions outside the school to which many Puerto Rican and other minority children refer their behavior and which support their knowledge-seeking attitudes and efforts to learn. Indeed, if minority children had only the majority society to which to refer for appraisal and evaluation of themselves, the odds against learning would be overwhelming. It is important to keep in mind that minority communities do not accept the definition of low achievement applied to many of their children. In this connection, black scholars have pointed out the significance to black children of a reference group of others who are black.[18]

The controversy over desegregation of the schools is implicated in all of this. Desegregation is not an educational program. It provides opportunity for educators to act; it offers schools the opportunity to capitalize on what has been learned about the effects of the school environment on children's realization of their potential. Some enlightened educators have dropped the old images of race and poverty and emphasize the educational values in having children with many different perspectives of the world learn together. In this period of transition from one set of social norms to another, young children themselves are the only group who do not have to unlearn behaviors which have been deeply internalized from previous socialization.

In light of all of this, it becomes more important to adopt theories of education which view children in active terms, as reliable objects, even experts on some matters, and to stress their competence. During the transitional process, all those adults involved in the desegregation controversy are called upon to use interpersonal skills in ways for which they are unprepared by previous socialization. New criteria for the assessment of educational achievement are being established, and these measures must be publicly supported. The notion that changes in normative expectations are for the benefit of children described as disadvantaged or deprived is an erroneous one, unless it can be applied to all children. Such changes in institutionalized behaviors provide a greater space for free movement within and between social roles for all people. They can enrich and enlarge the lives of all children and adults, as they transcend barriers to self-realization associated with minority and majority group status.

Sex-Role Socialization

Sex-role socialization sets up another barrier to self-actualization for many children. We have discussed intelligence, the standards used to measure the worth of children, and the extent to which misleading classifications disadvantage all children. Nevertheless, such comparisons are not, in their immediate consequences, as painful for nonminority as for minority children. The majority group does not suffer from negative response on the basis of race or ethnic identity. Keeping in mind, then, that any additional barrier to self-actualization exacerbates stress for minority children who are already discriminated against, we turn our attention to the critical human problems created by sex-role socialization.

We have previously referred to role discontinuity, recalling Benedict's definition of cultural continuity; that is, that the child is taught nothing that it will have to unlearn later. In a rapidly changing society, many discontinuous role expectations illustrate the restraints which sex role socialization places on children's realization of self-potential. For example, a double standard for morality appears in the expectations of many adults that children remain relatively sexless and the tendency of many adults to assess their own worth and success in interpersonal relationships by the extent of their sexual activities in these relationships. In more concrete terms, little boys are not expected to play with dolls or to be interested in tender ministration to babies, but are expected as adults to marry and to help care for little babies. These are only two examples of inconsistency in role expectations for children, who must revise their behavior drastically—who must, indeed, reverse it—in order to make the transition to the role of adult. If children learn that sexual expression is dangerous and evil, there is no guarantee that they will unlearn this as adults. Yet the majority of adults are expected to enjoy sexuality, at least within the limits of a marriage relationship. Benedict comments:

It is not surprising that in such a society many individuals fear to use behavior which has up to that time been under a ban and trust instead, though at great psychic cost, to attitudes that have been exercised with approval during the formative years.[19]

   Benedict's observations provide insights into a number of problems inherent in the ambiguities of social role learning in childhood. These ambiguities are more obvious at a time when sex-role stereotypes are being challenged in the society.

   Traditional sex-role definitions have offered children of both sexes an extremely limited view of their own human potential. They define fixed patterns of behavior, discourage critical judgment, and present the child with an overwhelming number of oversimplified opinions of adult life. Sex-role stereotypes have been presented to children in a variety of ways, including the kinds of toys with which they are expected to play, the extent to which they are expected to participate actively or passively in play and work situations, and the adult models with which they are expected to identify. Children have been expected to accept the social definition of the comparative worth of masculine and feminine roles, and the normative behaviors with which each of these roles is associated. Lenore J. Weitzman and her associates have noted that "with regard to relative status, they learn that boys are more highly valued than girls. And with regard to personality differences, they learn that boys are active and achieving, while girls are passive and emotional."[20]

   Eleanor Maccoby examined sex differences in regard to intellectual functioning and found that girls fall behind boys as they become socialized although at first they are better achievers.[21] This finding implies that training for passivity restrains initiative of girls. Children who learn that they are expected to be inactive and dependent also tend not to expect active mastery and competence of themselves.

   Sex-role socialization begins at an early age. A study by Weitzman and her associates of sex-role socialization in books for preschool children illustrates the expectations which sex-role stereotypes have presented to very young children.[22] Their findings highlight the stereotypes which appear to be fairly pervasive in the experiences that boys and girls continue to have in later childhood years. The study revealed that: Women do not often appear as major characters in children's books; almost all children's books are written about boys or adult men and their exciting adventures, or, occasionally, about male animals; females are expected to admire males and to love, watch, and serve them; boys are active leaders and girls are passive followers. Boys engage in activities in a larger world; girls stay at home. Girls are dependent and often fearful, but boys are independent and self-reliant. Girls are also portrayed as smaller in size than boys; they are pictured as less competent and skillful; they have many mishaps and are often rescued by boys.

These stereotyped expectations have many implications for the development of self-regard in little girls. The comparative reference group implications are quite harmful for girls, who are viewed as weaker, less competent, less intelligent, less interesting, brave or heroic than boys. Quite often the best they can hope for, from this standardized point of view, is to be "pretty," and even conceptions of desirable physical appearance are so mindless as to exclude the majority of little girls, all nonwhites, and many other minority children. Although little boys are not devalued, they are put at a disadvantage by the conventional expectations of bravery, strength, and heroism in the face of their own needs to express tenderness, to cry when they are hurt, and their need not to have to be physically robust and proficient in athletics, and not to have their small mistakes held above all else because they are little boys.

Fairly similar findings resulted from another survey of sex stereotyping in grade school children's readers. This study found, for example, that

In the readers, there are many role models for boys to shop among, from which to select a skill, a trade, a profession. Men are shown in almost every conceivable role; for girls the Reader Seal of Approval is reserved for one form of service or another, with wife or mother the overwhelming favorite. A girl with any other designs on the future must consider herself some kind of misfit.[23]

Further, this survey found that all adults portrayed were mothers and fathers in nuclear families. Mothers were presented as "limited, colorless, mindless and dull";[24] in contrast, images of fathers conveyed the impression of fun, excitement, and problem-solving skill. Parents, in these texts, never had disagreements with each other, but the readers did not portray any closeness between husband and wife.

While all children are not overly influenced by children's books, they are all subjected, in one way or another, to sex stereotyping in their everyday lives. Such uncritical behavior has become institutionalized. It is taken for granted that little boys will want to play certain roles and that little girls will want to play complementary roles when they all grow up. Traditionally, little girls who wanted to identify with activities associated with all the freedom provided for little boys have been criticized; even today, many people are uncomfortable about affirmative actions which allow girls to engage in games that have traditionally been exclusively played by boys. Boys who want to engage in activities expected of girls have also been subjected to disapproval. Although neither boys nor girls have had freedom of choice with respect to expectations associated with their sex, sex-role socialization has placed particularly severe restraints on the self-actualization of girls.

Social work practice today is carried on in a context of changing social definitions of the roles of men and women. The changes in sex-role expectations that are occurring and that will continue to occur challenge many firmly held beliefs, deeply rooted in the feelings and social identity of adults. It is easier for little children to accept new criteria for self-assessment than it is for those whose socialization for a sex role allowed no room for questioning traditional expectations. Not all adults, even those now beginning in roles of teachers and parents, are totally convinced that self-options are important to people in the long run; neither are many adults fully convinced that the new options for men and women are worth the potential loss of temporary approval in the short run. Many people are simply frightened by the implications of such drastic change in ways of thinking about sex roles, and self-conscious about behaving differently within them.

It is not so much that people want to deny others the right to grow and to realize their self-potential. Many people are in agreement with ultimate goals of this nature, but prior socialization has made so many demands on them to conform that change is actually quite painful. Painful feelings are involved in a sense of loss of roles that they became convinced they wanted and learned to play, sometimes at great cost to the drive for self-actualization. And some women and men, for whom the choice of family and caretaker roles was relatively free, misunderstand the suggestion that for many others these roles are stereotyped and limited.

Joseph Pleck and Jack Sawyer, who discuss the male role and masculinity, believe with others on the forefront of the changes now going on that the individual's full humanity appears to be more readily and clearly realized by those who, having achieved knowledge and understanding of this situation, have been able to resolve self-doubts about their own womanhood and manhood.[25] All of this has many implications for social workers who strive to regard the worth of individuals positively and unconditionally. Aware of the need for change and of the cost in loss of human resources that sex stereotyping creates, social workers are nevertheless sometimes caught in the difficult problems of transition in their own lives. Few adults have escaped sex role stereotyping by implication. On this issue, social workers locate themselves on the boundaries of the social system, willing to deviate if need be to continue the effort to open the society further to change in sex role expectations. It is in adult responses to children that this change will take place.

Developmentally Different Children

We have been discussing barriers to self-actualization that are socially derived, that create differences which compare and devalue one group in comparison with another. These differences are based on irrational and illogical conceptions of differences attributed to children identified by certain demographic characteristics, such as race or sex or economic class. Another group of children, about whom social workers are increasingly concerned, differs from all others in physical and/or mental functioning by virtue of physical differences not easily susceptible to modification through environmental interaction. These are the children with whom we are particularly concerned in this section.

All general descriptions of infants and children in early years of life assume some standard of physical and mental functioning commonly regarded as applicable to all. Descriptions of babies and little children who deviate from this standard are usually given by the degree of deviation from it. There is very little frame of reference, however, for the highly unusual child. Those who deviate most from the average expectable child are frequently described as being "developmentally disabled." The largest majority of children in this group are identified by physical differences due to incomplete physical formation or maturation, or to accidents which have resulted in some sort of enduring and often irreversible damage to body parts.

Social workers are very much concerned with human beings who experience these kinds of differences from the majority of others, and with the attitudes of others toward such differences. Physically these youngsters and their parents need many special medical, psychological, and social services. Social workers who concentrate their services in medical settings learn a good deal about all these areas of special need and are sensitive to the need to understand and to work with children and their parents in all three areas.

Children whose body image is distorted by their injury or difference experience exceptional problems in accepting themselves as competent. Their disability frequently makes it necessary for them to be passive and/or interferes with the innate motivation to master the environment. These children are frequently dependent on adults to a much greater degree than are children within the norm. They have very few adult models with like differences, and they are frequently frightened, isolated from other children, lonely, powerless to change their situation. Although many of these children have only slight disabilities, and many are reared by very sensitive and thoughtful others in environments conducive to growth, most of them have a hard row to hoe in the world of the usual. Other children and many adults may be embarrassed and fearful of the physical anomaly; in their initial tendency to identify with the child, they experience a threat to their own body image. The greater the observable difference between the child and the majority of other children, the greater the tendency of others to avoid them.

In our discussion of childhood we have seen that children are frequently viewed by adults as smaller and incomplete editions of themselves. For these unusual children, physical incompleteness is often a reality, and their autonomy and initiative are restrained by beginning feelings of inadequacy which are likely to increase in later stages of development, even if they learn to compensate for the physical difference. It is important to keep in mind that developmental disability is socially defined, by most people, in terms of inadequacy.

The pressure on parents to conform to society's expectations and to produce an average, expectable child is no less than it is on the child to look, feel, and behave in accordance with normative expectations. Many parents experience as a severe shock the loss of the child they expected—that is, of the model or preconception they have formed of a physically complete child whose physical or mental maturation and growth will follow a relatively predictable pattern. All parents whose babies are born with developmental disabilities can be expected to engage in some grief work; they need protection and support to do so. Some parents initially deny the fact of the baby's difference because it is so difficult to accept. Unless these parents have the opportunity to move from the stage of denial, through other stages of grief, to acceptance of the difference, they may pursue medical help and magical cures to their own and to the child's detriment.

All these children need health care. Such care is critical; it is of the most urgent importance that the best health care be available to all children. The cost of care is often beyond the means of families, and is especially difficult for the majority of nonwhite and Hispanic families. Social workers are keenly aware of the necessity to engage in advocacy with regard to public policy in this matter.

The labels applied to developmental disabilities have the function described earlier in discussion of social reality. The label "mental retardation" is an example of one that by its very application implies a negative valuation based on standard comparisons. Many people do not clearly understand mental functions, and apply oversimplified generalizations to children thus designated. It would be better to see these children's thinking as qualitatively different rather than as "retarded," which implies a quantitative difference.[26] Social workers familiar with children who have been so identified will recognize the overlay of emotional problems that accompany this designation. Mental retardation is also often erroneously attributed to individuals who have suffered central brain damage or other neuromuscular injury, but whose mental processes are not essentially impaired.

Children who are developmentally different form another minority. They are affected in many ways by the dysfunctions in the schools and other socializing institutions we have been discussing. The socializing institutions of the society are dysfunctional for those children in a number of ways. Recent federal legislation requiring schools to provide education for the developmentally disabled child who previously was excluded has solved some problems and left others unsolved. It is important to continue to investigate and evaluate the effects on these children of social, educational, technological, and general medical innovations designed to bring them into the world of children.

Areas for Further Study

Understanding and evaluating current methods for assessing the well-being of children, and the environments in which they live, is an important professional requirement for social workers. Those aspects of children's socialization which we have been discussing, especially standards of measurement, sex-role training, and responses to developmentally disabled children, are anchored in assumptions of what is healthy for children and what contributes to their well-being. There is reason to believe that many of the methods of assessing the health of children need to be submitted to further inquiry.

The conditions within which children in this society are living out their childhood years are constantly changing. We have discussed changes in social mores and values and some of the behaviors which they challenge. Economic changes, changes in law and public policy, technological innovations including computer technology, and demographic trends also have considerable import for children now and in the future.

We do not understand the effects of these changes on our children. Some system is needed to assemble, organize, and evaluate findings on the effects these changes are having on children. Social workers are expected to represent the community's interest in child welfare through direct work with children, planning and development of child welfare programs, and through occasional opportunities to administer such programs at local, state, and federal levels. If social workers are also to represent the values associated with the rights of children to self-actualization, they must pursue a great deal more understanding of the effects of social changes on children's lives.

Adolescence

Adolescence designates that time in the life of the person between childhood and adulthood. During this time, the individual is no longer defined as a child and is not yet an adult. This is the period of youth, of transition from childhod to full adult membership in the society. Since these young people are neither children nor adults, they do not simply try to combine those relatively contradictory values and roles of childhood and adulthood to which we have previously alluded. They may develop values and whole complex sets of role behaviors of their own. Some may be free to experiment with social roles while others may be limited to stereotypical role behaviors. With others like themselves, most adolescents experience great loyalty and conformity. Peers become the most significant reference group for most young people. Firmly held beliefs and the feelings in which they have been anchored are frequently raised to consciousness and checked with peers, and social reality testing is encouraged and restrained by their mandates. The search for answers to the questions, "Who am I?" and "Where do I belong?" is implicated in behavior associated with close, often intimate, relationships with other young people and with uncertainty about commitment to adulthood.

The development of the youth culture appears to be more anti-adults than is often the case. There are few rites of passage from childhood to adolescence. Myths about adolescents can block people's reasoned concern for them. Many descriptions of their characteristics are given from the vantage point of adults who assume that all adolescents are the same and that there is an unchanging and thoroughly describable kind of adult world into which all adolescents will enter. This period of youth is frequently seen as a waiting period during which young people learn the technical and interpersonal skills of adults. These views are based on a perception of the society as an enormous family guided by repetition in traditions in which youth are on the way to becoming, with only slight variations, what their parents have become. But the world of adults is not a stable one, and the society is not structured as a magnified family. The society has been undergoing a tremendous number of technological and interpersonal changes, and many adults are genuinely confused about their world.

A great many adolescents in this generation will be trying to find an identity as persons separate from their sex roles, and there are few guideposts for them to follow. Some will be internalizing and making commitments to their own minority group's goals through conversion experiences which are not yet characteristic of the majority of people in earlier minority generations. Contemporary adolescents do not have any built-in compass to tell them where they are, or the direction in which they need to go to realize their human potential. The self-sense of the adolescent is vulnerable to loss of its own boundaries because of major changes in both physical and social reality.

Some Implications of Physical Reality

Physical maturation involves a great growth spurt for adolescents. The onset of accelerated physical changes marks the end of childhood. Hormonal and over-all physiological changes are stressful for most adolescents. The consequences of their biological maturation include more than physical differences in appearance to others; they include young persons' feelings about themselves. As children, adolescents were aware of their bodies in comparison with adolescents and adults. They were aware of the significance attached to physical size, relative strength, and various interpretations of secondary sexual characteristics. When they are physically changed, or changing, the expectations they have for their own physical growth are influenced by prior knowledge of what they learned about what is desirable and valued in the society. Their self-concept is influenced by the ways in which their own maturation compares with these expectations, and by social comparison with peers.

John A. Clausen investigated the social meanings which differential physical and sexual maturation have had for the behavior of adolescents. He reviewed literature on the inter-relationships among physical and cognitive development, social behavior, and temperament which have been studied over the course of the last thirty years. His findings about the traditionally valued attributes of youth are particularly pertinent for social workers. Clausen notes that his findings are not current.[1] Our own search for more current investigations which might present evidence of changes in the traditionally valued physical attributes of youth was unsuccessful. We have assumed, then, that the findings from the literature reviewed by Clausen may continue to reflect attitudes held toward physical maturation of adolescents.

Clausen found that boys who matured early were seen by both adults and peers as more attractive; these boys had less need to strive for recognition. Boys who matured late often suffered from feelings of inadequacy as a result of their disadvantage in many competitive activities. While early maturation was generally assumed to be desirable for boys, it was also suggested that an early maturer could be pushed into premature adolescence without enough time to make the transition from childhood, whereas the boy who matured later had a longer preparation and could handle changes more flexibly.[2]

As is the case with most observations of adolescence reported in the literature, the findings are primarily from studies of male subjects. We know that early and late maturation has, in the past, had different implications for girls than it has had for boys. Clausen's findings revealed:

The features of physique that lead to regarding a boy as attractive—masculinity of build and muscularity—are quite different from those that lead to regarding a girl as attractive. Early maturing girls tend actually to be seen as less attractive than their later-maturing peers. . . . Among the boys, being larger and stronger than one's peers is definitely to be desired. One can compete athletically and one can move in older circles. Early maturing boys may be as physically mature as the average of girls in their age class. Early maturing girls, however, will not only exceed most of their female age-mates in size but will be larger than many of the boys. Moreover, the physically mature girl . . . is far more likely to be regarded as a sex object by older boys, and to be pressured into different kinds of peer relationships with the opposite sex.[3]

On the assumption that young people who possess attributes that are valued will be regarded more positively by peers and will receive many more positive responses directed to body image, the plight of the adolescent girl was extremely difficult. The early maturing girl was placed at a disadvantage in several ways; not the least of these was the kind of feedback that made it very difficult for her to discover the differences between becoming a person and being a sex object. We have referred to the fact that later maturing boys were not as highly valued by peers as early maturing boys, and they had to work much harder for acceptance through compensatory activities.[4] They did have more space for free movement to seek recognition through other activities than did girls, and most of them could anticipate more recognition for physical competence as they matured.

The influence of social definition of the desirable physical characteristics associated with athletic body build is especially interesting in light of the changing emphasis in sex role socialization. Until very recently, women were systematically prohibited from engaging in athletics that could bring them much recognition. They were denied access to major athletics: roles as athletes were simply not available to the large majority of women. Motivated by the women's movement and "buttressed by court rulings and legislative mandates, women have been moving from miniskirted cheerleading on the sidelines for the boys to playing and playing hard, for themselves."[5] Recent evidence has emerged suggesting that the female physical structure is better fitted for many sports than is the male physical structure.[6] Nevertheless, traditional values of what is desirable have not yet changed the attitudes of the majority enough to make a critical difference in the way many young girls regard their bodies.

The point of this illustration is that what is favored by the society and seen as attractive is not in the adolescents but in the eyes of their beholders. What has been valued in the past, and taken for granted, has to be reexamined in the present; otherwise, people will go on seeing what it is expected that they see. Those adolescents who are seen as attractive get more positive support for believing they are valuable and important. They are seen as "good looking," and those whose attributes do not fit the stereotyped expectations for youth are somehow not considered to be as good.

Most adolescents feel uncomfortable in their bodies at times. Whether they are early or late maturers, both boys and girls encounter stressful problems associated with physical changes for a number of reasons that have to do with the normative expectations of the past. Many adolescents experience a great deal of uncertainty about becoming sexually competent. There is still conflict between their own intuitive interest in masturbation, in sharing sexual experiences with others, on the one hand, and the persistent normative expectations that these activities are wrong, even harmful to their bodies, on the other. The sexual imagery which takes up more of their conscious thoughts is also often guilt-producing. The traditional norms which block many adolescents' access to information about their own bodies, to information that masturbation is not harmful, and that they need not feel guilt over sexual imagery, are dysfunctional to the need these young people have to feel at home in their bodies. Some adolescents, deprived of the right to experiment with their own bodies, can reject all of human sexuality as bad and wrong; others may so overemphasize sexual feelings and actions as to measure their worth only on this dimension.

Some Implications of Social Reality

Psychosocial Adolescence
Psychosocial adolescence in this society extends over a prolonged period of time. It is generally defined by the inner striving for identity, the opportunity to experiment with a number of social roles before becoming committed to more enduring adult roles, and the struggle to let go of childhood dependency and to take on more and more responsibility for oneself and for others. In some societies, childhood and

adulthood tend to blend into each other without this interim period. According to Diana Baumrind, adolescence as it is defined in this culture does not exist in a large part of the world.

In Mexico boys frequently share responsibility for family support by age 13, and in Thailand or on the Jordanian desert, adult duties may be assumed even earlier. In societies characterized by monolithic ideology, adolescents may willingly accept the opportunity to participate meaningfully in a culture with shared values, and thus with little internal stress achieve a socially defined identity.[7]

In our society, the move from childhood to adulthood may extend through the teenage years and beyond. Ideally, all young people have opportunities of becoming educated, and the time to resolve their identity conflict between a purely social definition and a self-definition. Many of those young people who end their education with high school, or before, are not needed in the labor force, except during a war in which a majority of young men usually take on adult responsibilities with little preparation for the adult roles they will play in a war. The increasing technological changes in the society are presumed to require advanced education, although a great deal of advanced education is not directed to the development of technological experts.

What people in this society believe about adolescence, then, provides very ambiguous images to young people in this life phase, and it is unlikely that a large number of adolescents actually have a psychosocial adolescence as it is described in most of the literature. Our literature has tended to describe the adolescence of white males, generally from fairly affluent backgrounds, whose struggle for autonomy and whose right to reach their human potential are viewed by all of us as highly desirable, as indeed they are. But we cannot, then, generalize our understanding of this group to all other adolescents who do not have the same opportunities to engage in the struggle for an identity of their own and to reach their human potential. Social workers have as deep a concern for the rights of those whose human struggles have not yet been described as well. While the literature has many valuable insights, the social worker who would understand those critical human issues which affect the self-development of this age group must accept some additional givens.

Adolescents in this society are not homogeneous; there are many differences among individual adolescents and among groups of adolescents. Without taking account of the differences in opportunity, the majority of people identify all adolescents as "teen-agers" who are expected to be preparing themselves for adult responsibilities through acquiring an education presumed to be critical to learning the skills of adulthood. It is generally thought that all young people have a prolonged period of time in which to make a transition from the dependence associated with childhood to the independence associated with adulthood, from no sexuality to adult sexuality, and from play to work. There are no clear-cut rites of passage which young people can count on, and the society offers no certainty that all young people will be accepted as adults. For example, society offers no guarantee that adult roles which young people want and which they can play, including work roles, will be accessible and available to them. With this in mind, then, let us take a step back and look at some of the major expectations of this life stage.

The Search for Continuity
Erikson has been a major interpreter of identity crises. He describes a psychosocial adolescence as a moratorium between childhood and adulthood in which the majority of young people have time to experiment with different social roles as they emancipate themselves from childhood dependency and develop their identity as adults. Erikson is among those authors whose discussion of adolescence is primarily concerned with young males who belong to the majority group in the society. We will, therefore, concentrate on those aspects of his discussion of the search for identity which have potential applicability across differences in sex, race, age, and economic conditions.

The reader may recall our earlier introduction of Erikson's discussion of identity, including the concept of continuity—that is, the need of the young person to achieve an inner continuity through bringing together the present self with the self that one was in the past and the self one aspires

to be in the future. The problem of achieving an inner continuity between past, present, and future is complicated by an
ongoing reinterpretation of many values and expectations in a
changing society. As Erikson observes, cultural and historic
change can "break up the inner consistency of a child's
hierarchy of expectations."[8] He refers to an obvious concomitant of identity as "a sense of 'knowing where one is going'
and an inner assuredness of anticipated recognition from those
that count."[9]

We have discussed some of the implications of role discontinuity with regard to male and female sex roles, and we have
seen some of the potential effects of the value changes on the
adult society into which present-day adolescents will enter.
The adolescent girl, for example, whose consciousness of
identity raises the questions, "Who am I?" and "Where do I
belong?" has to find a way to separate her self from her sex
role. She is not as likely to find continuity of experience from
past to present, and she may not find wide acceptance for her
newly emerging self in the near future. Earlier, we also discussed the changing reference group within which young
people who are black are testing their social reality. In their
struggle for an identity with other people who are black, it is
necessary for many young people in this generation to move
quickly through a pre-encounter and encounter stage, to
repudiate those destructive characteristics with which most of
the expectations of the majority group were associated in the
past, somehow to immerse themselves enough in new orientations to black culture to develop and to internalize a sense of
pride in a new identity. These adolescents have to find a historical past which differs from their personal history, to bring
this distant past into the present reality and to synthesize it
with a current and future self-concept with which only a
limited number of adults in the black community and no
adults in the white community have had any experience.

The sense of identity which many Chicano, Native
American, Puerto Rican, and Asian American young people
wish to achieve will require a unique integration of past,
present, and anticipated self-conceptions. Some of these
adolescents will forge the first links between the past, present,
and future of the groups to which they belong.

Role Moratorium
Erikson describes the role moratorium, in part, as

a period of delay granted to somebody who is not ready to meet an obligation. . . . a delay of adult commitments. . . . a period that is characterized by a selective permissiveness on the part of society.[10]

Such a role moratorium continues to be available primarily to males from affluent backgrounds. These young people have frequently been granted time to experiment with many different roles, to discover, through trying on and discarding one role and another, what their contribution to society can be. They may continue to engage in a traditional psychosocial moratorium and use it as they make a transition to some specific role commitment in the adult society. For example, affluent young persons who wish to take a year off before or after beginning college education, to travel around the country, to live with a family in another country for a time, to try themselves out in a number of interesting and creative temporary jobs, may enjoy a role moratorium before making adult commitments.

Even maximum freedom to choose or to reject a wide range of accessible and available roles will not necessarily result in total commitment to existing adult roles. Many of these adolescents are aware of the discontinuity which exists in some critical areas of adult life, and of the uncertainty facing many adults who counted on traditional behaviors to endure from the previous generation to their generation. Awareness of this phenomenon makes the new generation of these adolescents somewhat uncertain of their own future. Some of them simply wish to fit into society, but they are faced with changes in the adulthood they expected. Kenneth Keniston observed a number of young people who remained uncommitted to some aspects of adult life, but who were willing to become part of the adult world without total commitment.

They are not rebellious (in fact they like their parents), but they feel estranged and distant from what their elders represent. They often wish they could model themselves after (or against) what their parents stand for, but they are sensible enough to see that older people are often genuinely confused themselves.[11]

These young people experience a sense of powerlessness to effect changes in the society as they know it, and they are not often encouraged by their significant reference groups to deal with their feelings, to test the reality of their powerlessness. They often seek a few close, intimate relationships with others like themselves. With these others they can escape the harsh implications of their less than full commitment to the adult world of affluence.

Role Foreclosure

Many adolescents are not free to experiment with roles that they can play and that they wish to play. Institutionalized responses to minority groups and to young women frequently block role experimentation. Joan Lipsitz has completed a two-year nationwide study of programs and research on early adolescence. She found that young people under fifteen are the only age group that has recently shown an increase in admission rates to mental hospitals, that suicide has become the fifth leading cause of death among this group, that alcohol and other drug abuse among young adolescents is increasing, that there is an increase in pregnancy in this age group, and that crime and violence are increasing. Lipsitz estimated that in the foreseeable future one youth in nine will be referred to juvenile court before the age of eighteen. She also found that youngsters from twelve to fifteen years old are greatly underserved and overlooked by adults in general and by educators and the human service professions in particular.[12]

Lipsitz's findings are hard to reconcile with the popular notion that 70 percent of youth experience a relatively peaceful adolescence. They are also extremely tragic in the sense of loss of human potential of many very young adolescents. The adolescents whom Lipsitz's findings describe are now at least a year or two older. They are members of the new generation of adolescents. All the events reported by Lipsitz are associated with role foreclosure in adolescence.

The beliefs and attitudes that lead to the outcomes which Lipsitz's study identifies have serious implications for adolescents' strivings to realize themselves as persons of their own, and at the same time to anchor themselves in social roles that define the position of a valued human being. We have suggested that many adolescents do not experience a psychosocial moratorium, that they sense themselves as submerged in the society, expected to take an adultlike perspective toward the role of child which they are seeking to abandon, and discovering that they are expected to be childlike in the role of a "not-yet-adult." In this situation, there are many potentials for despair. They are aware that many roles they have anticipated playing, many that they feel convinced they might play, and many that they sense they are presently equipped to play, are closed to them. This awareness leaves them highly vulnerable to self-appraisals of personal worthlessness and social meaninglessness.

In the following sections, we shall focus on the attempts of some adolescents to escape the implications of worthlessness. We shall also discuss their attempts to create roles that will resolve the ambiguities and contradictions inherent in their transient state and support their self-esteem in the face of the powerlessness they feel. With particular but not exclusive reference to twelve- to fifteen-year-olds, we shall discuss more explicitly some of the social implications of suicide, mental illness, drug abuse, crime, and violence associated with gang formation and function, and pregnancy.

Suicide at an Early Age
The unwillingness of some youngsters to go on living at all suggests at least as much about their environmental relationships as it does about them. Lack of hope for future change has been hypothesized as a distinguishing factor between those young adolescents who are suicidally depressed and others who also appear to have no goals for themselves. According to Tooley, depression in the young adolescent who is suicidal is based on "a lack of love for their lives and a lack of hope (or even thought) that they might feel quite differently in a year or two."[13] She suggests that adolescents need to have connections with their past in order to build hope for a future, connections with a very personal past which they may not specifically remember. She discusses the implications this can have for

continuity of identity. Others in the young adolescent's life can lay some foundation in which the developmental task of identity formation can be anchored, by recalling positive attributes of the young person as a much younger person. Tooley observes that most people reach adolescence with some belief in a past self that was acceptable and important although individuals may not have specific memories to substantiate this belief. It is in the interpersonal context that young adolescents need assurance that they were important in the past, that they are still important, and that they will grow and change into important and worthwhile persons in the future. Lipsitz's findings are the more alarming because this is an age group that needs special attention from others to think well of themselves in this early transitional period between childhood and adolescence. This young person needs a great deal of support to believe that, in Tooley's words,

once, in the past, there was a lovable and interesting person that I do not personally remember but I believe that I was. In the future, which is another great void of unknown possibilities, it seems possible that I could become a person lovable and interesting and totally different from every other human being, even though there seems to be nothing in my current perception of my life or myself that would support that possibility.[14]

Young adolescents are especially vulnerable to self-doubt and uncertainty. They need special recognition from those adults whose judgment counts in their lives. It is primarily those who have known them in the past who can give meaning to their past importance through recalling memories of their strengths and goodness. If they develop suicidal depression, then they also need help from competent and qualified therapists. It is important that social workers learn how to intervene directly with the social side of their hopelessness through work with them and with other important people in their lives, including educators and important groups of peers.

While it may be difficult to do, differentiating, in our own understanding, between the suicidal gesture and actual suicide attempts is similarly important. At this age, efforts to elicit extraordinary emotional responses from others, daring, and experimentation with drugs may lead to such gestures. These activities are not intended to result in death, and seldom do, but any extreme kind of daring and experimentation with life is exceedingly dangerous. Others can respond helpfully to such gestures if they do not ignore the urgency of the feelings these gestures express.

The Role of Mental Patient

Symptoms of extreme disturbance lead to the role of mental patient. There are not many residential treatment facilities within which adolescents can receive the kind of highly sensitive, humanizing individual and group responses which they need. Those that do exist are very costly, and they usually have long waiting lists. The adolescents who have access to such facilities, who thus can get into the hands of people especially equipped to respond to their unique individuality, come primarily from the most affluent communities and families in the society. Many adolescents to whom such treatment is unavailable go into large hospital systems where they frequently tend to lose further touch with themselves and with other people. Funding is becoming more scarce for hospital personnel who have the time and the skill to respond to the special needs of adolescents. Social workers who have worked with adolescents, and with the families of adolescents, share with other professionals a deep concern about this situation.

The dependency in the role of mental patient has very special significance for adolescents. On the one hand, it may be very much needed by an adolescent whose life is characterized by unusual self-doubt and uncertainty. On the other hand, it is a temptation for some adolescents to prolong the dependency inherent in the role, regardless of the social and emotional cost in the loss of other roles to play. Some of the reasons for this are associated with the ways in which the role is labeled and the consequences of having been labeled as a mental patient. The adolescent is quite often subjected to stereotypical responses from both adults and peers and may be powerless to explain the emotional confusion and suffering that led to hospitalization. Some young people expect of themselves what others expect of them as mental patients; it is a natural tendency under group pressure in any event, and the posthospital adolescent is especially vulnerable. Very young adolescents may fall into a pattern of stereotypical responses with peers to whom such behavior can be quite threatening and from whom such behavior elicits rejecting responses. At best, social reality is extremely difficult for young adolescents to test. They need a great deal of reassurance themselves before they can reassure anyone else about themselves. Their acceptance of a peer who has had a mental hospital experience may depend upon how they can be enabled to feel about themselves. Some adolescent peer groups can be very helpful to individuals who remain oriented to the patient role, simply by opening up new roles to play in the community. If potential peer groups can be helped to function according to their strengths, they soon become more interested in the experiences the "patient" has had than in labeling him or her. In this event, the young person has a chance to be identified as a person who has had the experience of being a mental patient rather than to be identified by the role of mental patient. The isolation from peers in the community, which frequently characterizes the human relationships of adolescents whose "patient" status becomes chronic, may not always be an effect of illness; for many adolescents it may be a cause.

Drug Abuse

The young person's perceptions of self and of others' selves are frequently difficult to sort out; the use of consciousness-altering drugs makes it less important for them to try. Most of those adults who respond to drug problems among adolescents have also taken drugs of one sort or another, but few have used them extensively enough in their own early adolescence to share the experience the young person is having. The responses of parents and of many educators to drug abuse, then, is often characterized by anger and frustration which increase the age and experience gap between them and young people. For some adolescents the effects of drug use are exceedingly difficult to reverse, and the role of "addict" may foreclose other role possibilities.

In their fear that young people who experiment with drugs will become addicts, many adults do not differentiate between experimentation and abuse. It is important to understand the differences between the abuse of drugs, experimentation with them, and continued use which does not necessarily lead to abuse. For example, studies have not proved that the use of marijuana leads to addiction. We know much more about the potential harm of alcohol, which is a legal drug for adults. Therefore, continued use of marijuana is not so likely to be addictive as is the continued use of alcohol. Studies of the use of hard drugs have proved them to be addictive and quite harmful. It is highly improbable that anyone can take hard drugs in moderation. Even experimentation with some substances in this category, such as PCP, can be extremely harmful.

Earlier generations of adults did take alcohol in their adolescence. Most of these adults have not become alcoholics, although a majority have continued to use alcohol. Many adolescents use alcohol to a greater extent than they use hard drugs. Although the normative expectations remain as they were, it has become commonplace for the great majority of adolescents to experiment with both marijuana and alcohol. Most adolescents have tried both drugs; fewer have continued to use them over an extended time, and not all of those will necessarily become addicted to their use.

Those young people who do get hooked on hard drugs develop problems which are tragic in their consequences. The struggle to become a person of one's own demands a great deal of caring about the self; it is difficult to engage in the struggle, and excessive use of consciousness-altering drugs forecloses the achievement. The effect of the addiction, in the early phase, is to make the achievement appear attainable but to block its attainment, and one doesn't care. Altered consciousness makes reality testing both unnecessary and impossible. Eventually, dependence on the chemical stimuli replaces concern for self-development and interest in the self or in other selves. As the addiction progresses, the young person no longer can achieve even the alteration of consciousness effects which characterized the earlier phases of the addiction. Overdose is often associated with this. Eventually, the young person must have drugs in order to prevent excruciating physical pain and many suffer permanent physical damage.

The availability of drugs to young people is an important aspect of this problem. Drugs are obviously being sold to many troubled and vulnerable young people; in minority communities characterized by poverty, traffic in drugs is harder for young people to escape than it is in other communities. Some highly organized adult groups outside these communities exploit young people within them, at times. Some of these young people are employed to sell drugs to their peers and to deliver them to buyers in and outside their own communities. Others, who cannot afford to be buyers and who have become addicted to hard drugs, are left to find money where they can, often through theft which may be combined with violence. The loss of regard and respect for the self is a result of the compulsion of addiction. The role of addict forecloses all other role possibilities; in a sense, it may be suicidal, ending life before these young people know what life is beyond the early adolescent years.

Youth Gangs

Crime and violence in early and in later adolescence are frequently associated with violent youth gangs. Before describing the destructive aspects of gang membership for some adolescents, we remind the reader that all youth gangs are not violent. What we call a "gang" often depends upon how we define the natural tendency of adolescents to find others like themselves with whom to experience some mutality of recognition. A gang is not necessarily a frightening or threatening form of group life. Most adolescents meet their own needs for recognition and emotional security through close association with peers. A gang provides others with whom to belong and with whom to identify, others with whom to share the same images of reality. The need for closeness and acceptance often pushes young people to locate reality for their opinions about the society solely in the opinions of members of their gang. In turn, the gang has some power over the individual. The psychological yearning to belong with others to whom one seems to count, who give a measure of positive regard, and who give love at times, is much greater than many adults can comprehend.

In these groups, adolescents give up a lot of their own autonomy. The social needs to maintain the group, to take group action, require uniformity of opinion and a willingness to suppress evidence that does not fit with what other members think and are willing to do. Many of these young people do not know their minds and hearts very well. This is not because they lack good cognitive abilities, but because they function at an action level which may preclude any thoughtful self-observation. It seems likely that the more action-oriented the gang is, the less self-observing are its members. When a gang member gets established in the gang, the role has less and less space for free movement within it.

The history of violent youth gangs is interwoven with the history of compact cities in which the very affluent and the extremely poor live close together. Where these extremes come together, youth gangs frequently violate norms associated with property rights and physical safety; they engage in crime and violence. These gang members do not belong to the affluent group. They most frequently share conditions of poverty, overcrowded housing, inadequate schools, low income, poor health care, and few job opportunities to which to look forward in the future.

Most people are familiar with the prototypical youth gang, still portrayed by the mass media. Walter Miller comments on this:

To millions of Americans who saw West Side Story, and to millions of others whose knowledge of teenage gangs comes mainly from television dramas, the typical gang consists of a large, well-organized bunch of tough but basically likable young hoods in leather jackets bearing names like Sharks and Jets. These fictional gangs spend most of their time defending their "turf," and their reputation for bravery, against assaults by rival gangs. . . . are receptive to peace parlays, community programs, and rap sessions by police mediators or social workers.[15]

Miller and his colleagues surveyed gang activity across the country and found that contemporary youth gangs in large cities

typically consist of small loosely organized groups of about a dozen teen-age males. Instead of confining their claims of control to local streets and parks, many gangs have taken over neighborhood schools and recreational facilities. Along with turf and prestige, today's gangs are mainly concerned with money . . . they shake down local merchants and make armed, guerrilla-style forays to carry out muggings, robberies, and burglaries.[16]

In a sense, the prototype of the violent youth gang was characteristic of many youth gangs before the middle 1960s. The fictional gangs were patterned after the gangs of that time. And those gangs were patterned after the larger society. They were, in many ways, a microcosm of the larger social system as it existed then. The gang members' energies were organized to maintain the gang system. The gang was organized by many rules and regulations; expectations of behavior were explicit, patterned after the best of pecking orders. The members did protect each other, and their warfare, patterned after warfare for territorial imperatives in the larger society, was carried on to protect "their turf." They were often responsive to social workers from a number of youth service agencies.

The gangs of today are also a product of the larger social system. This society remains powerful through an accumulation of the most sophisticated weapons in history. A large number of people view these weapons with considerable anxiety as a source of the destruction of humankind. Violent youth gangs have been able to obtain weapons of much greater sophistication than they had twenty years ago; they measure their power in terms of the number and quality of their weapons. And they still take over neighborhoods, including schools and recreation areas; they still "protect" turf, and they often behave like small guerilla bands.

The analogy is imperfect, of course, but it is important to recall that the large majority of these young people are among the most powerless people in the society before they engage in gang violence. They live in communities in which there has not been any guarantee of protection from harm. Gangs like theirs are traditional groups in such communities. According to Miller, "some police officials consider gang violence a serious problem only when it threatens the safety or property of respectable middle-class citizenry."[17] This implies that people who live in ghetto communities where most gangs are living, whose income is low, whose housing and schooling and health care are inadequate, are not "respectable," and that their safety does not matter. Although there has been an increase in violence to affluent people by young teen-age gangs, most of the victims of gang violence are still gang members themselves and members of their immediate neighborhoods. And the majority of people in the society pay little attention to gangs when they are killing each other and hurting their immediate neighbors.

This is a tragic situation for everyone; these are social conditions in which everyone loses. The situation illustrates the fact that the welfare of everyone is dependent on the welfare of everyone else. Gang members themselves and members of their immediate neighborhoods are the major victims of violent gangs, and more affluent people in the cities are also victims. The increased availability of drugs in low-income communities heightens the likelihood of role foreclosure for many young gang members, who may engage in more crime and violence for money to buy drugs, with or without the support of the gang group. There may be a connection between the smaller size of gangs, their relatively loose organization, drug addiction, and the kinds of crime and violence in which they are engaged, such as victimizing vulnerable elderly people.

Role foreclosure is associated with the ways in which juvenile authorities respond to young offenders. In detention centers and in prisons, the institutionalized roles of "juvenile delinquent" and "criminal" are reinforced. Those victims of juvenile crime apart from the young offenders themselves want to see them hurt in the same way they have hurt others, especially if they have been involved in killings outside the gang. In 1978, the year of a gubernatorial election, the New York legislature passed a bill under which thirteen-year-olds who commit violent crimes that result in death can be given life sentences in state prisons. The notion of rehabilitation was disregarded in this legislation, on the assumption that it has not worked. The strangely incompatible answer, then, is to treat thirteen-year-olds as adults! It is widely agreed that the large majority of adults in prison are not rehabilitated, and the further criminalization of the thirteen- to fifteen-year-olds in adult prisons is most likely. The measure taken by New York and the juvenile waiver now in effect in a number of other states are based on the assumption that they will deter further crime. Jerome Miller has shown that young offenders can be held with other juveniles in small, secure, locked settings which they cannot leave and in which there is enough highly specialized staff to avoid problems of further criminalization.[18]

To date, literature on imprisonment of adults and of youngsters does not reveal evidence to support the theory that it deters crime. In chapter four we discussed the implications, for changing behavior, of involuntary comparative reference groups; these implications are one major factor contributing to this lack of connection between imprisonment and crime deterrence. Despite the fact that imprisonment is not a deterrent, most people see it as a way of decreasing crime. This attitude reflects the fact that people want these youngsters to be hurt in some way. Many people are hurt and frightened by young adolescents, or share the hurt and the fear of loved ones. In a sense, violence begets violence, if only in thought or intention. Many people become extremely angry when they or their loved one, or others with whom they simply identify, are hurt. Their rage then threatens to unbalance or disrupt their usual line of defenses. For those who are hurt or share the hurt of close relatives, this can be a crisis characterized initially by bewilderment and disorganization of thought, going on to defensive denial and only gradually allowing for new understanding of the reasons such painful things occur, and of the fact that revenge, in itself, is no guarantee that the pain will end.

Many people are encouraged by the criminal justice system to believe that if youngsters can be hurt and frightened enough, they will obey the rules that protect the more affluent in the society. This does not work. If social justice is interpreted to mean that the rules and the regulations support the rich, protect the middle class, and punish the poor, we will continue to foreclose the chances for the safety and the life chances of many young people who are poverty-oriented, as well as of others in the neighborhoods in which they live, and of a number of more affluent people.

Sex-Role Socialization to Motherhood and Early Pregnancy

The adolescent girl whose prior socialization has emphasized sex-role training for motherhood faces much greater discontinuity during the teen-age years than does the adolescent boy. Traditionally, expression of sexual competence is generally acceptable for young males but not for young females. Girls have been expected to make a commitment to marriage prior to engaging in sexual intercourse, foreclosing any experimentation. In this sense, socialization of female children for motherhood has become counterproductive in a number of ways. Stereotypically, many girls are expected to be dependent on, and submissive to, males and to retain virginity, which is the bedrock of traditional marriage. In this way, they are expected to prevent what is presumed by many people in the society to be irresponsible motherhood rather than involuntary motherhood.[19]

Jessie Bernard has observed that very little attention has been given to the importance of sexual initiation of young women, whereas a great deal of literature deals with sexual initiation of young men. Indeed, early sexual experimentation, specifically sexual intercourse, elicits from many adults a certain positive recognition of the virility and masculinity of young males. The prevailing notion is that the young male's sexual initiation is a serious and important event; it is a gain in experience rather than a loss of virginity. In contrast, the sexual initiation of young women is not expected to be an important event unless it results in pregnancy outside legally sanctioned marriage. In that event, the young girl is often faced with severe criticism. According to Bernard,

the loss of virginity has been a far more serious turning point for women . . . loss of virginity in Western cultures has led almost universally to lowered status, if not disgrace.[20]

Early pregnancy outside a marriage commitment is a threat to irrational social restraints against sex education and contraception. Many attitudes toward this behavior deny that there is any irrationality involved. At the same time, an overwhelming majority of people in the society remain fascinated with child seduction, rape, and seductive young females,[21] themes which have been exploited by a thriving pornography industry. There has still been no general consensus on how rape occurs; the victim-blaming implications in the responses of legal authorities have restrained many young women from even reporting the fact that they have been sexually attacked. The work of such organizations as Women on Rape, directed to changing these conditions through social-emotional support services, continues to fight an uphill battle with legal authorities in many areas of the country.

Continuing attitudes toward sexual functioning of female adolescents thus illustrate the ambiguity and the conflict of expectations through which the young woman is supposed to find her way from an explicit childhood to an uncertain adulthood. In this context we can begin to understand how exceedingly important it is to change social institutions which trap young people into sexism. Young teen-agers who get caught in the roles they were socialized to want may themselves become unwanted. Most young females still have no role moratorium; their sexual experimentation may lead to role foreclosure. Social workers who provide social services to female adolescents learn to understand the implications that choice in the matter of taking on a motherhood role has for them. In work with teen-age parents social workers invest their energies, together with these young people, to open up educational and work roles. In this area, social workers often encounter attitudes which are deeply embedded in emotion. Despite the difficulties such attitudes present, many social workers are among those people who strongly advocate a new kind of socialization for a future in which marriage and/or motherhood may be freely chosen or rejected by growing adolescents to whom a number of other significant, productive, and creative roles are also accessible and available.

The Struggle Against Self-Compromise

In the first chapter, we discussed the alienated self. Existential writers have shown the association of alienation with estrangement from the self and other selves, characterized by the feeling of being a powerless object under the control of values and institutions. By capitulating, the person loses freedom of choice.

The notion that all adolescents do not have to capitulate is based on the premise that options are available and that all adolescents are clear about what their options are. This is not always the case. For example, when the standards by which adolescents are judged and consequent pressures toward conformity are expressed by sex-role socialization, they may have few, if any, options. In this event, then, adolescents are not necessarily conscious of having given up the right of choice, since in the first place so little choice may have existed that choice itself was not recognizable. Nevertheless, individuals are inherently driven to maintain and fulfill their human potential and often experience pressures to conformity as restraining forces on growth and fulfillment. The dilemma of wanting to choose freely and not having alternative options is compounded by implications it has for self-compromise, for dealing in bad faith with one's self, and many adolescents then experience alienation.

Adolescents are searching for space for free movement within which to realize more autonomy. They are not usually looking for adults who will stand behind them and in whom they can believe, although they need such adults. Their situation is often characterized by ambiguity and uncertainty. For some, adult relationships have not proved trustworthy, and for these adolescents, commitment to the adult world is viewed as requiring continued self-compromise. A great deal of what adults see as rebellion is reflected in the view that many young people have of adult life as characterized by personal inauthenticity, self-compromise for economic gain, and isolation from enduring and meaningful human relationships. When this view is most likely to be borne out in their relationships with significant others in their lives, they are likely to experience a sense of despair and come to feel like objects under the control of these adults. They are searching, then, for a way to get free of the oppressiveness of this control.

Freedom to Choose Love Objects
Erikson regards the need to find others in whom to believe as an important characteristic of adolescence. This need is in opposition to self-compromise. It is a need to find some enduring principles around which to organize one's life. Erikson views it as

the search for something and somebody to be true to . . . a seeking for some durability in change . . . in a sincerity of conviction . . . or in the genuineness of personalities and the reliability of commitments.[22]

This need becomes more critical as the society makes a transition from norms that were previously taken for granted to new normative expectations. In the current society, the shift from unquestioned ways of life and life styles to new life styles is not complete. Baumrind observes that

while adolescents have always played a large role in the ongoing development of their parents, acting as interpreters of the emerging values and life styles, parents have been able to bring perspective and experience to the generational dialogue.[23]

In the current society, however, many adults, as well as adolescents, are caught in its shifting, changing value orientations.

What perspective and experience can these adults bring to the emerging freedom of choice in love objects? We have discussed, with reference to sexism, some of the sexual problems and conflicts produced by sex-role socialization. For various reasons, many parents find it quite difficult to support the freedom of young people to experiment with sexual relations. It is much more difficult to support the young person's right to choose to love someone of the same sex. Myths about homosexuality persist and are supported by highly prestigious institutions which continue to apply legal, religious, and economic restraints. In their search for others in whom to believe and to trust, adolescents are more than ever dependent on peers who are on the same quest. Most adolescents find a great deal of warmth and safety with a few others like themselves with whom they can express loyalty and with whom they can test reality. With groups of peers in whose judgment they trust, adolescents can share doubts and uncertainties that remain hidden from adults. They can also achieve recognition for real abilities. They do not judge each other as adults judge adolescents; they compare themselves with others like themselves. Such relationships often lead to unconditional positive regard, and at times they lead to devotion and deep feelings of affection.

Whether or not these peers are members of the opposite sex, these feelings may also lead to love and fulfillment expressed in part by physical intimacy. Most adolescents who wish to express love to others of their own sex do not feel free to do so, despite the sincerity of their conviction that another person like themselves provides more support and a more authentic relationship than a member of the opposite sex. Many who do choose to love others of the same sex continue to suffer from guilt about the choice and also risk condemnation or rejection from significant others. Because their behavior deviates from traditional expectations in the heavily emotionally charged sexual area, these adolescents need a great deal of emotional support from social workers and others who believe in their right to join an emerging movement to create new sex roles for which people have not been socialized, and for which there is currently no secure place in the society.

The Need for Structure
In chapter four we indicated that the individual strives for orderliness and simplicity in perceptions of interpersonal relations. Experiences of incongruity and inconsistency create conflict, which makes it extremely difficult for the individual to create and maintain a consistent and congruent view of the self and the interpersonal environment. In the service of continuity between the past and the present, individuals will frequently give up the struggle to integrate both with an uncertain future. In this event, they refer current pressing needs to invest their life energies into a cause or project to a past frame of reference, one which was previously used to predict causal expectations among related events. In an uncertain present, it frequently seems to the individual easier to regress to a past in which things were simpler, less ambiguous and uncertain, in which one could find much more clearly defined rules and regulations, and absolute answers to questions.

The more inner chaos they experience, the less likely it is that adolescents can make sense out of the changing social structure, and the more likely it is that they will seek absolute answers, and unmistakably clear rules and regulations. This often means that the adolescent gives up the search for anything else. Such a structure is sometimes offered by highly charismatic leaders who represent ideals associated with strongly religious or political movements. While charismatic religious and political leaders are not necessarily inauthentic, they may recruit some young people whose regression to dependence on structure and submission to outside authority are the outcome of inability to maintain inner harmony in the face of severe adolescent identity crisis. It is also possible that this resolution may be a temporary one. The extent to which it is temporary is indicated by the degree of inflexibility the adolescent allows in playing out the role of devotee.

The tendency to join organizations that offer role models and a structure for channeling energies into cause-oriented activities is not always motivated by regression. What we have in mind are those organizations that, in their requirement for commitment of all the adolescent's emotional and social energies, emphasize the tendencies some adolescents have to go backwards instead of forward.

Adulthood

Social workers' knowledge of adulthood is ordered by expectations of adult behavior. By which expectations? What does the social worker value in adult behavior? What guides the social worker's understanding of adults with whom they work? Earlier we said that social workers have to answer the "Who am I?" question for themselves and that their answers will be, in some ways, determined by their knowledge of those with whom they work. It is important, then, for social workers to review what they know about the longest stage of human development, the stage to which they belong, and the stage in which they are most likely to see themselves in others with whom they work. Somehow, all that has come before is gathered together in this adult stage. Infancy, childhood, and adolescence are the past which contains the selves that adults were; each phase of adulthood is the present, in which the person has to continue to move toward the self the person wants to be. How does adulthood begin, and how do we know it has happened?

Unlike earlier life stages about which many developmental theories are presented, we have less systematically organized knowledge on which to draw for this stage. Most explanations of adult life do not deal with the developmental aspects of adulthood. Lillian Troll, who has discussed issues in defining development, as well as problems of conceptualization and method in studying it, has reviewed the notion previously held by many people that adulthood marks the end of development.

From this perspective, adulthood is "the end of the line," and everything that happened before is significant primarily because it got us there. Once there, we have no place to go but down.[1]

She has also noted that criteria for identifying changes in adulthood that are developmental raise questions about what changes occur, and what differentiates adults from adolescents or children.

We approach this chapter, then, with some islands of knowledge between which bridges have not yet been built. The explanations we offer are provided by a number of authors who have studied different aspects of adult behavior, and they include some of our own impressions of the propelling and restraining forces which determine the extent to which adults are free to move their own humanness ahead. We have selected certain issues which we see as important to social workers' knowledge as they bring their own life and practice experience to bear on formulating their understanding of this life stage, and as they increase their knowledge through further exploration of the insights available in a widely scattered literature.

Defining Adulthood

No sudden cut-off point in the search for identity defines the close of adolescence and the beginning of adulthood. The rapid onslaught of physical maturation and preoccupation with body image has presumably been lived through in adolescence. People may feel confident and good about themselves, or uncertain and frightened by the implications of compromises they have made during the teen-age years. They may become adults in good faith with themselves, or they may be pressured to conform to rules and roles that restrain further self-development. They may be so heavily influenced by past experience as to have no expectation of growing and changing. They may have made gradual transitional changes from one stage to the next without undue stress, and find the transition to adulthood smooth and easy. They may be so determined by social definition as to preclude much self-observation and assessment. They may simply do what is expected, engaging in routines and necessary work without much conscious thought about their own right to choose, or they may be denied freedom of choice by nature of extraordinary social, economic, and political forces over which they have no control.

Adulthood is generally considered to include all the years between adolescence and old age, but the threshold of adulthood is quite difficult to define. The end of the teen-age years serves as a rough marker. Theorists who explain human behavior in terms of life stages suggest that adulthood begins at age twenty or age twenty-one. But the notion which many people have, that the rights and responsibilities of adulthood are explicit and that the standards by which people are perceived as adults are clear, reflects a lack of reality testing. It is as though everyone thinks everyone else knows, but few people check to find out. In general, adulthood is the goal of children and adolescents. By physical changes alone, an individual may be perceived as an adult eventually, but adulthood is defined in social terms as well as in physical ones. Many adolescents may not be welcomed into the adult society, and some individuals continue to feel like children among adults long after they have reached maximum physical growth and are well beyond their early twenties.

Whether young people realize the goal of their striving to become adults and go beyond the threshold is largely dependent upon supports in their social environment. Adulthood may be defined differently for different adolescents, depending upon the expectations of the significant adults in their lives. It makes a difference whether or not these are adults who simply exercise control over the lives of young people, are adults whose love and support are conditioned by the expectations they have of themselves as models, or are adults who can offer unconditional positive regard.

A general social distinction between adults and children includes stable employment and marriage. Neither biological development nor chronological age is in itself a clear indicator that the person has become an adult. Legal definitions of the chronological age at which people can drive, drink, are drafted into or can enlist in the armed forces, may enter contracts, differ. Normative behavior associated with economic independence, productivity, and caretaker roles are more critical determinants, and there is a kind of social timing within which it is presumed that people will fulfill these expectations. It is expected that individuals will have resolved their identity problems enough to maintain patterns of behavior that will complement the larger society, that the roles they play will become the means for preserving the social order into which they were born and for which socialization during childhood and adolescence has prepared them.

Some General Implications of Role Expectations

Most young adults expect of themselves what the society expects of them, and self-assessment is frequently dependent upon how well one performs ascribed roles. "Acting one's age" is tantamount to fulfilling the role expectations of adulthood. The success of the actor, then, is primarily measured by performances of ascribed caretaker and provider roles and of an array of achieved occupational roles. The effort is to fulfill these expectations so as not to fail to be identified as a responsible person doing what is expected. In large measure, marriage, parenting, and socially valued work roles give people a feeling of inner assuredness and of recognition from others who count in their lives, a sense of knowing where they are going, and who is going with them.

Many individual differences exist in those people who take on traditional adult roles, but some of these roles provide little space for free movement toward self-actualization. When marriage roles are entered into freely, with awareness of choice in the partnership, the sense of identity is enhanced. The society continues to prescribe an idealized family model which emphasizes romance in marriage, and fairly inflexible distinctions between caretaker and provider roles, with regard to parenting and child rearing, which may function to weaken the marital partnership. For some young people, disenchantment and new identity conflicts arise when life goals are not shared. For others, caring is associated with mutuality of regard, allowing for growth and change in the partnership arrangement.

There appears to be a generally held belief in an average expectable environment within which all adults have equal opportunity to achieve economic independence if they work

hard enough. In fact, opportunities are quite unequal, especially for members of minority groups who do not have equal
access to preparation for, and fulfillment through, meaningful
occupational roles. In the last chapter we discussed the role
foreclosure experienced by some adolescents and the implications this may have for freedom to choose roles they want and
roles they could play in adult life.

Pressures toward conformity tend to propel people into
roles they do not wish to play and cannot play well. Some
people simply succumb to such pressures in bad faith with
themselves, thereby negotiating a working relationship with
hopelessness. The ideal family model leads many people to
emphasize the form of the relationship arrangements rather
than their potential for human fulfillment. Adults who have
made strong commitments to preserving traditional, normative
behavior frequently find new family forms difficult to accept.
The space for free movement in the role of parent is often
limited by social attitudes, such as attitudes toward single
parents and expectations of women, as well as by other events
over which people in the role have very little control, such as
low income, death of a spouse, chronic illness of children.

Growth and Change, Stability and Commitment

In order for people to continue to reach their human potential,
they need opportunities to grow and to change. Changes in
adulthood are sometimes viewed as disruptive; people tend
to regard themselves as unchanging. There is a general
psychological tendency toward consistency in self-perception.
Stability is broadly associated with enduring patterns of
behavior; this is one of the ways people define personality.
Changing life situations, however, frequently demand new patterns of behavior. Discontinuity in role expectations in adult
life often produces crises characterized by bewilderment and
disorganization. Resolutions of these crises demand changes in
expectations of the self and others, and the learning of new
ways of behaving, including new ways to protect the self
against stagnation and despair.

While stability is highly desirable, implying feelings of
safety, protection, and equilibrium maintenance, it is often

associated with sameness of environmental expectations. It may be a function of stability to remain in unchanging circumstances; in such circumstances one may have an unchanging sense of identity. Whether this leads to development and growth is unclear; a changing sense of self may be, but is not necessarily, fulfilling of one's potential. When people experience many changes, some of them outside their control and some brought on by choice, they may respond by calling on resources within themselves that were previously unknown to them. Changes in expectable ways of living one's life often moves a person toward self-actualization.

Growth and change are generally expected to occur during those life stages preceding adulthood; rapid growth during earlier stages of life requires a great deal of ability to change. Howard Becker observed that childhood and youth are generally viewed as the time when individuals can "make mistakes that do not count. Therefore, we would expect children's behavior to be flexible and changeable, as in fact it seems to be."[2] Adulthood, on the other hand, is perceived as a stage in which the person gradually acquires a number of commitments which demand more consistency. The critical events of adult life are expected to result in enduring commitments. The kinds of commitments which adults are expected to make complement the social organization of the society into which the individual is born and socialized through earlier life stages. But if we assume that the ways in which people were socialized as children and adolescents are the major determinants of their behavior as adults, we have assumed that any changes that occur in adulthood are elaborations or expressions of earlier life experiences, that the values of the society are internalized during earlier stages of life and are simply reinforced by social institutions during the rest of life. This conflicts with the expectations that adults will be autonomous and that they will be capable of observing themselves influencing others as well as being influenced by others in their past and in their present experiences.

Bernice L. Neugarten has discussed the need for criteria for identifying changes in adulthood which account for growth and the integration of life experiences toward greater levels of competence in problem-solving. Approaching the question of how changes occur, she implies that the self-observing function is more predominant in adulthood than in prior growth stages, and that experience is evaluated in the light of new information.

If confronted with the question of whether or not there are any "inherent" or "inevitable" changes in personality that accompany adulthood, there is at least one that would come at once to mind; the conscious awareness of past experience in shaping one's behavior. . . . It is not merely that experience is recorded; it is that the awareness of that experience becomes increasingly dominant.[3]

This is not to say that all adults use their self-observing capacity, but it does suggest that growth in adulthood occurs as adults actively assess and evaluate the influences that past experience has had, in the light of new experience. We have previously discussed the idea that people change their frames of reference as they encounter new experiences and find new ways of viewing themselves and others in ongoing life.

Emphasizing that it is the characteristics of situations that most heavily determine growth possibilities for adults, Becker conceives personal change in adult life as occurring through the processes of situational adjustment and commitment. Although we have not viewed adjustment as a criterion of self-actualization, let us look a little further into Becker's view of these processes as explanations for adult development. According to Becker:

The person, as he moves in and out of a variety of situations, learns the requirements of continuing in each situation and of success in it. If he has a strong desire to continue, the ability to assess accurately what is required, and can deliver the required performance, the individual turns himself into the kind of person the situation demands.[4]

At first glance, the process Becker describes is reminiscent of the development of Cooley's looking-glass self. It is as though people are totally determined by what others expect of them. The notion takes on another meaning, however, if we conceive of adults as able to make a great many situational adjustments and to make choices with regard to the extent to which they will invest energy in one or another situation. It is important to bear in mind that as Becker employs the term "situation," it refers to a much smaller unit of experience than the term "social role." Situational adjustment requires a great deal of flexibility if we perceive the person moving through many situations. Such movement requires a shifting of perspective, in the course of which resocialization may take place. Resocialization is an aspect of adulthood which provides new comparative reference groups as a basis of self-appraisal and the internalizing of new audiences.

The knowledge-seeking attitude which we have emphasized, in the chapter on childhood, as a manifestation of the drive toward self-actualization leads to further growth in adulthood. The extent to which adults have access to new experiences, then, operates to promote, or to restrain, knowledge-seeking attitudes. Many adults adjust to situations in relatively stable institutions in which little change is likely to occur. Some adults do not move between situations very much and their perspectives do not shift much. While situational adjustments help to explain many changes in people during adult life, the extent to which changes are growth-oriented has many determinants. The nature of the changes explained by situational adjustment will depend upon both the impact of the situation on individuals and their impact on the situation. Those situations which influence them in the direction of more flexibility and open mindedness are more likely to encourage growth. Adjustment may also simply require conformity with concomitant lack of freedom to test reality.

Let us turn briefly to commitment, the second process discussed by Becker as applicable to personal change in adult life. According to Becker,

a person is committed when we observe him pursuing a consistent line of activity in a sequence of varied situations. Consistent activity persists over time. . . . even though the actor may engage in a variety of disparate acts, he sees them as essentially consistent . . . they serve him in pursuit of the same goal. . . . the actor rejects other situationally feasible alternatives, choosing from among the available courses of action that suit his purpose.[5]

Commitment would appear, then, to be possible to the extent that alternative routes to a goal are open to the individual. The notion that adults are free to choose and to decide what they will do with their lives is somewhat overrated. Many restraining forces limit freedom of choice. This leads to the

question of whether as many people actually make commitments by their own choice as we tend to think. We know that a
great many people do not have an opportunity to experiment
with different patterns of behavior during adolescence; we
know also that there are many taken-for-granted expectations
of behavior that are age-related. Neugarten and Nancy Datan,
for example, in a discussion of age norms as a system of social
control, have observed that a prescribed timetable exists for
the ordering of life events, a time when the person is "expected
to go to work, to marry, a time to raise children."[6]

People do not necessarily choose to make commitments.
The timing of many life events and the events themselves are
institutionalized. Within this context, then, people have more
or less freedom of choice to make commitments. As we pointed
out in chapter four, many people cannot make commitments
to occupational roles due to the sheer unavailability of such
roles. Achieved occupational roles which allow for a great deal
of space for free movement within them have not been widely
available to a majority of young black people, to members of
other minority groups, and to women; commitment to jobs,
then, is much more limiting for those who must work in jobs
that do not allow for growth through situational changes. The
ascribed role of many women and ascription of the role of
"unemployed person" provide numerous restraints which
isolate the individual from other situational growth experiences. Role discontinuity factors, as well, limit the extent to
which people can find growth experiences in the roles to which
they are expected to become committed. Nevertheless, those
events of adult life which distinguish it from other stages of
development, such as, for example, marrying, beginning a
family, settling into an occupation, are expected to result in
lasting commitments.

Comparative Studies of Functioning in Adulthood

Becker advanced his generalizations about the processes
implied by personal changes that have been observed in adult
life largely on the basis of studies of individuals in situations
characterized by an emphasis on socialization for a chosen
career, for example, socialization for the medical profession.

Earlier we have referred to the fact that scientific efforts to advance understanding about adulthood have raised a number of issues of definition, conceptualization, and method. While there are theories which suggest explanations for changes in adults, many biases are introduced into these explanations. The effects of pressures to conform to expectations ordered by the structure of the society lead to assessment of growth and change by highly traditional categories of behavior. Almost all research on adults has been limited to white, middle-class samples. Interdisciplinary and cross-cultural investigations are relatively few. As we have noted, the literature tends to be widely scattered, and synthesizing findings is an ongoing task.

K. Warner Schaie has commented on some of the difficulties that confront students of intellectual growth and other cognitive functions in adults: "Much of the literature on aging and cognitive behavior has been concerned with describing how older individuals differ from their younger peers at a given point in time."[7] We have chosen to highlight Schaie's observation here since we believe it has applicability to efforts to identify growth-related changes in adult functioning other than their cognitive component.

The studies Schaie is referring to simply describe differences between groups of people of different ages; readers familiar with research language will recognize these as cross-sectional studies. They do not tell us anything about how the same people change over time. For this information, groups of people must be compared with themselves at different ages. Such comparison, for example, would be based on data gathered from a group of people born in the same year, known as an age cohort, when they were twenty, forty, and sixty years old. This is a longitudinal study. But even this approach is problematic as a basis for generalization because, for a variety of reasons, not everybody in the group studied at age twenty will survive to be studied at forty, and again at age sixty. Another major problem of generalization from longitudinal studies has to do with the time in history at which the measures are taken. Findings from a longitudinal study of a given age cohort cannot be generalized to other older or younger cohorts of people whose life experiences have occurred under different environmental circumstances. For example, people who became adults prior to the Vietnam war and the social unrest of the 1960s would be likely to view the world differently from those who were adolescents during those years and are now adults, as well as from those who will become adults in the 1980s.

One common assumption of an age-related change is that intellectual ability decreases with age, and that intelligence is at its highest point in the middle to late twenties. We have previously discussed problems associated with testing intelligence at any age. Nevertheless, intelligence testing continues, and it is of interest to note that recent findings indicate growth in intellectual ability continuing well beyond the middle years. The highest intellectual productivity is associated with people who have greater education; the greater the education, the greater the intellectual productivity and the longer it will endure.[8] Studies do reveal a decrease in response time to testing as people get older; the older people are, the less quickly they respond. Some evidence supports the idea that although older people respond more slowly to such testing situations, they are more reflective and simply bring more experience to bear on their responses. On a philosophical note, Troll observes that

speed and youth have been balanced against deliberation and maturity in humans' descriptions of themselves since the beginning of time. A change-oriented society can make the mistake of weighting the speed-and-youth part of the equation so heavily that it is in danger of losing the benefit of deliberation and maturity.[9]

It is not clear what changes constitute deliberation and maturity.

Documented evidence from studies of adult functioning, then, does not provide much in the way of systematic ordering of growth and change in this life stage.

Applications of Personality Theory to Adulthood

Erik Erikson's theory is probably the best known among those that present systematic formulations of the effects on adult personality of continuing life experiences. Erikson does view growth and change as occurring throughout life. The reader will recall that he postulates a sequence of psychosocial tasks which successively dominate life. The eight tasks which cover the life span are: (1) basic trust (infancy); (2) autonomy (early childhood); (3) initiative (preschool); (4) industry (school age); (5) identity (adolescence); (6) intimacy (young adulthood); (7) generativity (adulthood); (8) integrity (late adulthood). According to Erikson's view, these psychosocial tasks identify eight issues, each of which presents a central conflict to be resolved in each successive stage of development. Erikson's theory is that while a particular issue is the major conflict of a given developmental stage, the same issue is present, though not dominant, in preceding and in later stages. For example, problems associated with identity dominate adolescence, but the issue of identity is also part of childhood and of the stages of adulthood. In the same way, a beginning solution of the integrity issue is present in early and middle adulthood, but is not as dominant as it will be in late adulthood, which most people refer to as old age.

Developing Intimacy and Avoiding Isolation

In this chapter, we are concerned with Erikson's discussion of the tasks of early to middle adulthood. In his thought, the psychosocial task of young adulthood is the development of intimacy and solidarity, and the avoidance of isolation. Intimacy, as Erikson uses the term, implies a synthesis of fusion and separateness, letting another person into one's life and entering into another person's life, at the same time maintaining a self-sense. This suggests a capacity to fuse one's own identity with another identity, to commit oneself to emotional attachments, and to develop the ethical strength to abide by such commitments. Intimacy requires an identity firm enough to risk such absorbing affiliations without fear of losing one's own individuality. Since, In Erikson's view, identity is not necessarily firmly established for the young adult, a crisis of self-esteem ensues which the individual can resolve either by movement toward intimacy or by succumbing to a tendency to withdraw from interpersonal closeness, which Erikson describes as isolation. He describes isolation as a process of "distantiation," or "distancing," leading to impersonality in relationships. That is, some individuals come to form highly stereotyped responses to others, abiding by the culturally prescribed expectations of behavior for various relationships, but keeping a kind of emotional distance in all of them.[10]

Achieving Generativity and Countering Stagnation

The psychosocial task which Erikson views as dominant in the next phase of adulthood is the development of a sense of generativity, countering the tendency toward stagnation. Generativity, according to Erikson, is

primarily the concern for establishing and guiding the next generation. There are, of course, people who, from misfortune or because of special and genuine gifts in other directions, do not apply this drive to offspring of their own, but to other forms of altruistic concern and creativity, which may absorb their kind of parental drive.[11]

Stagnation suggests a lack of caring and concern for others, with specific reference to children and home. Erikson's description of stagnation also suggests an inability to give to others, an excessive self-indulgence, and a lack of involvement in outside activities or investment of interest in anything other than necessary routines.

The opposing themes of the crises which Erikson describes for the life stages are not intended to suggest a strict "either-or" dichotomy; this is of particular importance to the stages of adulthood. Although intimacy is the opposite of isolation, people who achieve intimacy may, nevertheless, experience feelings of isolation at times, and no matter how much people's lives may be centered on generativity, they still may experience moments of interpersonal impoverishment which is tantamount to stagnation with regard to growth and development. Erikson appears to be suggesting these opposing themes as a way of describing a continuing tension that produces stress on the basis of which people actively experience the demands of growth.

The reader will find in the literature a considerable amount of material from other writers who have reviewed the adult stages of life as they are originally defined by Erikson. Without paying specific attention to some of the other ways in which Erikson has discussed them, we have selected from all this material general categories of developmental crises that we see as useful in describing aspects of the life experience of all adults. Nevertheless, there is reason to take issue with Erikson's treatment of the resolution of identity for young women. Erikson presents it in ways that appear to emphasize passivity, a living through the male marital partner and through child rearing. In this view, the woman's resolution is expressed through ascribed roles; she is presumed to gain fulfillment through the achievements of husband and children.

The problem which this poses is similar to some of the problems discussed in previous chapters with regard to the psychoanalytic emphasis in Erikson's descriptive analysis. Mary C. Schwartz has reviewed the bias in a reflection on views expressed by Erikson.[12] In an article published some time after his original work on life stages, Erikson emphasizes the woman's development through the roles of wife and mother. His views of the resolution of the young woman's identity are expressed in the following:

Young women often ask whether they can "have an identity" before they know whom they will marry and for whom they will make a home. Granted that something in the young woman's identity must keep itself open for the peculiarities of the man to be joined and of the children to be brought up, I think that much of a young woman's identity is already defined in her kind of attractiveness and in the selectivity of her search for the man (or men) by whom she wishes to be sought.[13]

The statement suggests stereotypical notions of the social functioning of young women derived from sex-role socialization. It appears to be saying that the woman can delay the answer to the "Who am I?" question in deference to the uniqueness of her husband and children, and the ascribed roles she will play with them, and that her search for her self is secondary to her search for a man through whom she will be defined as a wife and mother. From this point of view, she appears not to have an identity of her own separate from her attractiveness to males and her wish to be identified through them. In our view, Erikson does restrict the resolution of the crisis of intimacy for the young, adult woman. He does not appear to be quite as restrictive in his original interpretation of the resolution of the generativity crisis, although he severely narrows the options to intimate fulfillment through parenthood of people who suffer from "misfortune," or "have genuine and special gifts in other directions."

We still find the major tasks of establishing intimacy in human relationships and realizing fulfillment through some form of creativity a fair description of the life experiences on the basis of which adults appear to grow and to change their perspectives on themselves and others. It is the kinds of relationships in which intimacy may take place, and the purpose of those relationships, in which we see need for much more flexibility and space for free movement than Erikson's original work appears to prescribe. We have said that the categories of experience which he proposes as critical to the human growth of adults can help to order the social worker's knowledge of this stage of life. However, it is important for the social worker to perceive the value to people of growing and changing through the establishment of intimate human relationships, without assuming that such growth occurs only through socially prescribed and restricted roles for men or women, or that there is only one ultimately fulfilling option for women. Intimacy between men and women in the marital relationship, leading to creation and care of children, may be ultimately fulfilling if it is freely chosen, mutually supportive, and respecting of the rights of both to realize their human potential. It need not be viewed as the only means to this end.

Gail Sheehy's Description of Adulthood

Daniel Levinson is one of the current scholars who have been interested in pursuing stages of adult development. His study of males from early to middle adulthood confirmed the notion of a sequence of psychological tasks.[14] Gail Sheehy has elaborated this approach in a lively discussion of those crises which she views as characteristic of adult life.[15] She has written a popular book on her work, and it is our impression that quite a large number of adults identify their own life experiences in the descriptions she reports.

Sheehy collected 115 life stories through in-depth interviews with middle-class Americans, eighteen to fifty-five years of age, most of whom lived in urban or suburban areas of large cities. She chose to study this group because, in her view, the educated middle class has the greatest number of options and the least number of obstacles to choosing their lives. They are not hemmed in by traditions, as are those born rich and socially powerful, nor do they enjoy the same stability. And they are not deprived of education or economic advantages, as are the near-poor working class, nor do they hold the prerogative of some members of that class who have kith and kin to call upon when they are in trouble.[16]

Sheehy's work was oriented by a view of adult life as a series of passages from one stage to the next—the twenties, the thirties, the forties. Influenced by previous life-span research, with special reference to Erikson's work, this author has broadened the base of our understanding of Erikson's general categories. She does this through documenting the ways in which adults develop and use intimacy to avoid isolation and handle the drive toward self-actualization through periods of self-absorption and generativity. She documents instances of life experience which illustrate the beginnings of despair and the renewal of the life force through integration of life experience. She emphasizes Erikson's view of crises as critical turning points accentuated by one or another conflict between the demands for growth, the potential of the person, and the person's vulnerability. Her review of the experiences people have in passing through each decade of adulthood, and her descriptions of the ways in which people make the passage from one stage to another and of the content of life experience with which they struggle, suggests an inner dialogue. We briefly review her findings here.

The turning points of the twenties take up the issues of young people letting go, or struggling to be free of, the family of orientation; questioning whether to blend into another person or to risk being separate; searching for a way to balance behavior that is expected with inner questions about the identity one wants to have; struggling with the notions that choices made early in this period may be irreversible, that one's own will power is decisive in determining the course of one's life, and that self-observation may threaten the outcome of it all.[17] The turning points of the thirties include the issues of redefinition of the self and the roles one wishes to play: experiencing vulnerabilities associated with wanting to undo decisions made in the twenties; blaming life partners for circumstances which appear to block further growth; experiencing life's problems as unexpectedly painful; and questioning one's own willingness to change.[18]

Sheehy describes a "deadline decade" between the thirties and the forties which begins the passage into mid-life. This includes the struggle to maintain oneself as a person of one's own in the face of life experiences such as separations from life partners, environmental crises such as unemployment, sickness, and the parenting of growing children.[19] The turning points of the forties continue these themes, accentuating a reconciliation of the fear of loneliness and stagnation with regenerative and creative forces, toward acceptance of one's own human potential.[20] Subsequently, the passage through middle age beyond the forties may be characterized by self-renewal, based on increasing self-observing abilities and reexamination of self-development. Earlier resignation, or a giving in to a sense of despair that reflects an inability to accept the loss of one's earlier dreams of what life might be, leads to inflexibility and concrete-mindedness and blocks the self-observing function and the integration of life experience. Such integration leads to self-approval, finally to freedom to be what one is and to an acceptance of one's own aging and mortality.[21]

Throughout her discussion of predictable crises of adult life, Sheehy compares developmental differences of men and women, in the context of changing values and expectations. Much of her work highlights the psychological implications of adult experiences of that group with which she dealt. One of her objectives was to discover internal changes in her subjects, and through describing their struggles to continue to grow, to make it possible for her readers to engage in more self-evaluation without blaming themselves or the significant others in their lives for the painful parts of these experiences.[22]

Sheehy's application of personality theory to the events of adult life, then, allows for consideration of some of the social forces which also act as determinants for many members of the majority group in this society. In order to evaluate the implications that personality theory has for ordering our knowledge of adult life, we need to consider further the effects on individuals of the roles that become available to them by virtue of social definition. Adult behavior is affected by the age-status system of the society, in which, as Neugarten points out, "duties, rights and rewards are differentially distributed to age groups which have been socially defined."[23] From this perspective, the significance of both biological maturation and chronological age for adult growth has to do with: (1) the sets of social supports and restraints that demarcate the range of activities and expectations in which adults engage; and (2) the psychological reverberations of congruence or incongruence between the role sequences of an individual's life and the socially prescribed sequences that complement the society in which the individual actor is engaged. With this in mind, let us turn to a consideration of one major organized form of group life of the majority of adults in the society, and its implications for their growth strivings.

The Family

We have said that the forces in organized group life that propel people to behave in prescribed ways and that restrain them from behaving in other ways are critical to the understanding of social reality. The ways in which many people view themselves as actors in organized social life is heavily influenced by social definition, and pressures to conform to prescribed expectations of behavior can make social reality testing difficult. Active searching for knowledge about what it is that people are conforming to and why they behave as they do as members of subgroups of the society is difficult for many adults because it raises questions about behaviors that have simply been taken for granted. Most adults do not think of themselves as having decided to conform to what is expected; they tend to take for granted that what is expected is the best they can do for themselves and for other people. The human relationship arrangements within which most of the "taken-for-granted" behavior occurs is the family. The expectations of the family are highly institutionalized; that is, these expectations are below the psychological sights of most people.

The family is a subsystem of the larger society, and family members are components of the family system. It is in this context that the events of family life and the behavior of family members are institutionalized and reflect the needs of the larger social system of which they are a part. Although there have always been differences among families with regard to the space for free movement they have to make choices about how their family life will be organized and the extent to which it will complement other components of the larger social system, the space for free movement is limited by the needs of the larger social system. For example, there has been a marked decrease in family size, which reflects the goals of the larger society. Smaller families reflect the choice of parents, but the trend toward increasingly smaller families has occurred during a historical time in the society in which more people were not needed. Trends toward enlarging the population threatened the balance of economic and social organizational forces in the increasingly technological and industrialized society, and as this occurred, it became easier for families to make choices about family size. In the same way, the greatly increasing numbers of employed women who are also parents reflect the choices of women, but such increase has also occurred when economic changes in the over-all system have made employment outside the home necessary for many women.

The Nuclear Family
Other changes occurring in the family subsystem have implications for the larger system of which it is a part. These changes are inconsistent with institutionalized expectations. The nuclear family is the model of the family subsystem. It includes a husband and a wife, joined in a legally sanctioned marriage, and their legally sanctioned offspring. This traditional model of family form complements all the other subsystems of the society. As changes occur in the traditional model, they tend to disturb many balances in other components of the social system. We see the reverberations of this process in diverse ways: in attitudes toward choices on the part of married adults not to have any children; in increasingly high divorce rates; in new patterns of intimacy outside traditional marriages; in changing roles of women and in same-sex relationships. As the behavior characteristic of these deviations from the model of the nuclear family increases, it presents a

threat to the traditional family as an institution. Many people view such deviations from normative expectations as under-mining the society's foundations. Many adults, socialized by traditionally held beliefs which remain anchored in emotion, and which underlie the ways in which they have ordered their lives, have committed much of their energy to perpetuating a traditional family form during their lifetime. Accepting dif-ferent beliefs and new ways of valuing human relationship arrangements requires new perspectives which are inconsistent with their own experience and activities. The social worker is called upon to assess the changes occurring in the traditional family institution in a more objective light.

Over time, many families have made creative adaptations of the traditional American family model. The maintenance of mutual caring and sharing of life tasks has required a great many more adaptations of, and changes in, institutional behaviors than are generally recognized. Many nuclear families which have fitted the traditional model have had access to other institutions in the society which have supported and complemented their efforts. Such families have usually been free of extreme economic pressures, of disruptions of family functioning by the death of marital partners, of separa-tions due to long-term illness, and of a myriad of other events associated with an increasingly complex, technological society. However, many adults in nuclear families have had little freedom of choice within which to use their creative energies toward developing their own family styles of living, and their adjustments have not allowed for much actual growth and development of their human potential.

The Idealized Family Model
The traditional nuclear family is viewed as the foundation for the organization of human relationships in the American society, despite the ways in which families have gradually changed the traditional form. We see this "ideal" traditional model acted out by television families who are settling the country, living on the prairie in their own hand-hewn cabin in sight of a few other families, and who need very few lateral supports, have no complex industrialized society, and solve all their own problems. The family members give all their

loyalties to each other. Individuals draw their strength from the family; that is to say that the strength is in the group, which provides all emotional, economic, and intellectual resources with few, if any, significant interpersonal influences from outside the family's boundaries. The social reality within which the majority of families live their lives, however, is inconsistent with this idealized family. In our highly mobile, rapidly changing society, the nuclear family has needed a much broader base of support. As a self-sustained economic unit, the nuclear family is rarely workable. Events associated with changing patterns of mobility, competition for jobs, increasing rates of unemployment, costs of housing, health care, education, and other urban living problems of a majority of people attest to the difference between the myth and the facts of family life.

Traditionally, beliefs and expectations about family life have made it difficult for the members of many families to perceive themselves as worthwhile. Exploitation of the myth has implicated a wide range of "oughts" and "shoulds" in the self-esteem of family members. American family life is described in advertisements which, reflecting economically based social control of family life, suggest that the best people can do is not good enough unless they learn to love apple pies and hot dogs and buy products whose relevance to their worth as persons lacks substantiation. The high value placed upon traditional family relationships is inconsistent with many other values. For example, the value of education for all people conflicts with the values that underlie provision of limited educational opportunities for some of the people. The expectations of education for women conflict with the traditional expectations that women will automatically experience fulfillment in ascribed caretaker roles which have very little space for free movement within them and which allow for limited autonomy. Neither men nor women have much education in the tasks of caring for and supporting the young. Sex role socialization of many males continues to preclude the valued behaviors of tenderness and understanding of human relationships, and conflicts with the ideal expectations of the father as a participant in the family's emotional relationships. The prescribed role of provider conflicts with the fact of unemployment for many men, and with the need for both parents to guarantee economic security for the family. The values of regard for older adults and of their right to continue to have enduring supportive family relationships conflict with the value of independent functioning as a result of maturation. This is illustrated in the conflicts implicit in caring relationships between younger and older adults. Ray L. Birdwhistell observes that

if the only legitimate personal relationships must come from *within* the unit, and if the young, as they mature, must leave the unit to set up another such unit, such an organization is, by necessity, short-lived and self-destructive, the elderly are left lonely and isolated, and the maturing young are guilty of destroying the unit by the act of maturation.[24]

Birdwhistell's views of the idealized nuclear family unit as dysfunctional over time are borne out in a large number of families.

The traditional nuclear family is expected to be formed on the basis of romantic love between the marital partners which is presumed to endure from the time of the marriage to the death of the partners. The expectation is that romantic love will fulfill all their sexual needs and their emotional needs to escape from the pressures of problem-solving in everyday living. The ideal of romantic marriage provides a model within which the marital partners have exclusive sexual rights to each other and the duty to satisfy each others' physical and emotional needs. Fidelity ideally extends to all deeply personal feelings among the partners. Many marital partners experience disenchantment when the ideal fails, and because of continued expectations of themselves to live up to an ideal model of romantic love which becomes more and more difficult, they experience a sense of personal failure. Earlier we discussed the problems of role discontinuity which affect many adult sexual relationships. Some adults whose earlier sex role socialization does not allow for role flexibility between the marital partners experience many conflicts over traditional expectations. Many adults experience isolation and stagnation in marriages at the point when romantic love no longer serves the need for fulfillment and productivity, and they are unable to reformulate the

original marriage contract. The ideal model of romantic love is
also generally believed to be the basis of parenting, which is
assumed to be its natural extension. The system of values
within which ideal parenting is conceived implies that the love
of the parents will be reflected in the extent to which their
children can grow. According to Birdwhistell, such a conception has defined parents

not only as legally, morally, religiously, and economically responsible
for their children, but also as finally responsible for the personalities
of their children. As personality became seen as a result of "proper"
child care and child care as the final responsibility of the parents, the
parents (particularly the mother) were regarded as the cause of
"bad" personalities.[25]

This is the view that children are simply the products of
parental influences. It is reminiscent of the authoritarian and
relativistic concept of the superego which Erich Fromm discussed.

We can see in this discussion of the traditional model of
the nuclear family the burden of expectations imposed on
families. Birdwhistell concludes that if we could lessen "the
pathology inherent in the present family ideal by unmasking
its impossible goals, we might have better access to the talent
and energy now so wastefully employed by so many unhappy
and dissatisfied people."[26]

Social workers concerned with the strengths of families
understand that as an institution, the traditional nuclear
family has been overburdened. The majority of families need
many more social resources on which they can depend for supportive services. It is important to understand the ways in
which adults who have maintained families through their own
creative efforts have been able to resist the impossible ideals of
the traditional model, as well as to keep in mind that there are
productive and fulfilling nuclear families, created by marital
partners primarily out of romantic love, which undergo many
changes. The changes made by these adults are likely to reveal
a process of resocialization which allows for their own growth
through the renegotiation of the partnership arrangement.

Those who continue to view the idealized nuclear family
as the keystone of American life fail to grasp the implications

such ideals have had for troubled human relationships. The notions that the American family is endangered, that it is eroding, and that we are losing the very underpinnings of the society are frequently informed simply by the expectation that the traditional nuclear family is the only model for family life. The social worker whose observations are informed by the concept of social reality will take another look at what it is that is being lost. Change implies a break with traditions that reflect the firmly held, emotionally rooted beliefs of people. In the process of change, new role behaviors emerge which have no previous tradition. Those who play out these roles may have few, if any, models to follow. For example, people who deviate from expected family roles as adults may not know where they are going; they may not be able to anticipate the outcome of their behavior. They may be experimenting with new human relationship arrangements. To the extent that they are free to choose options, they may do so thoughtfully, with regard for their own growth and development. The social worker is not asked to judge people's choices as "good" or "bad" from the point of view of traditional norms. Rather, the social worker is asked to try to understand the extent to which the choices people make are made in good or bad faith with their potential for realizing their human worth.

Alternative Relationship Arrangements

Changes in sex-role expectations challenge many firmly held beliefs which are anchored in the social identity of most adult people whose socialization for a sex role allowed no room for questioning traditional expectations of family roles. Differences exist between the expectations of many members of the current generation of adults and those of earlier generations. Understanding such differences calls for attention to the differences in the historical time in which the present adult generation has been socialized and in which adults who are now entering the middle years of their lives have been resocialized. Neugarten and Datan have observed that the social system is shaped by historical time, which subsequently creates a changing set of normative expectations.[27] Today's generation of adults has been influenced by a changing social order in an age in which the pressures to conform to formerly unexamined norms are being seriously questioned. These adults have grown up in an era which made it possible to test social reality more actively, and many of them have changed expected patterns of intimacy and of commitment to family life.

Perry London has discussed the "intimacy gap" between generations, with regard to differences in motivation. He views the 1960s as the time of the sexual revolution and contrasts three generations of adults.

Today's 35-year-old women were just reaching the age of sexual discretion in 1960 when the Pill came along. People above that age have been reared with more or less traditional aspirations, for marriage, home, family and career. They gave birth to the sexual revolution and find themselves, by the millions, leading lives today they would never have anticipated as high school students. They never thought they would get divorced, or move a dozen times, or run a household alone while holding a full-time job, or go back to school in their thirties to train for a career. In all these respects, they differ sharply from the next generation, for whom such things are more norms than deviations.[28]

London suggests that older traditional patterns of intimacy have been radically altered. He cites a marked decline in the number of nuclear families in the last two decades. "In 1976 alone, 42% of all new households in the United States were singles, and 13.5% couples."[29] Other evidence attests to the changed set of normative expectations that is influencing intimacy patterns and adults' commitments to the traditional, idealized, nuclear family form. Thirty-eight percent of marriages are ending in divorce; in at least a third of first marriages, couples are disappointed and disenchanted, and they act on this through legal divorce. Many more marital partners are separated outside legal divorce. Approximately 18 percent of all families are headed by single parents. Among female parents, more than one half expend their life energies not only in financially unremunerated work within their families, but in financially remunerated work outside their homes.

Alternative Intimacy Patterns and Family Commitments
A number of young adults are not making legally sanctioned commitments to marriage. They are entering into a variety of

patterns of intimacy, some temporary and some long-term. Some patterns provide mutual support, care of each other and of offspring. Other relationship arrangements are formed on the basis of specific needs; for example, people may share living space for economic reasons, for companionship, for meeting sexual needs. Some young adults who do enter into legally and/or religiously sanctioned marriages devise their own contractual agreements which they include in the marriage ceremony. Others draw up legal marriage contracts which state the terms of their expectations of each other.

It is widely assumed that relationship arrangements which do not include legally sanctioned marriage represent a lack of commitment between the partners. Although some of these arrangements do represent commitments in the general, though nonlegal, sense of that term, the relationships that express these arrangements include a great deal of freedom and experimentation when they are characterized by the participants' free-choice decisions. Occasionally, these relationships, entered into under peer pressure, do not represent free choices. When they are entered into freely and planfully, such relationships represent options to traditional marriage. Some serve as premarriage arrangements and lead to formally sanctioned marriage. If they lead to new partnerships and continue to be characterized by situational change, they tend to resemble some divorce patterns.

Single-parent families are also frequently a result of choice. The most obvious of such families, of course, excluding those created by one parent's death, is a result of divorce, which may or may not be freely chosen by one of the marital partners. Single parents may wish to remarry. If they do, they may add another single adult to the family unit, or another single parent with children, and blend the families together. Occasionally, single adults, single parents, and married parents join in a collective group living situation characterized by one or another of a variety of patterns of mutual support and caring relationships.

Single parenthood is characterized primarily by divorced, separated, or unmarried women and their offspring. Many fewer men than women are heads of single-parent families. Concern for children frequently predominates in the responses of others to one-parent families. Although it is widely believed that families without fathers make children more vulnerable and create more identity problems for them, systematically unbiased research has not supported such an assumption. It has been found that children in single-parent families have the same growth chances as do children in two-parent families.[30]

Nontraditional, two-parent families also have potential for mutual sharing and fulfillment of children's needs. Divorced parents who share caring responsibilities for children may be more successful than they were able to be under the pressure of circumstances that led to their divorce. Two parents of the same sex may also share successfully in the care of children. Depending on the nature of their sex relationship, they may be regarded by others in the community simply as sexual deviants, without regard for the quality of their caring relationships.

Many family relationship arrangements, then, may provide social, emotional, and economic support for people. Adults have potential for creating various relationship forms within which they can achieve mutual support, care of each other and of offspring, fulfillment of love and safety needs. It is important for the social worker to evaluate these forms of human relationships by the caring nature of the responses they offer to those people who engage in them, rather than by the form they take.

Most of the literature on which we have drawn in our discussion of the family thus far has dealt with white families who belong to the majority group of American families. Indeed, the tendency among a large number of family theorists interested in the psychological and social sciences, among interested non-professional people in the society, and among social workers is to generalize from information about mainstream white families to all families in the society. It is not possible to generalize this material to families in minority groups, who may have quite a different experience in the society. First- and second-generation Hispanic families, Asian American families, Native American families, and black families have all made a contribution to family life in this country, and have struggled with different dimensions of life experience in the process.

The uniqueness of the black family illustrates the significance of the differences in the family experiences of one major minority group. This does not preclude the importance of the differences in the family experiences of other minority groups in the society. We hope that students of social work will seek to understand in depth the family life of these diverse groups. This search will be aided by reference to a growing literature including Miguel Montiel's discussion of Hispanic families,[31] Eddie Frank Brown's discussion of American Indians in modern society,[32] and Kenji Morase's discussion of Asian Americans.[33]

The Black Family

The black family in this society has a special social history which reflects the forced entry of black people into this country, their enslavement, and the black family's survival. One of the consequences of slavery as an institution in the United States was that the historical continuity of the black family with its roots in Africa has been concealed not only from white people, but from many black people themselves. In spite of this, the sense of "family" was not lost to them. During slavery, the black family in this country was completely without the support or protection of legal, religious, and political institutions and almost totally subjected to the economic interests of white property owners and merchants. Without institutional protections within the society at large, the earliest generations of black families were subject to the arbitrary decisions and actions of individual slave owners and traders, who either denied the meaning and importance to black individuals of family life, or exploited the emotional and social significance that family ties had for them. Enforced separations of parents and children, husbands and wives, brothers and sisters, and kinspeople of whatever age, relationship, or family position were systematically carried out; the threat of such enforced separations pervaded the daily life of the early generations of black people, while the power to actualize that threat was an implicit part of the emotional relationship between the black family group and the individuals who owned it. Economic interests of white slaveholders similarly influenced their sexual exploitation of slaves,

particularly of girls and women, as well as their control of the
life chances of children born of such unions.

In the last decade, black scholars, including social work
educators, have begun to describe the history of the black
family and to identify its strengths as an enduring institution,
as well as its significance for the continuity of black people. A
growing body of evidence supports the view that, uprooted and
dismembered as they were, and without formal societal sanctions for their existence, black families continued to define
themselves in terms of kinship networks which took a variety
of forms, but which have perpetuated the sense of solidarity
and social support and the high value placed by a majority of
black people on familial ties into the present day.[34]

Andrew Billingsley has discussed the wide variety of
family forms encompassed by the black family. In his 1968
study of black families in American society, he found the
following. Thirty-six percent, or slightly more than a third,
were simple nuclear families composed of a legally married
husband and wife and their children under eighteen; approximately 20 percent, or one fifth, were married couples
without children; 6 percent were single-parent families.
Slightly over a fourth, or 26.7 percent, were extended families;
that is, nuclear-type families that had taken in other relatives
or sub-families, such as a young couple living with one
partner's parents. A fairly substantial number, perhaps a
tenth, were families augmented by nonrelatives, either on a
long-term or less permanent basis.[35] These data highlight the
bias present in much research on the black family, as exem-
plified in such reports as that by Daniel Moynihan, who
described female-headed families on public assistance as
representative of black families generally.[36] Moynihan's
assumptions are fairly characteristic of the distortions
introduced into many generalizations about black families by
many social scientists who, taking it for granted that black
families are not only problem-ridden but are the cause of the
problems they face, prove what they want to prove.

Many blacks have suffered from poverty combined with
racism. As can be seen from Billingsley's work, the majority of
black families have maintained very close ties despite the
degrading conditions imposed upon them by the two forces of

poverty and racism. Despite the myths of failure in child-rearing, developed largely from the responses of white people to black ghettoized people in the impacted areas of large cities, black families have provided as much, if not more, nurturing and caring responses to children as have white families who have been under less strain. The absence of societal supports and the inconsistency in responses in daily living from whites have made heavy emotional demands on black caretakers and present special difficulties and dilemmas for many of them. Parenting in the black community demands unusual strength and devotion in championing and advocating for children within white institutions, such as the school. The task of demonstrating devotedness to children's welfare is often very heavy for parents who are overburdened by the necessity of protecting themselves from social and psychological assaults.

Many members of the black community are more concerned with the quality of the family relationships than with the form of the relationship arrangement.[37] Most black families have been adept at developing mutual support systems among themselves and between families in the absence of other supports from the larger society. The significance for many black parents and children of extended family and interfamily ties, of friendships and other family links to the black community is considerable. Because such affectional bonds are, characteristically, not formalized, the degree to which they function as child support networks and as resources to parents is frequently overlooked. For example, in our previous discussion of infancy and early childhood, we reported Rossi's observations of the constructive effects of multiple mothering of infants. Black families living in poverty make up a considerable proportion of the working poor, and the need for sharing for survival reasons has both an economic and a social-emotional support base. Social workers who observe extended and augmented family forms in this group of black people need to understand the implications such family forms have for mutual support of caretakers. What is frequently assessed as a disorganized family is actually a relatively well-organized human relationship arrangement among people who protect each other from exploitation, who share in the care of children, and whose caring is frequently marked by a more egalitarian approach to child care than is usual for the majority of people in the society. It is important for social workers to dispel the myth of disorganization, with its underlying implications of weakness. Many agency policies and practices have been based on this myth and have been detrimental to the integrity of the black family. Adoption and placement practices have, at times, perpetuated the breaking up of black families. A number of studies of achievement values among black parents have been similarly biased by institutionalized racism.

Billingsley provided the first systematic critique of black family structure. In addition to documenting the actual forms of family life in the black community, his findings helped to dispel the myth of the matriarchal home as a dominant characteristic. The myth of matriarchy reflects a lack of reality testing of the historical base of economic security in which the fact of working women was an adaptation to extreme economic pressures that required both parents, and at times all members of the family, to work, simply to survive. The severe effects of unemployment on a large proportion of black families, and the greater availability of occupations for women, albeit primarily menial occupations in the past, had less to do with sex-role orientations than with economic survival.

Researchers who have been unaware of value differences between black and white families have perpetuated misconceptions of the black family. The definition of family strengths, for example, is a value judgment in the frame of reference of the dominant white group in the society. Some of those black adults who are oriented by white middle-class values have also lost touch with historically significant value differences.

Changing Occupational Values

Our discussion of family forms and family roles has called attention to one of the major dimensions of the social identifications of adults. Work roles function for adults as another major basis for such social identification. The traditional role expectations for adult males and adult females as family members, and the idealization of the nuclear family form, are systematically linked to issues of social provision for the economic base of family life. One of the major reasons that families cannot follow the old rules is the absence of economic self-sufficiency. Economic security is one of the anchorages of adult life. It is apparent that the normative expectations for the provider role by which the traditional nuclear family was regulated could not be met by unemployed males who were unable to fulfill it. Changing values about the roles of women in the dominant society have brought about some changes in expectations of female adults, both within and outside families.

Women are no longer viewed exclusively as caretakers or as homemakers, since there is at least a fifty-fifty chance that they will work outside the home. But there is still some uneasiness about this institutional change. For example, if women with children work outside the home, they are assumed to be "working mothers." Society tends to reserve the term "work" for activities that involve a direct exchange of money for labor, and the general expectations are that the male partner in the relationship will be the "working" partner. Fathers are not referred to as "working fathers"; if they are not working outside the home, they are assumed to be unemployed. Few families have successfully reversed the traditional role expectations of mothering and fathering, and there is some question whether the ascribed mothering role would work any better for the majority of fathers than it works for the majority of mothers. Although sociobiologists suggest that parenting is biologically more natural for females than for males, this is not born out in cross-cultural studies of human behavior. Urie Bronfenbrenner notes the similar potential for parenting of men and women. He observed societies in which males were continuously related to young children and found males to be as able as females to care for them. He observed that adults learn the critical caring responses from children.[38]

As traditional values change, there are still many adults who continue to view new work roles for women as creating problems for their children. This influences children's own interpretations of their mother's role. Mothers do not necessarily create problems for their children by working outside the home. They work in order to solve family problems.

Mothers may choose to work as a means of fulfillment, and as a result they are likely to have more meaningful relations with their children, or they may work to guarantee the family's economic survival.

There is a need for change in other components of the social system within which the changing roles of women are taking place. Ultimately, we need to create changes in traditional work schedules to allow for more flexibility in work patterns for both women and men. Child rearing and child care are role behaviors which have simply been ascribed; we need to recognize them as achieved roles in terms of creative work. There is a great need for resources, for child care education, for child care centers to support the growth of children and to allow continued growth and development of the adults in their lives. The society needs to change traditional normative expectations, to increase respect for all forms of work regardless of the sex of the worker.[39]

Technological changes have made many previously available occupations obsolete. That dominant group in the society that has had the greatest amount of freedom of occupational choice has developed a generation of adults whose previous life experience has included the human rights revolution of the 1960s. This is the same generation of adults who have developed new patterns of intimacy. All these factors have come together to create more active reality testing about existing values in the world of work. Those who continue to have less freedom of choice in the determination of how work will affect their lives, and whose occupational choices are so severely limited as to preclude the development of new work contracts in regard to their own aspirations, have relatively little power to change these values.

Daniel Yankelovitch has reported that the usual method of creating jobs through economic growth will not supply the number of jobs that will be needed by people in the future, and it is likely that government statements about unemployment rates do not take into account the potential demand for work.[40] To this point, there has been no national policy which would make it possible for everyone to work who wants to work. Legislation to this end is delayed by a number of factors, including the cost of creating the jobs that are needed and will be needed, and the inability of most legislators either to comprehend or to get support for the social changes that the provision of meaningful work for all adult people would require.

The social-psychological welfare of people is implicated in work incentives for those who now hold a large number of the jobs that are available, and a lack of other identity anchorages, as well as disparity in the wage structure, increases workers' needs for economic rewards. Studies of the general dimensions of well-being define it as

a sense of self-esteem and conviction of one's worth as an individual; a clear-cut sense of identity; the ability to believe that one's actions make sense to others as well as to oneself; a set of concrete goals and values; feelings of potency and efficacy; enough stimulation to avoid boredom; a feeling that one's work is reasonably stable; and an overall sense of meaning and coherence in one's life.[41]

These factors are reminiscent of our discussion of motivations of behavior toward self-actualization. They also reflect a generally held view of the mature adult. "Success" in adult life, with regard to ideal models, might also be defined, in part, by such characteristics, but the general social assessment of success of the majority group in the society appears to be based more on economic holdings or accumulation of wealth than on self-actualizing characteristics. Many people in the society continue to behave as though one always has full control over the kind of job one achieves. We have seen that all work roles are not achievement roles, that many adults are victims of unemployment, low-paying jobs, or work situations that have in them no space for free movement for creativity. Many adults whose work situation does not allow for any incentive come to expect of themselves what is expected of them, and they are blamed for lack of incentive and creativity.

Since the social identity of the person is intimately tied into work roles, this takes on a very important meaning for the social worker. It is not only a matter of having a job for which one receives enough compensation to survive economically in the highly competitive society. It is a matter of how much the work one does contributes to one's social and psychological well-being. Social workers need somehow to free themselves

enough from the competitiveness that exists in the work structure to take the broad perspective within which the social
welfare of people is defined by the kind of work they do. From
this perspective, comparison of employment rates for minority
people and women with the rates of employment of majority
groups and of men, and the perpetuation of these rates of
employment, leads to the conclusion that the way many people
fare in the society is determined without reference to their real
abilities and potential for human growth and development.

Some evidence exists that people in the society are becoming more aware of the need for continued institutional change
in the work structure; a number of social and political forces
are directed to changing the work structure. Work values are
changing: discontent among groups of workers who are critical
to the stability and continuity of large organizations is
frequently associated with jobs that offer little prospect of personal growth. This has begun to stimulate questions about the
current incentives of jobs in large, impersonal companies.
Some members of the new adult generation are demanding
more right to self-determination and refusing to accept those
dimensions of self-compromise that characterize some of the
traditional attitudes toward work. On the one hand, legislation
directed to providing work is critical to the economic survival
needs of people; on the other hand, changes in the work structure of the society are needed at many levels of the social
system as it is now designed.

Some Functions of Human Liberation

The extent to which adults can enter the middle years and
experience a renewal of their life force depends, in part, on the
ways in which they have been free to follow the urgings of their
drive for self-actualization. The historical time in which they
were born and during which they were originally socialized,
and the extent to which life conditions have allowed for changing frames of reference and resocialization, are major determinants of the expectations they hold for themselves as
adults and of the options which remain open to them.

Adult crises function to disrupt self-continuity, and there
is a kind of relocating of self-potential that makes it possible

for people to negotiate these crises in relatively good faith. These negotiations are characterized, on the one hand, by a need for commitment to socially prescribed performances, and on the other by a yearning for freedom from the heavy influences of restraining forces on creative capabilities. In the transition from traditional social norms to newly emerging expectations which have not yet been supported by a general normative consensus, many social and psychological mountains have to be climbed. Adults are being asked to employ many skills in negotiating their crises which have not previously been practiced and which they have not had much opportunity to learn. Earlier assumptions about human behavior which were simply taken for granted have been challenged by those adults who are willing to try new ways of valuing differences. The courage to affirm their own humanness seems to be more available to those adults who have been able to resolve uncertainties about their own essential worth.[42] This resolution appears to depend on the opportunity to be free to choose to behave in ways which were restrained by some aspects of past conditioning. The freer adults are from restraints on their own self-actualization, then, the more likely it is that they will support the liberation of others from continuing social restraints which block the realization of their human potential.

Most adults who are members of groups that are actively seeking changes in stereotyped attitudes toward differences from traditional values have undergone changes in their own attitudes toward themselves and toward others like themselves. Many of them are responsible for the network of organized social movements which accentuate the rights of people to deviate from traditional expectations. Other adults, uncertain of the implications for social change which these movements have, tend to see all behaviors which deviate from social norms as an expression of some basic personality disturbance in those individuals who advocate them. The social worker needs to bring knowledge of the function of deviance to bear on their understanding of social movements. Those who see deviant behaviors as a breakdown in the social system want to eliminate them. But survival of the system is also dependent upon the support that deviant activities can derive from forces within the system. Those who support system change work to open further the boundaries by deinstitutionalizing social roles which are dysfunctional for people in the society. The social worker's understanding and respect for differences reflect this knowledge and preclude stereotyped attitudes toward those who deviate from expected behaviors. It is apparent that some adults need to find new ways to push their humanness ahead. Following is a discussion of some of the critical areas in which freedom of choice in adult life is restrained by institutionalized expectations.

Freedom to Choose Same-Sex Relationships

Adults have not been free to choose same-sex relationships without being subjected to destructive responses from the majority of people in the society. The taboos against such relationships are deeply rooted in myths about sexuality. Despite the sampling errors in early research which equated homosexuality with mental illness, and general acceptance in the psychiatric community of the findings of later studies which indicated no significant difference in the incidence of emotional disturbance between homosexual and heterosexual adults,[43] the belief persists that same-sex relationships are a form of emotional aberration. Many adults appear to be very much threatened by same-sex relationships and may displace or project their own unacceptable homosexual urges onto other adults for whom loving and caring relationships for others of the same sex are a natural expression of their human relationship feelings. Those for whom same-sex relationships are the preferred way of expressing their need for mutual sharing are frequently endowed with exploitative sexual motivations.

Same-sex relationships serve the same life functions of mutuality and support as do other forms of affectional relationships. The caring responses and responsibility-taking of adults who have same-sex relationships are not sex-linked. The human talents and resources of many of these adults are likely to continue to be blocked until pressures to conform exclusively to heterosexual relationship forms are reexamined by more knowledge-seeking, less vulnerable adults whose identity is firmly established. Traditional rules and regulations governing human relationship options in the larger social system reflect a historical need of the society for creation of the young.

Although these sources of pressures to conformity do not discriminate against adults who marry and who do not become parents, either by their own choice or for other reasons, they are frequently applied negatively to people who engage in same-sex relationships. Some decrease in the oppression of adults who engage in these relationships is apparent in the growing number of adults who support the liberation of others from continuing social restraints which block their human potential. Respect for difference in relationship choices in this connection demands a great deal more willingness on the part of a much larger number of adults to become aware of their need to deal with their own uncertain reactions, anchored in pressures to conform to traditional expectations.

Freedom from Racism
In an earlier discussion of social role, we illustrated the extent to which racism is destructive to the human potential of black people, and the extent to which conditioning of the majority group in the society propels them toward the role of pawn or patron. Role inflexibility and a lack of reality testing, then, have been supported by the society's need to maintain an underclass that could take up the slack of unemployment and provide a negative comparison group, especially for those members of the majority group who are most uncertain of their own identity. We have also seen, in the destructive behavior of some minority adolescents, an illustration of some of the wider implications of the inequality of opportunity and the dehumanizing characteristics of racism. We have suggested that white adults who perpetuate inhumanity suffer a loss of their claim to integrity. Integrity cannot be achieved through dehumanization of others; the drive toward self-actualization demands more. It is our impression that some aspects of excessive despair from which many adults suffer reflect an inability to free themselves from role inflexibility. The inner balance which is maintained at the cost of justifying racism restrains growth. The more that adults are liberated from the pressures of society to conform to destructive behavior, the greater will be their potential for continuing to liberate themselves from residual aspects of past conditioning, and for respecting others' rights to free themselves from destructive

relationships. The changing reference groups within which many young black people are testing their social reality, immersing themselves in new orientations to black culture, and finding a historical past to synthesize with a current and future self-concept characterize a search for continuity in identity in their own adulthood. This is expressed in the major interpersonal relationships they form, in care of the young, and in efforts to continue to change racist institutions. Since racism complements some of the unavowed goals of the society, these adults are involved in major work for social change.

Freedom from Sexism

Many of the expectations of adults have been linked to sex. According to Matina S. Horner:

Cherishing, care, competence and responsibility are human, not sex-linked responsibilities and attributes, and neither expressive nor instrumental competence is a sex-linked trait by biological prede-termination even though both have been treated as such. Intragender pluralism is certainly as great, if not greater than differences between sexes. Given that people tend to differ from each other as indi-viduals, perhaps more than men and women do as groups, to imply or attribute sex differences in areas where one's gender is an irrele-vant variable or criterion, as is commonly done, is not only damaging and unethical, but is now as it has been in the past very wasteful of a vast reservoir of human talent and resources.[44]

The shifting values of the society with regard to making it possible for women to accept and to use their human potential represent a transition from one set of normative expectations to another. As in any transitional period, adults face some dif-ficult choices. The courage which will be necessary to affirm the humanity of women in the face of deeply entrenched attitudes will be more available to those adults who have been able to identify themselves clearly, and whose continuing self-esteem does not depend primarily on conforming to either the male or the female stereotypically defined behaviors. As components of the social system, changes in women's behavior will demand complementary changes in the behavior of men. Most men are also caught to some extent in the constraining forces of sexism, and the extent to which male and female adults can find workable options to traditional human relationship expectations will determine the time it takes to lower, and finally to remove, the barriers to freeing up human resources which are now wasted. [45]

Older Adults

The previous chapter has called attention to the conception of a social timing which orders many life events for adults and within which it is assumed that they will establish economic independence, become caretakers and productive members of the society. Whether they play out the roles these adult activities define in the expected ways, or work to change the social order of things, they are counted as adults.

From the perspective of such assumptions, aged persons are not usually viewed as adult people. It is not assumed that they will be productive members of the society, and there are few, if any, roles which they are expected, as aged persons, to enact. Even those adults who have been able to resolve doubts about their own essential worth cannot count on socially supported opportunities to continue to grow once they have become identified as aged persons.

Adulthood is the goal of children and of adolescents, but older adulthood is rarely, if ever, the goal of anyone in this society. Every life stage prior to this last one is characterized by some sort of anticipation of the future. Socialization during earlier stages is presumed to prepare people for succeeding stages. Younger people talk about what they want to be, about how they want to live their adult lives; adults struggle for more space for free movement in the roles they play and often create new roles within which they can reach more of their human potential to liberate themselves and others from inflexible expectations. The roles they play become the means for preserving or for changing the social order of the society, and each generation of adults may influence the ways in which those who follow them are socialized for adult roles. But in this future-oriented society, people have very little socialization for the later years of adulthood. This stage of life is generally characterized by many role losses, including loss of responsibility and of social supports for continued participation in the affairs of the community. Role discontinuity, economic decline, loss of recognition, of authority, and of freedom to make decisions about their own lives are correlates of other losses in this life stage.

At some time or other, all people who survive long enough will be viewed socially as "aging" or "aged." Although people do want to live out their lives, very little value is attached to aging as a goal, or to the status of late adulthood. Indeed, most people who are oriented to youth devalue aging and old age. Changes in the appearance or activities of aged persons which deviate from the ideals of youth, that is, from what many people in the society have learned to believe is "good" and "beautiful," often evoke negative responses. Aged persons, then, are frequently seen as deviants,[1] as people who are "unusual" and have something "wrong" with them. Many people in late adulthood do experience decline in physical and mental powers, but these experiences are highly variable, and not all aging people show the same physical characteristics. Overgeneralization and stereotypical reactions to older people reflect the need to use them as a negative comparison group in a youth-oriented society.

The ways in which aging persons are viewed in the society present many problems for them and for their beholders. The more that aged adults are isolated and devalued, the less likely it is that they can go on valuing themselves, and the less likely it is that they can actively test reality. Those who endow aged persons with negative characteristics will not be able to view themselves positively when they grow old.

Although we have alluded, in the previous chapter, to some of the social and psychological implications of aging, we shall consider aging in later adulthood in more detail in this chapter. We have selected for discussion a number of issues to which we believe all social workers' attention should be drawn. These issues underlie the social worker's concern with preserving the human dignity of aging persons and with liberating them from dehumanizing social constraints. Social workers need to understand their own relationship to aged persons and to their own aging process, whether they are currently young or old.

We shall highlight some of the most critical social problems with which older adults struggle, and with which they need help. An emerging literature on social gerontology contains many new insights which go beyond what we shall discuss here. Whether or not their professional efforts engage them directly in working with aged persons, it is important for social workers to study this stage of life. The issues with which we are concerned, and many insights becoming available in the social gerontological literature, need to become part of the social worker's perspective. If one is to participate in providing social and emotional resources to people and to work for change in those institutionalized behaviors which continue to devalue them, it is important to get a perspective on human growth as a process that continued throughout life.

Definitions of Aging

There's no one answer to the question of when "old age" begins, nor is it possible to generalize the time at which earlier adulthood ends and older adulthood takes place. Some people define "aged" by the state of a person's appearance; one may have a "general physical image of 'old' and the closer an individual approximates your image, the more likely you are to perceive that person as 'old.'"[2] Some people define others as old when they reach a certain age and have no identifiable tasks in the work structure or in families. This implies that they have lost their social identity, and are identified simply by chronological age. But chronological age, in itself, is an arbitrary criterion reflecting more about the expectations of others in the society than about the person who is being defined.

Until quite recently, mandatory retirement regulations were applied to people in the work force at the age of sixty-five. At this age, legal regulations for income tax exemptions and eligibility for Social Security benefits, called "old age" insurance, do apply to people. Legal and economic definitions, however, are themselves variable. For example, as Robert C. Atchley has noted,

under federal law, workers are classified as "older" after age 45. Widows are eligible for Social Security at age 60. The minimum retirement age under Social Security is now 62. . . . Department of Labor Employment projects for older workers start at age fifty-five. The Department of Housing and Urban Development uses sixty-two years old in determining whether people are eligible for "elderly housing."[3]

In this context, the definition of aging is associated with the occupational structure, which has heavily influenced people's definitions of older adults. Such definitions are arbitrarily based on the assumption that at a particular chronological age, people are no longer able to function in their jobs. In a number of occupations, professional sports, for example, one's career may end at a much earlier age without the implication that the individual is aging or is elderly. Recent legislation raising the mandatory retirement age from sixty-five to seventy is in part a response to the irrelevance of chronological age to ability to function on the job. According to Atchley,

when the question is how well some one can function on a job or at what minimum age one can be expected to responsibly handle an important position, we are dealing with people's expectations and with age as a relative concept.[4]

When laws specify eligibility or ineligibility for certain rights and privileges, they reflect the prevailing conceptions of competence.

The general notion that retirement gives people the right to rest and enjoy leisure is based on the experience of a relatively small group of people in the society, and even for this group the idea is that their competence is in the past. For a large number of people, retirement from an occupation results not in enjoyment of leisure and rest but in serious economic and role losses which lead to financial and social dependency with associated self-devaluation. In later discussion, we shall see the implications these consequences have for self-definition of many aged persons.

Richard Kalish has noted that those who define aging by physical criteria tend to emphasize "body posture, gait, facial features, hair color and hairline, voice, skin resiliency, general body contour, and ability to hear and see."[5] Definition by such criteria, however, is also unreliable. Tremendous variations occur in the biological functioning and in the general health status of older adults. The term "senescence," which identifies the period of time during which decrements in physical functioning occur, simply means to grow old, in the same way that "adolescence" means to grow "up." Variations in senescence of biological and organic processes occur not only between people, but within the same individual.

According to Kalish, "organic changes become translated into behavior, and you might think of 'old' in terms of forgetfulness . . . slower reaction time, altered sleeping patterns, slower motor behavior."[6] None of these reactions, however, can be generalized to all older people in terms of time. Physical changes tend to occur over a number of years; they are rarely sudden. The incidence of serious physical decline and extreme vulnerability identifies a group of people known as the "frail elderly." The majority of aging people are relatively well.

Many people have believed, and continue to believe, that the climacteric, which generally runs its course during the fifth and sixth decades of life, signifies the ending of adulthood. Applied to women, this term describes the menopause, or ending of reproductive capacity; applied to men, it implies reduced sexual activity. While extreme age may be accompanied by decline in sexual ability and interest in sexual activity, this does not describe the majority of aging persons. Troll has observed that menopause is now considered simply an event of middle age. She notes that

It is less significant not only socially but also psychologically in the life of a woman. . . . If women are anxious during these years, it is more likely to be about changes in their families than about changes in their bodies.[7]

Menopause does not change the sexual capacity of women; the climacteric is not a dependable criterion for less sexual activity in either sex. Nevertheless, many people, particularly those who associate sexual ability with physical vitality, assume that older people lack sexual capacity. The continuation throughout adulthood of a great many taboos associated with sexuality becomes the bases for stereotyping aged persons. Erroneous conceptions of the climacteric may be the basis of the common expectation that aged persons cannot have active sexual lives.

Efforts to learn from self-reports of adults who are identified by others as old do not provide much basis for differentiating a point at which individuals become older adults. Such self-reports, by people beyond the fifth decade of their lives, reveal that in general, the younger people are, the more they perceive the generation just ahead of them as old, and many people beyond the age of seventy do not see themselves as aged. The self-perceptions of aging persons are influenced by the way some members of younger generations view them. We are left, then, with few guidelines for identifying the onset of later adulthood in this society. The society provides no formal rites of passage from earlier to later adulthood, and few, if any, explicit expectations and responsibilities to define new role behaviors for the aging and aged person.

Defining Aging as Deviance
Some people in the society define older adults by stereotypes associated with the use of the aged as a negative reference group by which younger people compare themselves. Some common stereotypes of aged persons are that they are "odd," "peculiar," and "crazy." Such labeling is a function of assigning older people to the role of deviant. Let us look more closely at the process through which such assignment is made, since it is critical to understanding the ways in which older adults are very often defined.

At first glance, those who stereotype and subsequently discriminate against aged persons appear to be compensating for their own fears of inadequacy. They appear to be projecting the deficits they suspect they have themselves. But the process is more complicated; it is a reflection of the larger social system's expectations. The reader may recall that it is in those instances in which people cannot adequately put themselves in the shoes of the other, in which no set of social expectations exists to explain the behavior being evaluated, that the behavior is likely to be labeled "odd" or "abnormal." The phase of life identified as late adulthood has no stage directions, no acceptable or expectable script fitting a designation of life tasks through which people in this life stage can further the goals of the society. The aged person's life is relatively unstructured by social expectations, and from the point of view of all the specific regulations and directives for every other stage, there is very little with which younger people in the society can identify, or with which they want to identify. Through all the preceding phases of life, people in the society are socialized into expecting their own and other people's behavior to complement social norms. In the previous chapter, for example, we noted that marriage or some life partnership arrangement, parenting or another form of caretaking and giving to the young, and occupational roles give people a feeling of assurance and recognition within a relationship network of others whose roles they complement in one way or another. Whether or not adults work to change social institutions and, thereby, change the roles that contain institutionalized behavior, they either fit into already established structures or develop new ones within which their energies are directed.

We have seen the cost of social change illustrated in efforts to change the ways in which roles are usually played. Without accustomed ways of doing things, people can become quite anxious. In this sense, having roles to play binds anxiety; expected activities that are presumed to contribute to the common good make one feel "good," give one a sense of engaging in some sort of meaningful behavior. "Acting one's age," then, is a way of fulfilling the expectations people have of one's role behavior. One may question the stage directions, and sometimes change them, but one needs some sort of structured activities on which one can count, some place to go with the other actors in one's life. When there are no stage directions, no productive or complementary roles to play, and when the person no longer has control over the way she or he lives life, living can become aimless and frightening. It is the experience of aimlessness and fear with which most younger people cannot identify, which most of them see as deviant from anything they have learned to anticipate in their future. In the labels they apply to this experience, they imply that it is "bad" and "wrong." They define aging persons as they define other deviants, in negative terms.

Social Structural Implications of Growing Old

In the sense that all people are likely to experience themselves as aging persons, the aged are not a minority group. Everyone is, at some time in her or his life, likely to be involved in this ill-defined experience for which there appears to be little, if any preparation. Medical advances have brought considerable increase in life expectancy for most people. Demographers have reported a lowering of the birth rate and an increase in the number of elderly persons in the society; in 1977, one in every nine persons in the United States was older than sixty-five, and that number will continue to increase.[8] These human beings are faced with potential normlessness, loss of social identity, economic deprivation, and a generally devalued place in the society.

We cannot, however, design strategies for the systematic integration of aged persons within the society, in socially valued roles, unless we look more closely at some of the social structural implications of growing old in this society.

Responses to Aging
All human behavior occurs in an organizational and institutional context. The context of human life is socially structured by shared images and symbols which are elements of action systems. For example, the ways in which people perceive the actors in a family express the shared symbols of the family as a subsystem. We have seen that individuals in a family define their organization as a family through their performance of family roles, and that social role performances are also the means by which the family subsystem in the society is defined. We identify the boundaries of the family system through

observing the point at which people no longer play roles associated with the expectations of family members. At every level of organized activity, we can assess the extent to which individuals are enacting roles which fit the expectations of that level of organization.

When we look at society from the point of view of age grading, we are looking at a system of social stratification, with an underlying assumption that if we know in which stratum to place ourselves and others, we know something important about how we are alike and how we differ, in expectations and prerogatives, and about how we should view such likenesses and differences. Our assumptions about the justness or injustice of the distribution of these expectations and prerogatives comes, through the course of our socialization, to be closely linked to our conceptions of the roles by which people legitimatize or challenge the grading system. As we have noted, we also come to associate certain constellations of roles with particular strata. For example, when we think of age strata, we might think of an individual whose central role set included roles of daughter, part-time domestic worker, and student as an adolescent but not child or middle-aged adult; or of an individual whose central roles included son, small business owner, salesman, and political campaign manager as an adult but not as an adolescent. We tend to identify ourselves on an age continuum when we become aware that we have made a transition from one set of roles to another, and frequently it is when people have gone from one set to another that they are considered to have made the transition from one life stage to another.

Socialization for Age Roles

People are socialized according to the expectations for their behavior at each successive level of organized social life, from infancy through adulthood. This implies that people learn enough about what will be expected later to perform acceptably in a variety of social roles. We have discussed the effects of role discontinuity in which they have not been prepared to share the symbols of those action systems they subsequently enter, or to perform the expected role behaviors. We have also discussed the differences in ascribed and achieved roles with regard to differences in the space for free movement to endow role behaviors with one's own creativity. We tend to expect that as individuals advance in age they will carry more achieved than ascribed roles. Since conformity to the expectations for achieved roles tends to be associated more strongly with social rewards than conformity to the expectations for ascribed roles, we tend to feel that our expenditure of life energies has been justified, or that expectations of such expenditures are justifiable, when our expectations of reciprocity are met. This is to say that we come to expect that the availability of social rewards is relevant to the resources with which we have provided others.

Preparation for major complementary role behavior is carried on for all stages of life but the last one. Role changes that people make throughout life from infants to toddlers, to nursery and preschool and school-age children, to adolescents, to adults, are usually associated with social rewards, including authority, responsibility, recognition, and autonomy. We have emphasized the lack of rewards available to some groups in the course of this social schedule of human events, and we have discussed the need for changing inflexible expectations of behavior; nevertheless, that social content which identified existing role expectations was clear in preceding life stages, as were the possibilities of influencing changes in the expected role behaviors. In general, the age grading and the social timing which characterize social supports for forming new human relationship arrangements and taking on increasing responsibility apply to these life stages. Generally, people can play many roles that are expected and can count on a considerable amount of reciprocal behavior without having to consider consciously how to behave or what response will be forthcoming.

Role learning, as we have suggested, is not always consciously undertaken. Those early frames of reference developed through internalizing the values of significant reference groups change on a gradual run, as do the perceptions of people as they seek more and more knowledge of the world. At any one point in the process of growing and changing, the life stage just ahead may call up images laden with expectations; one goes from "little" to "big," from a relatively acceptable "here" to a more desirable "there," to the next life stage as a step forward into the future for which everyone is somehow preparing or wanting to prepare.

For what is the aged person prepared? For what is the aged person preparing, and when is anyone prepared for aging? What are the social rewards, and where are the social supports? What kind of freedom and which responsibilities can people anticipate? What opportunities are there to go on learning and growing? The answers to these questions raise to our consciousness a wide range of institutionalized restraints that depreciate the aged, undermine their human worth, and exclude them from the mainstream of social life.

Devaluation of Aging
According to Irving Rosow,

Older people arouse strains of social conscience. They have done the world's work and met the demands of life, only to fall prey in their later years to growing deprivation and dependence. They have not necessarily failed, so they are not personally responsible for their fate. Diffused in our midst with a quietly insistent presence, they personify uncomfortable issues of social justice.[9]

Devaluation of aging is associated with the values on which the majority of people place their priorities. These values reflect the goals of the larger social system, and the roles that people carry have related value components. It is expected that those who play them will internalize these values so that their personal value priorities are congruent with the central and dominant value priorities of the society their roles help to sustain.

Kalish lists those characteristics most valued in society: achievement and potential for achievement; productivity of goods and services; ability to carry on human relationships successfully; independence and self-sufficiency; ability to enjoy life; knowledge and awareness; capacity for grasping technology; physical attractiveness, sexual capacity, and physical vitality; influence and power; material wealth.[10] Let us examine this set of valued characteristics from the point of view of prevailing expectations of what the behavior of aged individuals will demonstrate.

Achievement and productivity. Aged individuals are no longer expected to achieve. Those aged persons who have carried highly sanctioned achieved roles throughout middle life may sometimes continue to pursue them into their seventies and eighties; the majority of elderly persons, however, have no chance for achievement in the work force. Society offers very little systematic encouragement for use of creative energies, for mobilization of the life force, or for the drive for self-actualization. Production of noneconomic goods is assumed, like virtue, to be its own reward.

Ability to carry on human relationships successfully. The ability to carry on human relationships successfully requires continued relationship networks within which to experience sharing and which support expectations of reciprocal and complementary role responses. When we discussed the traditional nuclear family in the previous chapter, we considered some of the implications of caring family relationships for elderly people. Pressures toward mobility of family members increase the pressures toward segregating and isolating aged people and promote separation between generations. While increasing longevity is reflected in a growing number of three- and four-generation families, these are far from being the norm. Many elderly people experience both aloneness and loneliness in the separation from those who have been closest to them. And as we shall see later in discussing role losses, most older adults experience a diminution of the number of significant others with whom they have developed meaningful relationships.

Independence and self-sufficiency. The overwhelming majority of aged persons are not independent and self-sufficient. Atchley observes that

because of the decline in income, old age creates a progressive loss of independence for many Americans. Americans are taught to prize independence and guard it. No matter that the demands of job and family often reduce independence to an illusion, people still crave the illusion. Objectively, social independence means having enough money to get by, having a household of one's own, and having good enough health to be able to get around. Money generally goes first, usually as a result of retirement but sometimes as a result of illness in the family. Health goes next, and with it the ability to keep up a household and to get around.[11]

Some aged people experience dependence and lack of self-sufficiency as assaults on their integrity. Fear of dependency is viewed as a causative factor in the increasing suicide rates among eighty-year-old people.[12]

Ability to enjoy life. Social and psychological constraints on people in their aging years greatly influence their ability to enjoy life. The mix of pleasure and pain to which people have become accustomed is frequently tolerable to the extent that they are free to exercise options and choose among alternative life circumstances. People can choose to enjoy change when they have a part in the decisions that lead to changes to which they can feel committed. For a great many elderly people, the narrowing of options and the tendencies of others to exclude them from decision-making limits the scope within which their abilities to enjoy life may be exercised.

Knowledge and awareness, capacity for grasping technology. Although technology changes rapidly in this society, most adults have little encouragement to continue to learn complex technological material. Aged persons' technological knowledge is frequently outdated and not highly valued. In nontechnological societies, such individuals often receive respect for their accumulated knowledge, and are revered for having wisdom, for having had an opportunity to integrate more knowledge than young people have. In this society, the reverse is most often the case.

Physical attractiveness and vitality, sexual capacity. Physical attractiveness is a relative factor; it depends upon what others behold as attractive. Beauty is in the eyes of others first; then it is internalized by the growing individual and becomes the prototype of what is prized as "attractive." During their lifetimes, many aged persons have had the opportunity to examine and to change some of their own values. Many people learn to value differently as they become more seasoned by life experience. This would suggest that many old people have had the opportunity to develop their own ways of giving merit to physical appearance, and that they might well put high priority on their own appearance. But holding an opinion that differs from most others can be threatening and extremely difficult; aged people, no less than younger persons, depend upon others' opinions for ideas about what reality is. When most others do not acclaim old age and identify it negatively by physical differences from youth, aged persons frequently experience difficulty in maintaining values that differ from those of the majority.

Earlier we have pointed out the expectation that aged persons will not have active sexual lives, and have discussed the persistence throughout adulthood of many taboos associated with sexuality. The distorted view of this real human capacity as characteristic only of the young, and as socially meritorious only through its expression in biological reproduction is implicated in the perpetuation of stereotypical behavior toward aging persons.

There is no question that for the majority of people, physical vitality decreases with age, although many aged persons are quite vigorous. Older people can expect to become less so as they get older, and as a group, they are not as physically active as younger people. This decrease occurs gradually, and is so varied that there is no way of generalizing its timing or rapidity.

Influence and power, material wealth. The close association between wealth and social power in this society needs no documentation. The majority of older persons have no material wealth. According to Atchley:

A small but highly visible minority of retired Americans have ample incomes, but most are struggling to make ends meet. Social Security pensions are the main source of retirement income in America, yet the level of these pensions is generally inadequate. . . . As people grow older, they not only fall below the poverty line but also fall well below their previous incomes and the national median income for all families. . . . Single women, widows, older retired people, and blacks are very likely to be drawing grossly inadequate pensions. . . . Many older women were widows of workers, which means that they were drawing reduced pensions based on their dead husbands' incomes, and many single women over sixty-five were neither working nor entitled to Social Security pensions.[13]

Many older adults struggle simply to survive; two thirds of all retired Americans live below the poverty line.[14] Some have financial assets other than income, such as home ownership, but such assets are rarely large enough to be of much significant help. Most live on inflexible incomes. As Atchley points out, there is considerable discrepancy between a few older people who have substantial accumulations of material assets and the great majority, who have a very low level of current income, let alone other material wealth.

We have been considering some of the social structural implications of growing old in this society. Margaret Clark expresses the nature of the questions which the social order presents to both aged and younger people, as follows:

One may reasonably conclude that the accession to the status of old age in American society represents a dramatic cultural discontinuity, in that some of the most basic orientations . . . must be changed at that stage of the life cycle. Abrupt changes in the demands made on the aging individual require marked shifts in value orientations. Yet, as we know, values are among the most tenacious of human sentiments. They are the building blocks, not only of self-esteem, but also of the very definition of reality.[15]

Minority Aging

The life conditions of aging persons who are members of minorities reflect the multiple consequences of the discrimination which characterizes their social history in the society. All the problems that face aged adults in the society are compounded for black, Mexican, Puerto Rican, Asian, and Native Americans. They are likely to have even fewer social institutional supports than are available to other aged persons. For example, exclusion of agricultural workers from Social Security coverage accounts for significant losses for many minority elderly. "Mexican Americans and Puerto Ricans, who comprised a large segment of the agricultural labor force through the 1960s, were excluded from coverage under the Social Security Act."[16]

Information about the income levels of aged black persons reveals the cumulative consequences of discrimination in education and in the work force throughout their lives. Thus Atchley reports,

Black workers . . . have Social Security pensions that reflect the effects of job discrimination. One-quarter of the men and one-fifth of the women who draw the minimum benefits are black.[17]

According to Donald Davis,

Even if every racial barrier were immediately eliminated for aged black workers, the mass of aged blacks would still face a disastrous economic future. Their limited educational attainment in part was the starting point of a vicious cycle which failed to prepare them for skilled jobs or for upgrading opportunities. Although we have observed a higher educational attainment of young adult blacks in recent years, the educational levels of middle-aged and elderly blacks are very low.[18]

Black and other minority aged persons, then, are not only likely to have an extremely low income, they are also least likely to have money from savings or other financial assets as they grow older.

In addition to more severe economic losses, health problems are much more serious for minority persons. The death rate of minority aged is disproportionately high. Fewer non-whites than whites live to age seventy-five; older minority people have a greater incidence of death from the major terminal diseases and from accidents. The shortage of health personnel and medical services generally available to minority groups in inner city ghetto areas means that many more minority than majority aged people spend the end of their lives in public custodial-care mental hospitals because of the lack of skilled nursing home facilities and unwillingness on the part of some of these facilities to take minority patients.[19] Social workers frequently are the major links between minority aged and those public health services that are accessible. The well elderly among minority groups are more likely than their nonminority counterparts to live in inadequate housing, suffer from a lack of transportation and fewer institutional supports than do other aged persons.

Aged members of minorities, then, suffer multiple jeopardy. The last stage of life is more hazardous for members of our society whose opportunities have always been limited. A past history of low-income employment, or unemployment, frequently associated with loss of Social Security benefits, and of poor health which increases their vulnerability to health problems in late life, severely limits their expectations at this stage of living. For them, the general devaluation of aging means that they are likely to experience even greater dependence on public support, and fewer sources of recognition of their critical needs for respect and dignity, than other aged members of society.

Role Ambiguity, Role Discontinuity, and Role Losses

Earlier we have questioned what social rewards and social supports aged people can anticipate. It is apparent that on the most important value dimensions of the American social system, aged people symbolize a position that is viewed as deviating widely from major economic and social goals. Having been socialized in earlier life stages to organize their energies in roles that support the achievement of these goals, they find themselves, in old age, redefined as incompetent, or as representing what others are being socialized *not* to become, *not* to want, *not* to aspire to.

The valued characteristics of the society have, as we have seen, little, if any, association with the life conditions of its aged adults. The values we have discussed are goals of a youth-oriented society with emphasis on the future. No major role expectations of aging persons are associated with the society's central goals, and no clear-cut expectations are held for people once they are socially defined as aged.

Role Ambiguity
While the transition from childhood to adolescence and from adolescence to adulthood is frequently difficult to define, the transition from middle to late adulthood to aged is almost impossible to locate. Certainly those ceremonies which mark the retirement of the worker, when they do occur, do not make a distinctive change in the persons; other local ceremonies, such as ninetieth birthday or sixtieth wedding anniversary celebrations, may recognize past accomplishments but hardly presage expectations of new roles. The roles of grandparents are undertaken by many adults at relatively early ages, before they are perceived as belonging to that group of older adults who are socially defined as aged. The paucity of socially valued roles specifically for aged persons leads to a sense of meaninglessness and aimlessness for many older adults, who experience

a great deal of uncertainty and doubt as to their essential value to the society. Most older adults experience a relaxation, or loosening, of expectations that they will conform to existing norms; many encounter a "What can you expect at their age?" response which is reminiscent of attitudes toward much younger people.

The social norms that guide the behavior of aged persons are not explicit. Somehow it is implicit that aged persons have roles to fill. As Rosow points out,

norms are . . . left implicit when appropriate standards are simply ambiguous and there are few guidelines by which to structure and give direction to a role. That is, when expectations are weak, unclear, and indefinite. This may reflect either a normative vacuum or sheer vagueness. . . . Certainly, for the aged, norms are not explicated because of ambiguous standards—not because they are self-evident or vary in their form across situations. Old and young alike are simply unclear about the proper role for the elderly.[20]

Very few people examine the lack of standards by which to live as an elderly person. It is as though people think everyone else knows how aging is structured socially, but no one checks to find out what norms guide the life energies of people who are aged.

Role Discontinuity and Role Losses

Lack of preparation for being aged leads to a great deal of role discontinuity. For a very large number of aged persons, giving up the central roles in their lives is not a matter of choice. Many would like to continue in the work force; many who retire would like to take up activities for which they previously had little time but find their free choice limited by insufficient money and by other people's perceptions of them as aged. Frequently they find that they have been disqualified and reidentified by characteristics which fit neither their real abilities nor their expectations of themselves. They are expected to have completed their important life tasks, to have been rewarded and recognized, and no longer to need support and recognition.

Many writers suggest that women have an easier time than men in adapting themselves to decreasing role responsibilities. The notion is that the social schedule which regulates maturation of offspring and declining responsibilities as home-makers occurs more gradually and does not present as many precipitous and unplanned role changes as does retirement for men. This does not describe the life conditions of a majority of women. It may apply to women whose functioning in a nuclear family includes a highly satisfying parent partnership, continuation of domestic roles with the same life partner, and no sudden decline in family income. According to Philip Jaslow, however,

employment may tend to provide the older woman—perhaps more than any other—with a source of dignity, self-esteem, a means for retaining a youthful self-image, opportunities for social participation, or any other integrative or supportive function which has been suggested for older men.[21]

Jaslow studied morale among older women, using a multistage area probability sample of 2,398 women, obtained in 1968. His findings were based on responses of noninstitutionalized women aged sixty-five and older. The sample included women employed at the time the sample was obtained; retired women, who were unemployed at the time of the study but had previously worked continuously for at least five years; and women who had never been in the work force. He found that

employed women had higher morale than the retirees, with the exception of those women with annual incomes of $5000 or more, among whom the retirees had better morale than the workers. Women classified as never having worked were found to have the lowest morale as a group. Small but statistically significant differences remained when the intervening effects of age, income and health were simultaneously isolated, indicating that the group differences in morale stemmed in part—but not entirely—from the fact that the working women tended to be the youngest, the healthiest, and financially better off, while the women who had never worked tended to be the oldest, poorest, and in the worst health.[22]

An analysis by Gayle B. Thompson of data from the larger parent national sample on which Jaslow drew revealed that variation in morale of male workers and retired males could be almost entirely attributed to systematic group differences in income, age, and health status.[23] These researchers have raised questions regarding current knowledge of both men's and women's responses to retirement and suggest a continued need for inclusion of female subjects in research projects.

A large number of aged persons experience role losses. These include loss of family roles due to death of a spouse, of occupational roles due to retirement, of provider roles due to decrease in income, and dependence. Such losses are associated with decreases in group memberships; often their impact is to block people from forming meaningful new human relationships. All elderly persons are likely to suffer the loss by death of some of their contemporaries. This is a loss of meaningful others with whom people have shared important parts of their lives, with whom they could remember their own personal history and the social historical time within which they have lived. For some aging persons, peers who have not shared parts of their own past life experience do not function as positive reference groups. Many aged persons refer their behavior to younger groups of people for judgment and appraisal, reflecting earlier socialization to youth and the expectations of behavior to which it led them. Since they do not have any clearly identified age norms, they tend to be guided by those that do exist for younger people.

The expectations that older people have of themselves are frequently influenced by loss of complementary role expectations. Most aged people have no power positions to hold onto. Both role loss and role discontinuity are involved here. Older persons' authority, defined by their knowledge and competence, is lost since it is simply not accepted by other people. Rosow observes that

those with superior power and authority are almost invariably younger persons—adult children or relatives, various professionals . . . or other middle-aged groups. . . . In the course of their adult lives the aged have normally been in authority over those younger than themselves, but seldom have they been subordinate to them. Thus, when they become subordinate to younger persons, the customary intergenerational roles are reversed. Superior responsibility, power, and often competence then reside in the younger rather than the older group. There is absolutely no systematic precedent for this in the life experience of the aged.[24]

Earlier we have referred to the fact that aged members of minority groups have fewer institutional supports than the

majority aged. Loss of valued roles, then, further complicates
the lives of many minority elderly who were socialized in other
cultures to expect increased recognition for their attainment of
old age. Consequently, the loss of complementary role expectations is experienced as an acute source of stress for many
elderly persons in minority communities. In Hispanic, Native
American, and Asian groups, aged persons, by tradition and
custom, normally commanded more respect with increasing
age. They often held important roles in the family and in the
community, associated with the transmission of culture. The
effects of urbanization in American society and the loss by
many younger minority people of identification with the culture which these aged persons symbolize have devalued their
position in the life of the family and the community. Increasingly, these aged persons have had to deal with interpersonal
problems of role discontinuity in regard to the roles for which
they were socialized.[25]

Social Reality

Absence of new reference groups which could function as
standards of comparison for self-appraisal and as a source for
new value preferences, norms, and attitudes increases many
aged persons' sense of difference from other people.
Throughout all periods of life, reference groups serve individuals as a way of finding out how similar or different they
are in relation to others. We have discussed some of the ways
in which such groups serve individuals as a basis for reality
testing. There are many pressures on aged persons to conform
to others' views of aging.

   Aging people do not wish to conform to the stereotyped
notions of others. It is likely that younger people who hold
stereotyped ideas about aging do not attempt to find out what
aging means to aging people. Younger people whose relationships with aged persons include continued caring frequently do not endeavor to find out how close or far away their
own views of the world are from the views of those older
persons about whom they care. For both older and younger
people, then, social reality is likely to include behaviors which
they do not want to know about.

The psychological tendency for groups of people to experience the world in relation to some frame of reference they all share characterizes groups of aged as well as younger people. This may account for the tendency of aged persons to share their past experiences with each other, and with younger people. Unable to share images of a social future, many aged persons come not to give value to themselves in the present. When people in this age group do seek actively to test the reality of others' opinions of them, they often find, more by inference than by open admission, that others do devalue them as contributing members of the society. Viewed by many others as relatively nonproductive, dependent, lacking in currently prized knowledge and influence, some aged persons view themselves in the same way.

People are generally not aware of the extent of this degrading attitude, and of the existence of agism, which has some characteristics in common with racism and sexism. According to Margaret I. Kuhn, agism is characterized by

built in responses of our society to persons and groups considered to be inferior. . . . [deprivation] of status, the right to control their own destinies and to have access to power, with the end result of powerlessness . . . social and economic discrimination and deprivation of the contributions of many competent and creative persons who are needed to deal with our vast and complex problems. . . . individual alienation, despair, and hostility.[26]

Agism is institutionalized in this society; behaviors that express it have happened again and again until they are below the sights of most people. It is the major source of social restraints on the liberation of aging people. In spite of a slowly evolving social movement directed to consciousness raising and to active change in social institutions which perpetuate agism, people are slow to support the effort to liberate aging persons from conditions which block their continued growth and self-actualization. Many aged persons have experienced powerlessness at a number of levels, and their energies are frequently drawn off by efforts simply to survive economically, by accelerated physical decline brought on through lack of good health care. These aging people can easily become involuntarily isolated from others. In fact, the idiosyncratic behavior which is sometimes observed in aging people may be more the effect of isolation, lack of group support, of others with whom to test reality, than evidence of chronic and irreversible disease.

Social Influences on the Self-Concept in Aging

Many pressures are brought to bear on aged persons to devalue themselves. The life conditions of the most disadvantaged aged persons frequently constitute conditions in which they suffer from either a general loss of social response, or social response which perpetuates stereotypes. Such isolation often leads to self-compromise. Kuhn observed the kinds of responses which people who needed nursing care, for example, could expect in some situations.

In nursing homes probably the ultimate indignity is to be given a bedpan by a perfect stranger who calls you by your first name. Too often institutional managers, along with staff, regard and treat the residents as children, incapable of making sound judgments or managing their lives. So successful is this benevolence that retired residents soon become children.[27]

The perpetuation of agism can distort many areas of human relationships. The onset of mental confusion about self-boundaries among some aged persons is highly likely to be, at least in part, a consequence of avoidance of painful knowledge about the way the self is viewed by others, especially by those on whom aged persons have to depend for help. At times, an aged person may become critical of those on whom that person depends for help, suspecting them of depriving him or her of rights and personal belongings. When this is obviously an inaccurate description of the motivation of the immediate caretakers, the behavior is frequently diagnosed as "paranoid." In these instances, it is less important to label the behavior than to understand the psychological vulnerability of an aged person who can no longer defend against the painful feelings associated with the social responses of a majority of people toward all aged persons.

Protection of self-esteem, of love and respect for oneself, presents problems for a large number of the well elderly. Some people undergo considerable denial of their own aging. Rosow studied the opinions of a large number of aging persons in this regard. He reports that

only one third of the sample regarded persons over sixty-five as still productive and useful, but fully five-sixths felt that they were still useful themselves. Similarly, while five-sixths agreed that older people who denied that they were old were "usually just kidding themselves," more than one-half then insisted that they personally were not old.[28]

For many people, the consequences of identifying oneself as aging appear quite painful. There are many "jokes" about people who do not want to admit to their age, who want to be viewed as young. The extremely profitable cosmetic industry depends to a considerable extent on the negative attitudes of many older people toward their physical appearance. Younger people frequently "compliment" older people by telling them they do not "look their age" or "act their age." That they look "youthful," engage in "youthful" activities, have a "youthful" spirit, are all considered complimentary remarks by the aging. It is as though there is nothing good which is intrinsic to aging. No further growth is expected of aging persons by most people in the society. It is no wonder that some elderly persons deny their age. This denial is an effort to block out real threats to self-esteem.

People may also defend against knowledge of their essential worth and creativity. Consciousness of their own drive to fulfillment can create feelings of vulnerability. Among aging people, the courage to withstand the pressures to conform to what a majority of people expect of them requires the ability to tolerate loneliness, to behave according to one's own ability to continue to grow and to create new forms of activity, to do the unexpected, to affirm something about oneself which is likely not to be generally accepted.

The greatest danger of all lies in the tendency to confuse irrational responses to rational circumstances with rational responses to irrational circumstances. In a sense, all aging persons have to defend themselves against the irrational tendency of others to place on the elderly themselves the responsibility for those conditions of life that block their ability to reach their human potential. Under irrational social conditions, the behavior which many aged persons find necessary to realize their authenticity may be identified as "odd" and deviant, and perhaps at times as "sick." Such behavior may in fact be, in large measure, a response to growth, to tension maintenance, so that learning can continue. Our understanding of human behavior must include the right of people in old age to react to irrational circumstances such as expectations of their worthlessness by changing them in the service of their need to go on growing and believing in their own self-worth.

In the previous chapter, we referred to Erikson's identification of the psychosocial task specific to old age as the development of a sense of integrity, and the mastery of a sense of despair. In view of the social influences on the person's conception of the last stage of life, the expectations that one can achieve an integration of all that has gone before appear to be almost too demanding to be achieved. It is remarkable that so many aged persons do engage their energies in the task of integrating their life experiences and not giving in to the pressures to despair.

Erikson suggested that integrity is associated with acceptance of one's life as one's own; in a sense, this means that no one else could have lived that life in just that way. The last life task requires a great deal of self-observation and acceptance of the self and of one's accomplishments, no matter how they were judged socially. One is, in a way, the final judge of one's human worth. In the last stage, it is likely that one can finally be in touch with the self one was, the self one wanted to be, and the self one has become. The theme of Erikson's discussion leads to the statement:

Although aware of the relativity of all the various life styles which have given meaning to human striving, the possessor of integrity is ready to defend the dignity of his own life style against all physical and economic threats. For he knows that an individual life is the accidental coincidence of but one life cycle with but one segment of history; and that for him all human integrity stands or falls with the one style of integrity of which he partakes. The style of integrity developed by his culture or civilization.[29]

Precisely this readiness to defend the dignity of the last stage of life underlines the remarkable ability of many aged persons to achieve integration. In this stage, the need to keep good faith with the self, to maintain a sense of one's own essential worth, and to continue to believe in the worth of all other human beings, to somehow see oneself as part of all humankind, requires a great deal of psychological work. For those older adults whose life experiences have allowed for freedom to search for knowledge, for use of their self-observing capacities and of their drive to self-actualization, this joining of themselves with all of humankind would appear to be less of a struggle. For those who have experienced oppression and whose life experiences have been characterized by active struggle against the social restraints on human potential, the struggle for personal integration would also appear to be less than for those who have succumbed to the pressures to conformity, who have not actually worked to change very much at all.

It is also left to the elderly themselves, in large measure, to work to change the very conditions which make the achievement of this life task difficult during the aging years. Those who carry on their fight against oppression of elderly people may include persons who have not previously challenged institutionalized behavior. For these persons, and for all aging people, integrity demands the challenging of attitudes toward aging which have become institutionalized, and it requires that they work to change these attitudes. The integrity of younger people is of course involved in this, as is the integrity claim of all human beings who directly or indirectly contribute to perpetuating dehumanization of people in this last stage of life.

Aging persons need a great deal of social support to undertake the task of integration. The expectation that they will actively continue to work for liberation from social restraints in their later adulthood contradicts the expectation that they will disengage.

Some Implications of Disengagement
For many aged persons, loss of social roles and meaningful relationships is associated with disengagement. It is important to keep in mind that most elderly persons are not encouraged to continue active participation in the society. Robert J. Havighurst, Bernice Neugarten, and Sheldon Tobin describe both social and psychological disengagement:

The decreased social interaction that characterizes old age results from the withdrawal by society from the aging person; and the decrease in interaction proceeds against the desires of most aging men and women. The older person who ages optimally is the person who stays active and who manages to resist the shrinkage of his social world. He maintains the activities of middle age as long as possible and then finds substitutes for those activities he is forced to relinquish; substitutes for friends and loved ones whom he loses by death.[30]

Aging has also been characterized by relatively complementary disengagement of the society from the individual and of the individual from the society. This describes the point of view of those who support a theory of disengagement. According to Havighurst and his associates:

It is suggested that the individual's withdrawal has intrinsic, or developmental, qualities as well as responsive ones; that social withdrawal is accompanied by, or preceded by, increased preoccupation with the self and decreased emotional investment in persons and objects in the environment; and that, in this sense, disengagement is a natural rather than an imposed process. In this view, the older person who has a sense of psychological well-being will usually be the person who has reached a new equilibrium characterized by a greater psychological distance, altered types of relationships, and decreased social interaction with the persons around him.[31]

Any theory of disengagement which sees it as voluntary is subject to question in light of the social restraints on active participation in the society imposed upon a majority of aging persons. When psychological disengagement is generalized as a natural and inevitable process of aging in this society, it operates to perpetuate agism. It is important to look at the many variations among the group generally called "aged." For many of them, social restraints are a source of despair. The pressures to disengage come from the society and are not initiated by the person.

In later stages of aging, it is highly likely that some aged persons experience reduced energy output, that lower activity levels are preferred, and less active participation may well be a matter of choice. The point is that older adults need freedom to choose that pattern of activity or disengagement which best fits their expectations of themselves and others. The willingness of some older adults to adjust to the general expectations that they will simply disengage from further active participation in society is a way of dealing in bad faith with their innate abilities to continue to grow through life experience.

Kalish points out that for many older adults, increased activity may be predictive of increasingly higher, and decreasing activity of lower, morale:

The majority of both popular and professional opinion supports the idea not only that involvement and activity are helpful in successful aging but that they may even help in maintaining survival itself.[32]

Havighurst and his associates found that freedom to disengage has a great deal of meaning to many adults. They sampled the responses of a stratified probability sample of middle- and working-class white adults from one metropolitan, mid-West city. Their findings suggested that to one individual disengagement may mean

freedom to indulge in material comforts, to indulge passive . . . needs to take on a . . . carefree life. For another this may mean freedom to pursue . . . important social values and to devote more time to the examination of philosophical and religious concepts. For still another . . . freedom to choose the work and community roles that symbolize his sense of worth and to remain highly engaged.[33]

Adults who have experienced more freedom of movement in their earlier adult lives, or who have worked to liberate themselves and other people from restraints on human abilities, are more likely to continue to have, or to struggle to get, more freedom of choice in older adulthood. As we have noted, adults find it extremely difficult to dissociate themselves from the values of the society or to change earlier response patterns to stress.

Attitudes Toward the Ending of Life

A great many people tend to live as though they will never die. In general, awareness of death has been discouraged in our youth-oriented society. Although the ways in which people come to the end of their lives are more than simply the out-

come of the ways they have lived their lives, their views of
death are very much influenced by what they have learned to
expect of themselves and of others. For example, advances in
medical science, the funding of research to develop cures
for terminal illnesses, and the attitudes of most medical
professionals are all directed toward eradicating disease and
prolonging life. Paradoxically, this presents the person who
does not surmount dying with a sense of having somehow
failed to live. Melvin J. Krant observed that all the emphasis
on medical advances and the preservation of life imply an
official policy in the health care system suggesting that death

is an evil to be overcome. . . . While, in effect, this position seems
generous toward relieving human suffering, the inherent implication
that all disease, including even the aging process, can be eradicated,
places a burden on all dying people, or individuals with serious terminal illness, in the sense that in some fashion they are out of keeping with national expectancy.[34]

Of course, the emphasis on perpetuating life and relieving
suffering is an exceedingly important goal for the society. But
it is also important to enable people to accept the naturalness
of death. There is a lack of preparation and very little understanding of the meaning of death. We do not provide very
much encouragement for knowledge-seeking about death
among children or adults, although most people experience
death through the loss of loved ones in the course of their lives.

A growing concern to address this lack in our socialization
is reflected in the literature and in many efforts of people in
the human services to communicate their insights. Elisabeth
Kübler-Ross observed five stages through which people antici-
pating death are likely to progress. These are: (1) denial; (2)
protest; (3) attempts to ward off death through bargaining; (4)
depression; and (5) acceptance.[35] It seems likely that the more
people have been able to come to terms with other losses, the
more they will be able to accept the ending of their own lives.
According to Kalish,

People often assume that death is more frightening for the elderly than
for the young, perhaps because of its imminence. The evidence,
however, indicates just the opposite. Although older people think
about death more frequently, they are less afraid of it.[36]

In our view, the extent to which elderly people can handle the ending of their own lives with acceptance and view death as the last of a long series of growth experiences is dependent on a great many things. We can suggest only some of the implications of this experience.

In order to understand the meaning of death, we must consider much more than the moment when death occurs. It has meaning with regard to individuals' lives and the extent to which they have been able to realize their human potential. One's human dignity is implicated in one's self-worth. Discussing the concept of death with dignity, Krant observes:

Such a concept implies, in our culture, that an individual has a sense of stature and a sense of control of his destiny. To feel helpless, hopeless, damaged, deformed, or alien is synonymous with feeling powerless, out of control, and distanced from those people and those objects in life which provided a sense of stability, safety, security, and ultimately a sense of being a dignified human being.[37]

The extent to which aged persons can experience dignity in death is dependent on their own preparation, on their ability to celebrate the lives they have lived, on their willingness to accept the ending of physical life and the continuity of their contributions to others. All these factors are encouraged by others who function to enhance the right of dying persons to know that their death is imminent, and who recognize their right to make decisions concerning the conditions of their care. It is clear that most people do know when they are dying, but medical personnel, family members, and friends often do not want to confirm this knowledge. In a sense, this denies dying persons the opportunity to share the experience and denies them support for their own continued integration of this event into their lives. They need an opportunity to review their lives. Kalish suggests that this life review

can be extremely helpful in enabling the older person to see his life as an integrated whole rather than as a series of episodes, to reflect upon his accomplishments and to deal with feelings of nostalgia and regret.[38]

When the person ends life in the care of strangers in the impersonal atmosphere of hospitals or nursing facilities, attention to needed integrating experiences is less likely. Individuals also need to be able to control the extent to which those responsible for their care respond to terminal suffering through the use of "heroic measures" to prolong life. The "living will" is a statement which many aged persons might wish to make while they still have their health and can clearly think through the implications of their care as they end their lives. Such a statement has been formalized by the Euthanasia Educational Council.[39]

As members of society become more aware of death as a natural part of human experience, attitudes toward the ending of life are much more likely to include respect for the dying person's right to end life with dignity.

Implications for Social Workers

From the social worker's perspective, aging is developmental. Human development begins at the beginning of life and continues to the end. From this perspective, each life stage is characterized by gains and by losses. The extent to which individuals can continue to realize their potential for human functioning will depend on the balance between the gains and the losses. The elderly person, no less than the younger, continues to grow to the extent that the gains outweigh the losses.

We have discussed the nature of the losses which aging people experience, and they outweigh the gains for the majority of people in this stage of the life cycle. If social workers maintain their commitment to the value of human life, they cannot afford to view elderly persons differently from the way they view human beings in other life stages. Working for the rights of people in this age group to grow is as important, for example, as working for the rights of any other age group. Programs that attempt to respond to the losses that children experience emphasize replacement of caring persons, provision for financial support including day care and income supplements to families, education and emotional support that encourages active mastery of the environment, health care, and a number of other special human services. Acceptance and expectation of the need for increased services for children have been much more strongly emphasized than expectations and acceptance of need for services by aging persons. Society has provided fewer resources for them in the past, and many of the services that do exist reflect a lack of planning related to need.[40]

Aged persons need support to function independently; they need support groups in order to continue active participation in the society; they need freedom from social and psychological stress to continue to realize their human potential, to exercise freedom of choice with regard to the degree of their disengagement from activity and their need to integrate their life experience; and they need protection of their integrity as their lives come to an end. It is critical that social workers have knowledge of existing services and resources for older adults and that they advocate changes in social policy toward the continued development of resources and services. Of critical importance are opportunities for meaningful employment in full- or part-time work that allows opportunity to use their skills, subsidies for housing and housekeeping or house maintenance services, increased health care, and a wide range of educational and supportive social services. Social workers need to become aware of the planning and policy implications of community housing programs for supporting the integration of aged persons into the community.[41]

Social workers need to become knowledgeable about those interdependent social support systems within which people function, including family, friendships, the community of neighbors, professionals, and occupational, religious, and self-help networks. The interconnection with others on which supportive groups are based remains critical to the life force of aging persons. Their ability to function, to experience their strengths, to continue to remain in touch with themselves and their own drive to grow depends on the quality of their social support systems, especially in times of crises.[42] Many losses that elderly people experience are intensified by lack of replacement systems in the supportive network structure by which their social energies were directed. It is important for social workers to enable older adults to replace "natural" networks when this is needed. Such replacement systems can take many forms. For example, although a great deal of intergenerational conflict may exist in families, a growing number of two-generation families want a third-generation experience and welcome the introduction, on a friendship basis, of an elderly person whose original family is not available.

When intergenerational conflicts do occur, their causes cannot always be generalized. The expected patterns of behavior and the cultural values of Asian and of Puerto Rican Americans, for example, often reflect normative expectations with regard to intergenerational behavior and priorities different from those of dominant American groups. Younger people currently migrating and moving into the society, as for instance those from Taiwan and other cultures, may experience the separation of generations quite differently from the majority.

Social workers have become more active in work with aged persons toward mobilizing their energies to change institutionalized restraints which perpetuate agism. Older adults need to participate in the planning of programs on their own behalf. Community center programs and day center services of all kinds need to make use of the skills and strengths of the elderly people they serve and for whom they are designed. Older people may be very helpful as volunteers in such programs, but they must also be seen as having the same needs as younger people to have their investment of interest, ability, and energy recognized through financial rewards. In the struggle against agism, many aged persons can join with each other to expose dehumanizing conditions, explore new life styles, and advocate change, in the tradition established by the Gray Panthers.[43] Learning to collaborate with others in the planning and delivery of social services to aged persons, social workers have found that this work requires "new combinations of method and modalities and collaboration with other human service professionals in recently designed service milieus."[44]

An important recent development is the hospice program, designed by the National Hospice Organization for persons in late stages of terminal illnesses. Hospice programs provide services when it becomes apparent that death is imminent. Their objective is to help people deal with their own death in a relatively pain-free environment of acceptance and serenity.

The program may be implemented in the home of the aged person, in a combination of hospital and home care, or in a specially designed hospice setting.[45]

In their work with aged persons, social workers make the bridge between the individual and the social reality. Their task is to help redefine a set of expectations which organize, for older adults, social contributions that complement new goals. Pressures to conform to the existing social reality make this task very difficult. Those goals to which it is directed include recognition and support for the rights of aged persons to continue to grow, to free their life force, to integrate their own life experiences, and to share in the work of liberating others from restraints on self-actualization.

Many social workers are collaborating with others who are engaged in this effort. Without this kind of work, devaluation of aging will continue to result in a loss to the society of a great many accomplishments associated with moving humanness ahead.

Chapter 11

Summary and Reflections

The purpose of this book has been to introduce a body of knowledge on which social workers can draw to inform their practice. This purpose led us to select four organizing concepts, to develop them in some depth, to connect them with each other, and to link them to stage-specific life experiences.

Our selection of the explanations we have offered was based on the following premises. The organizational and institutional arrangements within which people live largely determine the ways in which their human energies are directed. Knowledge which is fundamental to social work practice must be weighted on the social determinants of human problems and their psychological implications. The explanations on which social workers draw must link knowledge of social organization to knowledge about individuals. The concepts we have selected have the propensity for organizing the social worker's knowledge of human welfare. They provide a perspective which directs the social worker's attention to human needs and aspirations, and to humanizing and dehumanizing processes. This perspective also makes it possible for social workers to locate some dimensions of social change to which it is critical that they direct their interventions.

We do not pretend that this is all the knowledge the social worker needs in order to become a compassionate and effective practitioner. These few concepts simply provide a scaffolding on which students can build more knowledge. The understanding of human behavior to which this knowledge leads also is intended to provide an integrated theoretical grounding that can be further elaborated by the social worker for use in practice. We hope that the students and the practitioners who have this framework to which to refer will want to seek more knowledge, to explore other theoretical approaches, as they deepen their commitment to social work.

Social workers direct their interventions to the interface between the individual and those human relationship arrangements which express the expected behaviors of the society. These expected behaviors predetermine a social schedule of life events which may encourage the individual's internal motivation for growth, or may discourage it. Social restraints may inhibit the individual's freedom to choose to behave in accord with the drive for growth. Social workers need to be clear about the freedom of choice issue which such restraints pose. In order to work with individuals, social workers need to develop a perspective that allows them to understand behavior from the viewpoint of those others with whom they work as well as from their own. Social workers experience others in relation to themselves. The more one can draw self-boundaries, the more one will encourage others' freedom to understand where the social worker ends and they begin. The answer to the "Who am I?" question is found, in part, through self-observation which requires the ability to learn to formulate a conception of oneself-as-actor influencing, as well as being influenced by, others.

Social workers learn to understand the language of behavior from the study of individuals in groups through which they are joined to society and by which their social identity is often defined. The individual neither defines the society nor is entirely defined by it. The restraining and propelling forces which the person encounters in the search for self-realization are mediated by those groups to which the individual belongs or has belonged.

The more similar people are to each other, the more likely they are to compare themselves with each other in making their self-appraisals. When pressures to compare with others unlike themselves cannot be overcome, people may not be able to make accurate evaluations of themselves. The availability of others who view them as equals increases the ability of individuals to make accurate self-appraisals and encourages self-assertion. Self-assertion has been extremely difficult for many minority groups in the United States in the face of pressures to use the majority group as a comparative reference. Widely held negative attitudes toward minority groups are expressed in responses which denigrate minority group members.

The concept of social reality links the self-concept and the impressive influences of reference groups to the broader organizational and institutionalized content of social system transactions. It directs the social worker's attention to the ways in which the larger social system influences perceptions of reality in order to maintain the complementary transactions among its component groups. It explains the institutionalized basis of human behavior and the reasons that it is necessary to account for system dynamics in working for social change.

The concept of social role explains the means by which the organizational and institutional arrangements that largely determine the direction of human energies are maintained. The roles which people play in their lives are frequently used to define their social identity. Social roles are learned through reference groups, and they influence the individual's perception of social reality.

In large measure, social workers direct their energies to changes in institutionalized role behaviors. Social workers frequently occupy positions at the boundaries of the social system, and they endeavor to keep these boundaries open. In their work with community groups, social service organizations, and government agencies, social workers strive to change dysfunctional institutionalized responses to social psychological needs of people. The introduction of new orientations to human needs frequently requires a break with traditions which reflect the institutionalized beliefs of people. Energies that are so organized and directed are not easily disengaged. People expect to have their energies structured by role behaviors which perpetuate established rules and regulations. Structure binds anxiety; it protects self-consistency. People often resist social change and will not participate in it unless the social forces which support traditional behaviors no longer support those behaviors. Social workers who promote change in role behaviors which are dysfunctional for the consumers of social services need knowledge of the forces in society which propel and which restrain people in institutionalized roles from changing them. Social workers need to develop skills to harness the energy of people for whom institutionalized roles are dysfunctional, toward action for change. Social workers also mobilize support for existing groups who are working for change in dysfunctional institutions.

Our discussion of life stages has highlighted a number of issues which we believe are critical to the social worker's perspective. We have placed more emphasis on those social forces which restrain human growth than on those that propel it. We have used a problem approach which precluded discussion of some of the more positive outcomes of maturation for those people in society who have the greatest number of guarantees of protection for their human rights. We have examined the pressures to conform to social definition in the light of changing social institutions. Our approach proceeded on the following premises.

There is no overarching theory of human development which includes explanations of biological, psychological, and social functioning. A number of theories exist, each orienting the social worker to some, but not all, critical factors in the growth and development of individuals. From the point of view of many social theorists, behavior expected in successive life stages is a product of what people have learned to believe is expected. The society has a model of successive life stages, a social agenda which is taken for granted and remains relatively unquestioned. It is simply expected that the individual will internalize existing conceptions and expectations of life stages and fulfill them. These expectations maintain some institutionalized behaviors which are dysfunctional for many people. Some social definitions, for example, tend to perpetuate racism, sexism, and agism.

Many psychological theorists continue to explain human problems from the point of view of differences between individuals and neglect the social organizational context within which their behavior occurs. Traditional depth psychologies tend to look for the causes of human problems within individuals. These explanations have been highly influential in encouraging expectations of behavior associated with instinctual tension reduction. The taboos associated with sexuality and the embarrassment which is widely associated with body function have their origins in a general consensus that behavior is instinctually determined.

Most contemporary theorists agree that behavior is motivated by some form of self-actualization, by a drive to reach human potential. It might be expected, then, that the society would project a model of life stages which emphasizes the forwarding of human potentials. But the model of expectations for successive life stages often appears to block the drive toward self-actualization. Perhaps this is associated with the assumption being voiced in contemporary society that self-actualization is self-aggrandizing, somehow hedonistic and destructive of support for the good of all. On the contrary, the more people are free to reach their own human potential, the more they will respect the rights of others to do so. All human beings have self-actualizing tendencies which promote humanization. The more that people are liberated from restraints on their own actualization, the more they will liberate others. The resistance to acceptance of this premise does not necessarily reflect a need to deny others the right to grow and to realize their self-potential. Many people are in agreement with ultimate goals of this nature, but prior socialization has made so many demands upon them to conform that change is quite painful. There is an essential sadness in the tendency of some people to draw the boundaries of human experience so narrowly as to elect to view themselves and others in rigid and overly moralistic ways. Self-actualization leads to opening the boundaries of one's view in order to take in the wonder of one's own and of others' human potential.

In illustrating restraints on the development of human potential, we have emphasized those institutionalized behaviors which perpetuate racism. The dehumanizing effects of institutionalized racism have placed many restraints on the opportunities for the development of human potential of a majority of nonblack as well as a majority of black people in the United States.

We have not elaborated to the same extent on the ways in which such institutionalized behavior characterizes the continuing devaluation of a number of other minority groups. All groups of people who suffer from oppression experience devaluation of their human worth. This devaluation takes on many subtle variations which emerge differently according to the social-historical background of minority groups and the form of oppression to which they are subjected. It involves a generalized assignment of values to differences, to the advantage of the majority and the disadvantage of the minority.[1] This process is used to justify the exclusion of many minority groups from full participation in the society. It is imperative that social workers further their own knowledge of the variations in the social-historical context out of which discrimination emerges. An increasing volume of literature, a number of well-organized courses in ethnic studies, and ongoing study and action groups within the social work community provide opportunities for further in-depth exploration of these variations.

We have taken the position that all people have the right to claim their own integrity. Human beings who perpetuate institutionalized behaviors which block others' human rights have forfeited their own claim to integrity. In the process of liberating others from such restraints people free themselves as well. Respect for differences implies social support for the integrity of all groups in society, and increases the opportunity to learn from the variety of human experiences that differences represent.

We have emphasized the need to continue to support those forces in the social system which promote the opening of its boundaries. The system can absorb deviance from established expectations, and change can be accomplished within this social system. At times, the complexity of the work for change can lead the social worker to despair of being able to make meaningful changes in the balance of forces which perpetuate dehumanizing social conditions. But social change is cumulative, and all changes in dysfunctional restraints, at any level of human transactions, are meaningful. It is important to test the social reality within which resistance to change is simply taken for granted. In the face of many influences to the contrary, it is necessary for social workers to maintain their commitment to change. This commitment is based on the belief that all people have the drive to grow and to reach more of their human potential, that they can change their social institutions, and that they have the right to do so. Social workers' attitudes toward social change are grounded in the belief that injustice to any group of people is a threat to justice for all people, that everyone's welfare is dependent on everyone else's human welfare.

Notes

Introduction
1. Ronald Federico, *The Social Welfare Institution: an Introduction* (2d ed.; Lexington, Mass: Heath, 1976).
2. Paul D. MacLean, "A Triune Concept of the Brain and Behavior," in Donald R. Campbell and Thomas J. Boag, eds., *The Clarence M. Hincks Memorial Lectures, 1969* (Toronto: University of Toronto Press, 1973).

1. Social Influences on the Self-Concept
1. William James, "Psychology" (*American Science Series; Briefer Course;* New York: Holt, 1915), p. 216.
2. *Ibid.*, p. 179.
3. Charles Horton Cooley, *Human Nature and the Social Order* (1st ed. rev.; New York: Scribner's, 1922), p. 182.
4, *Ibid.*, pp. 183–84.
5. Morton Deutsch and Robert M. Krauss, *Theories in Social Psychology* (New York: Basic Books, 1965), p. 184.
6. *Ibid.*, pp. 183–84.
7. George Herbert Mead, *Mind, Self and Society* (Chicago: University of Chicago Press, 1934), p. 135.
8. *Ibid.*, p. 155.
9. *Ibid.*, p. 202.
10. Ruth L. Monroe, *Schools of Psychoanalytic Thought* (New York: Holt, Rinehart and Winston, 1955), pp. 579–80.
11. Calvin Hall and Gardner Lindzey, *Theories of Personality* (New York: Wiley, 1957), p. 468.
12. Percival M. Symonds, *The Ego and the Self* (New York: Appleton-Century-Crofts, 1951), p. 4.
13. Ernest R. Hilgard, "Human Motives and the Concept of the Self," *American Psychologist* (1949), 4(9):376.
14. *Ibid.*, p. 379.
15. Gordon W. Allport, *Personality* (New York: Holt, 1937), p. 320.
16. Franz Alexander, *Fundamentals of Psychoanalysis* (New York: Norton, 1963), p. 21.
17. Abraham H. Maslow, *Toward a Psychology of Being* (New York: Van Nostrand Reinhold, 1968), p. ii.

18. *Ibid.*, p. 23.

19. Gordon W. Allport, "The General and the Unique in Psychological Science," *Journal of Personality* (1962), 30(3):405–22.

20. Maslow, *Toward a Psychology of Being*, p. 26.

21. *Ibid.*, p. 190.

22. *Ibid.*, pp. 192–93.

23. *Ibid.*, p. 193.

24. Carl R. Rogers, *Client-centered Therapy* (Boston: Houghton Mifflin, 1951), p. 483.

25. Hall and Lindzey, *Theories of Personality*, p. 478.

26. Carl R. Rogers, "A Theory of Therapy, Personality, and Interpersonal Relationships, as Developed in a Client-centered Framework," in Sigmond Koch, ed., *Psychology: a Study of a Science* (New York: McGraw-Hill, 1959), p. 224.

27 Stanley D. Rosenberg and Bernard J. Bergen, *The Cold Fire* (Hanover, N.H.: University Press of New England, 1976), p. 1.

28. Albert Camus, *The Rebel* (New York: Vantage Books, 1956).

29. Rosenberg and Bergen, *The Cold Fire*, p. 2.

30. Soren Kierkegaard, tr. Walter Lowrie, *Fear and Trembling and the Sickness unto Death* (Princeton, N.J.: Princeton University Press, 1968), p. 201.

31. Rosenberg and Bergen, *The Cold Fire*, p. 3.

32. Erik Erikson, *Identity and the Life Cycle*, Psychological Issues, Vol. I, No. 1 (New York: International Universities Press, 1959), p. 120.

33. *Ibid.*, p. 118.

34. Grace Ganter, Margaret Yeakel, and Norman Polansky, *Retrieval from Limbo* (New York: Child Welfare League of America, Inc., 1971).

35. *Ibid.*, pp. 27–28.

2. Reference Group Behavior

1. Herbert H. Hyman and Eleanor Singer, "An Introduction to Reference Group Theory and Research," in Edwin P. Hollander and Raymond G. Hunt, eds., *Current Perspectives in Social Psychology* (3d ed.; New York: Oxford University Press, 1971), p. 67.

2. Franz Kafka, *The Trial* (New York: Knopf, 1937).

3. Dennis H. Wrong, "Freud and Society," in Alex Inkeles, ed., *Readings on Modern Sociology* (Englewood Cliffs, N.J.: Prentice-Hall, 1960), p. 88.

4. Francis X. Sutton *et al.*, *The American Business Creed* (Cambridge: Harvard University Press, 1956), p. 264.

5. Wrong, "Freud and Society," pp. 95–96.

6. Abraham H. Maslow, *Toward a Psychology of Being* (2d ed.; New York: Van Nostrand Reinhold, 1968), p. 22.

7. Helen H. Lynd, *On Shame and the Search for Identity* (New York: Science Editions, 1965), p. 35.

8. Maslow, *Toward a Psychology of Being*, p. 12.

9. Lynd, *On Shame and the Search for Identity*, p. 33.

10. *Ibid.*, p. 35.

11. *Ibid.*, p. 95.

12. Tamotsu Shibutani, "Reference Groups as Perspectives," *American Journal of Sociology* (1955), 60:564.

13. Manford Kuhn, "The Reference Group Reconsidered," *Sociological Quarterly* (1964), 5:7.

14. Franz Alexander, *Fundamentals of Psychoanalysis* (New York: Norton, 1963), p. 84.

15. Erich Fromm, *Man for Himself* (New York: Rinehart, 1947).

16. Gordon W. Allport, "The Psychologist's Frame of Reference," *Psychological Bulletin* (1940), 37:24.

17. Fritz Heider, "Perceiving the Other Person," in Hollander and Hunt, eds., *Current Perspectives in Social Psychology*, p. 309.

18. *Ibid.*

19. Daniel Katz, "The Functional Approach to the Study of Attitudes," in Hollander and Hunt, eds., *Current Perspectives in Social Psychology*, p. 338.

20. *Ibid.*, pp. 336–42.

21. *Ibid.*, p. 336.

22. *Ibid.*, p. 337.

23. *Ibid.*

24. *Ibid.*

25. Harold H. Kelley, "Two Functions of Reference Groups," in Guy E. Swanson, Theodore M. Newcomb, and Eugene L. Hartley, eds., *Readings in Social Psychology* (New York: Holt, 1952), pp. 412–13.

26. *Ibid.*

27. Kafka, *The Trial*, p. 199.

28. Donald T. Campbell, "Common Fate, Similarity and Other Indices of Aggregates of Persons as Social Entities," *Behavioral Sciences* (1958), 3(1):15–25.

29. Samuel Stouffer *et al.*, *The American Soldier: Adjustment During Army Life*, (Princeton, N.J.: Princeton University Press, 1949), Vol. 1.

30. Robert K. Merton and Alice Kitt, "Contributions to the Theory of Reference Group Behavior," in Robert K. Merton and Paul F. Lazarsfeld, eds., *Studies in the Scope and Method of the American Soldier* (Glencoe, Ill.: Free Press, 1950), pp. 40–105.

31. Kenneth Keniston, *The Uncommitted* (New York: Dell, 1967), p. 447.

32. Leon Festinger, "A Theory of Social Comparison Processes," *Human Relations* (1954), 7:125.

33. William E. Cross, Jr., "The Negro-to-Black Conversion Experience," *Black World* (1971), 20:13–27.

34. *Ibid.*, pp. 15–16.

35. *Ibid.*, p. 17.

36. *Ibid.*, pp. 18–20.

37. *Ibid.*, pp. 21–22.

38. *Ibid.*, p. 23.

39. Miguel Montiel, "Chicanos in the United States: an Overview of Socio-historical Context and Emerging Perspectives," in Miguel Montiel, ed., *Hispanic Families* (Washington: National Coalition of Hispanic Mental Health and Human Services Organizations, 1978), p. 37. See also Rodolfo Acuna, *Occupied America: the Chicano Struggle toward Freedom* (San Francisco: Canfield Press, 1972).

40. Montiel, "Chicanos in the United States," p. 37.

41. Elena Padilla, *Up from Puerto Rico* (New York: Columbia University Press, 1958).

42. Joseph P. Fitzpatrick, "The Role of Language as a Factor of Strength for the Puerto Rican Community" (paper delivered at Conference on the Puerto Rican Child in his Cultural Context, Barranquitas, Puerto Rico, 1965), cited in Joseph P. Fitzpatrick, *Puerto Rican Americans* (Englewood Cliffs, N.J.: Prentice-Hall, 1971), p. 149.

43. Kengi Murase, "Social Welfare Policy and Services: Asian Americans," in Dolores G. Norton *et al.*, *The Dual Perspective* (New York: Council on Social Work Education, 1978), p. 40.

3. Social Reality

1. Fritz Heider, *The Psychology of Interpersonal Relations* (New York: Wiley, 1958), pp. 22–27.

2. *Ibid.*, pp. 53–56.

3, *Ibid.*

4. Leon Festinger, "A Theory of Social Comparison Processes," *Human Relations* (1954), 7:117–40.

5. Solomon Asch, "Studies of Independence and Conformity: a Minority of One against a Unanimous Majority," *Psychological Monographs*, No. 416 (1956), 70(9).

6. Harold H. Kelley, "Two Functions of Reference Groups," in Herbert H. Hyman and Eleanor Singer, eds., *Readings in Reference Group Theory and Research* (New York: Free Press, 1968), pp. 77–83.

7. Festinger, "A Theory of Social Comparison Processes," p. 131.

8. Leon Festinger *et al.*, "The Influence Process in the Presence of Extreme Deviates," *Human Relations* (1952), 5:327–46.

9. Stanley Schachter, "Deviance, Rejection and Communication," *Journal of Abnormal and Social Psychology* (1951), 46:92–99.

10. Leon Festinger and John W. Thibaut, "Interpersonal Communications in Small Groups," *Journal of Abnormal Psychology* (1951), 46:92–99.

11. Festinger, "A Theory of Social Comparison Processes," p. 137.

12. *Ibid.*

13. Fritz Heider, "On Perception, Event Structure and Psychological Environment: Selected Papers," *Psychological Issues* (1959), 1[3]:66–67.

14. *Ibid.*, pp. 82–84.

15. Marvin E. Shaw and Philip R. Costanzo, *Theories of Social Psychology* (New York: McGraw-Hill, 1970), p. 187.

16. Robert B. Zajonc, "The Process of Cognitive Tuning in Communication," *Journal of Abnormal and Social Psychology* (1960), 61:159.

17. Leon Festinger, *A Theory of Cognitive Dissonance* (Stanford, Calif.: Stanford University Press, 1957), p. 57.

18. William A. Scott, "Conceptualizing and Measuring Structural Properties of Cognition," in O. J. Harvey, *Motivation and Social Interaction* (New York: Ronald Press, 1963), p. 269.

19. Shaw and Costanzo, *Theories of Social Psychology*, p. 173.

20. Morton Deutsch and Robert M. Krauss, *Theories in Social Psychology* (New York: Basic Books, Inc., 1965), p. 33.

21. *Ibid.*

22. *Ibid.*, p. 68.

23. Festinger, *A Theory of Cognitive Dissonance*, pp. 32–83.

24. *Ibid.*, pp. 12–15.

25. *Ibid.*, p. 13.

26. *Ibid.*, p. 14.

27. *Ibid.*, pp. 18–24.

28. *Ibid.*, pp. 34–36.

29. Nelida A. Ferrari, "Institutionalization and Attitude Change in an Aged Population: a Field Study in Dissonance Theory" (D.S.W. dissertation, School of Applied Social Sciences, Case Western Reserve University, 1962).

30. Irving Sarnoff, "Psychoanalytic Theory and Social Attitudes," *Public Opinion Quarterly* (1960), 24:225.

31. *Ibid.*, p. 260.

32. Norman A. Polansky, *Ego Psychology and Communication* (Chicago: Aldine Press, 1971), p. 28.

33. Margaret Yeakel, "Ordinal Position and Response to Stress in Hospitalized Children" (D.S.W. dissertation, School of Applied Social Sciences, Case Western Reserve University, 1963).

34. Jules V. Coleman, "Social Factors Influencing the Development and Contain-

ment of Psychiatric Symptoms," in Thomas J. Scheff, ed., *Mental Illness and Social Process* (New York: Harper and Row, 1967), p. 159.

35. Abraham Maslow, *Toward a Psychology of Being* (2d ed.; New York: Van Nostrand Reinhold, 1968), p. 60.

36. *Ibid.*, p. 61.

37. *Ibid.*, p. 60.

38. *Ibid.*, p. 28.

39. Gordon Allport, *Becoming* (New Haven: Yale University Press, 1955), p. 68.

40. William Ryan, *Blaming the Victim* (New York: Random House, Pantheon Books, 1970).

41. Sarnoff, "Psychoanalytic Theory and Social Attitudes," p. 255.

42. William Gordon, "Basic Constructs for an Integrative Conception of Social Work," in Gordon Hearn, ed., *The General Systems Approach: Contributions toward an Holistic Conception of Social Work* (New York: Council on Social Work Education, 1971), p. 9.

43. Harold H. Kelley, "Attribution Theory in Social Psychology," in Marshall Jones, ed., *Nebraska Symposium on Motivation* (Lincoln, Nebr.: University of Nebraska Press, 1967), p. 196.

4. Social Role

1. Theodore R. Sarbin, "Notes on the Transformation of Social Identity," in Leigh M. Roberts, Norman S. Greenfield, and Milton H. Miller, eds., *Comprehensive Mental Health* (Madison, Wis.: University of Wisconsin Press, 1968), p. 102.

2. Dorothy Emmet, *Rules, Roles and Relations* (New York: St. Martin's Press, 1966), p. 175.

3. Herman Stein and Richard Cloward, eds., *Social Perspectives on Behavior* (New York: Free Press, 1958), p. 171.

4. Raymond G. Hunt, "Role and Role Conflict," in Edwin P. Hollander and Raymond G. Hunt, eds., *Current Perspectives in Social Psychology* (New York: Oxford University Press, 1971), p. 279.

5. Ruth Benedict, "Continuities and Discontinuities in Cultural Conditioning," in Stein and Cloward, eds., *Social Perspectives on Behavior*, p. 245.

6. Sarbin, "Notes on the Transformation of Social Identity," p. 105.

7. *Ibid.*, p. 107.

8. *Ibid.*

9. *Ibid.*, p. 106.

10. *Ibid.*, p. 108.

11. William Ryan, *Blaming the Victim* (New York: Random House, Pantheon Books, 1971).

12. Erving Goffman, "Normal Deviants," in Thomas J. Scheff, ed., *Mental Illness and Social Processes* (New York: Harper and Row, 1967), p. 267.

13. David Mechanic, "Some Factors in Identifying and Defining Mental Illness," in Scheff, ed., *Mental Illness and Social Processes*, p. 26.

14. *Ibid.*

15. Scheff, ed., *Mental Illness and Social Processes*, p. 4.

16. Kai T. Erikson, "Notes on the Sociology of Deviance," in Scheff, ed., *Mental Illness and Social Processes*, p. 294.

17. *Ibid.*, p. 295.

18. *Ibid.*

19. *Ibid.*, p. 298.

20. "The New White Person" (paper prepared by the Center for Social Change, Oakland, Calif.).

21. *Ibid.*

22. William E. Cross, Jr., "The Negro-to-Black Conversion Experience," *Black World* (1971) [20]:13–27.

23. Grace Ganter, "The Socio-Conditioning of the White Practitoner: New Perspectives," *Journal of Contemporary Psychotherapy* (1977) [9]1:28–32.

5. Linking the Concepts

1. Abraham H. Maslow, *Toward a Psychology of Being* (2d ed.: New York: Van Nostrand Reinhold, 1968), p. 13.

2. *Ibid.*

3. George J. McCall and J. L. Simmons, *Identities and Interactions* (rev. ed.; New York: Free Press, 1968), p. 221.

4. *Ibid.*, p. 200.

5. Jaber F. Gubrium and David R. Buckholdt, *Toward Maturity* (San Francisco: Jossey-Bass, 1977), pp. 7–8.

6. Robert M. White, "Competence and the Psychosexual Stages," in Marshall Jones, ed., *Nebraska Symposium on Motivation* (Lincoln, Nebr.: University of Nebraska Press, 1960), p. 97.

7. *Ibid.*, p. 98.

8. Karen Horney, *Neurosis and Human Growth* (New York: Norton, 1950).

9. Harry Stack Sullivan, *The Interpersonal Theory of Psychiatry* (New York: Norton, 1953).

10. Erich Fromm, *The Heart of Man* (New York: Norton, 1968).

11. Erik H. Erikson, *Identity, Youth and Crisis* (New York: Norton, 1968).

12. White, "Competence and the Psychosexual Stages," p. 100.

13. Marie Jahoda, *Current Concepts of Positive Mental Health* (New York: Basic Books, 1958).

6. Infancy and Early Childhood

1. Lois Barclay Murphy and Alice E. Moriarity, *Vulnerability, Coping and Growth* (New Haven, Conn.: Yale University Press, 1976), p. 50.

2. Henry W. Maier, *Three Theories of Child Development* (New York: Harper and Row, 1965), p. 16.

3. Erik H. Erikson, *Identity and the Life Cycle*, Psychological Issues, Vol. I, No. 1 (New York: International Universities Press, 1959), p. 52.

4. Robert White, "Competence and the Psychosexual Stages," in Marshall Jones, ed., *Nebraska Symposium on Motivation* (Lincoln, Nebr.: University of Nebraska Press, 1960), p. 100.

5. Erikson, *Identity and the Life Cycle*, p. 63.

6. Kay M. Tooley, "The Remembrance of Things Past: on the Collection and Recollection of Ingredients Useful in the Treatment of Disorders Resulting from Unhappiness, Rootlessness, and the Fear of Things to Come," *American Journal of Orthopsychiatry* (1978), 1(48):175.

7. White, "Competence and the Psychosexual Stages," p. 102.

8. *Ibid.*, p. 109.

9. Erikson, *Identity and the Life Cycle*, p. 67.

10. *Ibid.*, p. 68.

11. *Ibid.*, p. 71.

12. White, "Competence and the Psychosexual Stages," p. 117.

13. Erikson, *Identity and the Life Cycle*, p. 77.

14. White, "Competence and the Psychosexual Stages," p. 125.

15. *Ibid.*, pp. 122–23.

16. Bettye M. Caldwell, "What Is the Optimal Learning Environment for Young Children?" *American Journal of Orthopsychiatry* (1967), 1(37):8–21.

17. Ulric Neisser, *Cognition and Reality* (San Francisco: Freeman, 1976), p. 11.

18. Charlotte Buhler, "The Reality Principle," *American Journal of Psychotherapy* (1954), 8:260–75.

19. Robert White, *Ego and Reality in Psychoanalytic Theory*, (Psychological Issues Monograph, Vol. III, No. 3 (New York: International Universities Press, 1963), p. 50.

20. Jean Piaget and Barbel Inhelder, *The Psychology of the Child* (New York: Basic Books, 1969), p. 20.

21. *Ibid.*, pp. 4–27.

22. White, *Ego and Reality in Psychoanalytic Theory*, p. 50.

23. Buhler, "The Reality Principle," pp. 641–42.

24. Jean Piaget, *The Origin of Intelligence in Children* (New York: International Universities Press, 1952).

25. Jerome Bruner, "On Cognitive Growth," in Jerome Bruner *et al.*, *Studies in Cognitive Growth* (New York: Wiley, 1966), p. 1.

26. *Ibid.*, p. 2.

27. White, "Ego and Reality in Psychoanalytic Theory," pp. 134–35.

28. Norman K. Denzin, *Childhood Socialization* (San Francisco: Jossey-Bass, 1977), pp. 6–7.

29. Annaliese F. Korner, "Mother-Child Interaction," *Social Work* (1965), 3(10):47–50.

30. Louis W. Sander, "Issues in Early Mother-Child Interaction," *Journal of the American Academy of Child Psychiatry* (1962), 1(1):141–66.

31. Therese Benedek, "Parenthood as a Developmental Phase," *Journal of the American Psychoanalytic Association* (1959), 7:389–417.

32. Alice S. Rossi, "Transition to Parenthood," *Journal of Marriage and the Family* (1968), 2(30):26–39.

33. Alan B. Knox, *Adult Development and Learning* (San Francisco, Calif.: Jossey-Bass, 1977), p. 377.

34. David R. Burgest, "Racism in Everyday Speech and Social Work Jargon," *Social Work* (1973), 3(18):24.

35. Knox, *Adult Development and Learning*, p. 378.

36. Anne Rice, "Factors Associated with the Right to Be Legitimate" (master's thesis, Temple University School of Social Administration, 1974), p. 4.

37. Harry D. Krause, "The Bastard Finds His Father," in Albert E. Wilkerson, ed., *The Rights of Children* (Philadelphia: Temple University Press, 1973), pp. 148–49.

38. Andrew Billingsley, *Black Families in White America* (Englewood Cliffs, N.J.: Prentice-Hall, 1968), p. 61.

39. William Ryan, *Blaming the Victim* (New York: Random House, Pantheon Books, 1971), p. 111.

40. René Dubos, "Environmental Determinants of Human Life," in D. C. Glass, ed., *Environmental Influences* (New York: Rockefeller University Press and Russell Sage Foundation, 1968), p. 139.

41. U.S. Department of Health, Education, and Welfare, Children's Bureau, *Infant Mortality: a Challenge to the Nation* (Washington, D.C.: United States Government Printing Office, 1966), p. 1.

7. Childhood

1. Robert White, *Ego and Reality in Psychoanalytic Theory*, Psychological Issues Monograph, Vol. III, No. 3 (New York: International Universities Press, 1963), p. 192.

2. *Ibid.*, p. 193.

3. Joseph Church, *Language and the Discovery of Reality* (New York: Random House, 1966), p. 26.

4. *Ibid.*, p. 27.

5. Erik H. Erikson, *Identity and the Life Cycle*, Psychological Issues Monograph, Vol. I, No. 1 (New York: International Universities Press, 1959), p. 86.

6. Robert White, "Competence and the Psychosexual Stages of Development," in Marshall Jones, ed., *Nebraska Symposium on Motivation* (Lincoln, Nebr.: University of Nebraska Press, 1960), p. 127.

7. Margaret Yeakel and Grace Ganter, "Some Principles and Methods of Sampling," in Norman A. Polansky, ed., *Social Work Research* (rev. ed.; Chicago: University of Chicago Press, 1975), p. 93.

8. Harry Stack Sullivan, *The Interpersonal Theory of Psychiatry* (New York: Norton, 1953).

9. George Herbert Mead, *Mind, Self and Society* (Chicago: University of Chicago Press, 1934).

10. Norman K. Denzin, *Childhood Socialization* (San Francisco: Jossey-Bass, 1977), p. 20.

11. Albert E. Wilkerson, *The Rights of Children* (Philadelphia: Temple University Press, 1973), p. viii.

12. Arthur Jensen, "The Differences Are Real," *Psychology Today* (1973), 7(7):80.

13. Philip J. Scrofani, Antanas Suziedelis, and Milton F. Shore, "Conceptual Ability in Black and White Children of Different Social Classes: an Experimental Test of Jensen's Hypothesis," *American Journal of Orthopsychiatry* (1973), 43(4):541.

14. William Ryan, *Blaming the Victim* (New York: Random House, Pantheon Books, 1971), p. 53.

15. Robert Rosenthal and Lenore Jacobson, *Pygmalion in the Classroom* (New York: Holt, Rinehart and Winston, 1968).

16. Ryan, *Blaming the Victim*, pp. 56–57.

17. Joseph P. Fitzpatrick, *Puerto Rican Americans* (Englewood Cliffs, N.J.: Prentice-Hall, 1971), p. 151.

18. Alvin F. Poussaint, "The Black Child's Image of the Future," in Alvin Toffler, ed., *Learning for Tomorrow* (New York: Random House, 1972), pp. 56–71.

19. Ruth Benedict, "Continuities and Discontinuities in Cultural Conditioning," in Margaret Mead and Martha Wolfenstein, eds., *Childhood Socialization* (1st Phoenix ed., Chicago: University of Chicago Press, 1963), p. 30.

20. Lenore J. Weitzman et al., "Sex-Role Socialization in Picture Books for Preschool Children," *American Journal of Sociology* (1972), 77(6):1131.

21. Eleanor E. Maccoby, "Sex Differences in Intellectual Functioning," in Eleanor E. Maccoby, ed., *The Development of Sex Differences* (Stanford, Calif.: Stanford University Press, 1966).

22. Weitzman *et al.*, "Sex-Role Socialization in Picture Books for Preschool Children," pp. 1125–50.

23. Women on Words and Images, *Dick and Jane as Victims: Sex Stereotyping in Children's Readers: An Analysis* (Princeton, N.J.: Women on Words and Images, 1972), p. 25.

24. *Ibid.*, p. 26.

25. Joseph H. Pleck and Jack Sawyer, *Men and Masculinity* (Englewood Cliffs, N.J.: Prentice-Hall, 1974).

26. Grace Ganter, Margaret Yeakel, and Norman Polansky, *Retrieval from Limbo* (New York: Child Welfare League of America, Inc., 1971), p. 21.

8. Adolescence

1. John A. Clausen, "Differential Physical and Sexual Maturation," in Sigmund E. Dragastin and Glen Elder, Jr., eds., *Adolescence in the Life Cycle* (New York: Wiley, 1975), p. 25.
2. *Ibid.*, pp. 33-34.
3. *Ibid.*, pp. 34-35.
4. *Ibid.*, pp. 35-36.
5. B. J. Phillips, "Comes the Revolution," *Time*, June 26, 1978, p. 54.
6. *Ibid.*, p. 60.
7. Diana Baumrind, "Early Socialization and Adolescent Competence," in Dragastin and Elder, eds., *Adolescence in the Life Cycle*, p. 118.
8. Erik H. Erikson, *Identity, Youth and Crisis* (New York: Norton, 1968), p. 159.
9. *Ibid.*, p. 165.
10. *Ibid.*, p. 157.
11. Kenneth Keniston, "Social Change and Youth in America," *Daedalus* (1962), 91(1):164.
12. Joan Lipsitz, *Growing up Forgotten* (Lexington, Mass.: Lexington Books, 1977).
13. Kay M. Tooley, "The Remembrance of Things Past: on the Collection and Recollection of Ingredients Useful in the Treatment of Disorders Resulting from Unhappiness, Rootlessness, and the Fear of Things to Come," *American Journal of Orthopsychiatry* (1978), 1 (48):175.
14. *Ibid.*, p. 176.
15. Walter Miller, "The Rumble This Time," *Psychology Today*, May, 1977, p. 52.
16. *Ibid.*
17. *Ibid.*, p. 58.
18. Jerome Miller, in MacNeil/Lehrer Report, "Juvenile Justice," WNET/WETA, July 20, 1978.
19. Jessie Bernard, "Adolescence and Socialization for Motherhood," in Dragastin and Elder, eds., *Adolescence in the Life Cycle*, p. 231.
20. *Ibid.*, p. 244.
21. *Ibid.*
22. Erik H. Erikson, "Youth, Fidelity and Diversity," *Daedalus* (1962), 91(1):6-7.
23. Baumrind, "Early Socialization and Adolescent Competence," p. 138.

9. Adulthood

1. Lillian Troll, *Early and Middle Adulthood* (Monterey, Calif.: Brooks/Cole, 1975), p. 1.
2. Howard S. Becker, "Personal Change in Adult Life," *Sociometry* (1964), 27:52.
3. Bernice L. Neugarten, ed., *Middle Age and Aging: a Reader in Social Psychology* (Chicago: University of Chicago Press, 1968), p 139.
4. Becker, "Personal Change in Adult Life," p. 44.
5. *Ibid.*, pp. 49-50.
6. Bernice L. Neugarten and Nancy Datan, "Sociological Perspectives on the Life Cycle," in Paul Baltes and K. Warner Schaie, eds., *Life-Span Developmental Psychology* (New York: Academic Press, 1973), p. 59.
7. K. Warner Schaie, "Age Changes and Age Differences," *The Gerontologist* (1967), 7(2): part 1, p. 128.
8. Troll, *Early and Middle Adulthood*, pp. 30-31.
9. *Ibid.*, p. 44.

10. Erik H. Erikson, *Identity, Youth and Crisis* (New York: Norton, 1968), pp. 135–36.

11. *Ibid.*, p. 138.

12. Mary C. Schwartz, "Sexism in the Social Work Curriculum," *Journal of Education for Social Work* (1973) 9(3):65–70.

13. Erik H. Erikson, "Inner and Outer Space: Reflections on Womanhood," in Robert Lipton, ed., *The Woman in America* (Boston: Houghton Mifflin, Riverside Press, 1965), p. 19.

14. Daniel J. Levinson, "The Psychological Development of Men in Early Adulthood and the Mid-Life Transition," in David F. Ricks, A. Thomas and Merrill Roff, eds., *Life History; the Search in Psychopathology* (Minneapolis: University of Minnesota Press, 1974), Vol. 3.

15. Gail Sheehy, *Passages* (New York: Dutton, 1974).

16. *Ibid.*, pp. 16–17.

17. *Ibid.*, pp. 84–118.

18. *Ibid.*, pp. 138–204.

19. *Ibid.*, pp. 242–72.

20. *Ibid.*, pp. 274–332.

21. *Ibid.*, pp. 342–55.

22. *Ibid.*, p. 15.

23. Neugarten and Datan, "Sociological Perspectives on the Life Cycle," p. 59.

24. Ray L. Birdwhistell, "The Idealized Model of the American Family," *Social Casework* (1970), 4(51):196.

25. *Ibid.*, pp. 196–97.

26. *Ibid.*, p. 198.

27. Neugarten and Datan, "Sociological Perspectives on the Life Cycle," p. 57.

28. Perry London, "The Intimacy Gap," *Psychology Today* (1978) 12(11):40.

29. *Ibid.*

30. Elizabeth Herzog and Cecelia E. Sudia, "Family Structure and Composition: Research Considerations," in Roger R. Miller, ed., *Race, Research and Reason: Social Work Perspectives* (New York: National Association of Social Workers, 1969) pp. 145–64.

31. Miguel Montiel, ed., *Hispanic Families* (Washington: National Coalition of Hispanic Mental Health and Human Services Organizations, 1978).

32. Eddie Frank Brown, "American Indians in Modern Society: Implications for Social Policy and Services," in Dolores G. Norton *et al.*, *The Dual Perspective* (New York: Council on Social Work Education, 1978) pp. 68–76.

33. Kenji Morase, "Social Welfare Policy and Services: Asian Americans," in Norton *et al.*, *The Dual Perspective*, pp. 34–48.

34. Robert Staples, ed., *The Black Family: Essays and Studies* (2d ed.: Belmont, Calif.: Wadsworth, 1978).

35. Andrew Billingsley, *Black Families in White America* (Englewood Cliffs, N.J.: Prentice-Hall, 1968), pp. 16–21.

36. Daniel P. Moynihan, *The Negro Family: the Case for National Action*, United States Department of Labor, Office of Policy Planning and Research (Washington, D.C.: U.S. Government Printing Office, 1965), pp. 29–44.

37. Audrey Pittman, personal communication, December, 1978.

38. Urie Bronfenbrenner, "The Erosion of the American Family," *Psychology Today* (1977) 12(10):45.

39. *Ibid.*

40. Daniel Y. Yankelovitch, "The New Psychological Contracts at Work," *Psychology Today* (1978) 12(11):46–50.

41. *Ibid.*, p. 47.

42. Matina S. Horner, "Toward Women as Equal and Essential Participants," in *The Nature of a Humane Society*, Symposium sponsored by the Southeastern Pennsylvania Synod of the Lutheran Church in America (Philadelphia: Fortress Press, 1976), pp. 135–37.

43. Margaret Yeakel and Grace Ganter, "Some Principles and Methods of Sampling," in Norman A. Polansky, ed., *Social Work Research* (rev. ed.: Chicago: University of Chicago Press, 1975), pp. 93–94.

44. Horner, "Toward Women as Equal and Essential Participants," p. 135.

45.*Ibid.*, pp. 138–40.

10. Older Adults

1. Wilbur H. Watson and Robert J. Maxwell, *Human Aging and Dying* (New York: St. Martin's Press, 1977), p. 2.

2. Richard A. Kalish, *Late Adulthood: Perspectives on Human Development* (Monterey, Calif.: Brooks/Cole, 1975), p. 3.

3. Robert C. Atchley, "Aging as a Social Problem: an Overview," in Mildred M. Seltzer, Sherry L. Corbett, and Robert C. Atchley, eds., *Social Problems of the Aging* (Belmont, Calif.: Wadsworth, 1975), p. 5.

4. *Ibid.*

5. Kalish, *Late Adulthood: Perspectives on Human Development*, p. 3.

6. *Ibid.*

7. Lillian Troll, *Early and Middle Adulthood* (Monterey, Calif.: Brooks/Cole, 1975), p. 28.

8. U.S. Department of Health, Education, and Welfare, Office of Human Development Services, Administration on Aging and National Clearing House on Aging, *Facts about Older Americans 1978* (Publication No. OHDS 79-20006).

9. Irving Rosow, *Socialization to Old Age* (paperback ed.; Berkeley, Calif: University of California Press, 1977), p. 2.

10. Kalish, *Late Adulthood: Perspectives on Human Development*, p. 75.

11. Atchley, "Aging as a Social Problem," p. 10.

12. *Ibid.*

13. *Ibid.*, pp. 6–7.

14. Lucille Duberman, *Social Inequality: Class and Caste in America* (Philadelphia: Lippincott, 1976), p. 271.

15. Margaret Clark, "The Anthropology of Aging," in Bernice L. Neugarten, ed., *Middle Age and Aging* (Chicago: University of Chicago Press, 1968), pp. 441–42.

16. Ismael Dieppa and Miguel Montiel, "Hispanic Families: an Exploration," in Miguel Montiel, ed., *Hispanic Families* (Washington: National Coalition of Hispanic Mental Health and Human Services Organizations, 1978), pp. 6–7.

17. Atchley, "Aging as a Social Problem," p. 7.

18. Donald Davis, "Growing Old Black," in U.S. Senate, Special Committee on Aging, *The Multiple Hazards of Age and Race: the Situation of Aged Blacks in the United States* (Washington, D.C.: United States Government Printing Office, 1971), p. 60.

19. *Ibid.*

20. Rosow, *Socialization to Old Age*, p. 52.

21. Philip Jaslow, "Employment, Retirement, and Morale among Older Women," *Journal of Gerontology* (1976), 31(2):213.

22. *Ibid.*

23. Gayle B. Thompson, "Work versus Leisure Roles: an Investigation of Morale among Employed and Retired Men," *Journal of Gerontology* (1973), 28(2):343–44.

24. Rosow, *Socialization to Old Age*, p. 138.

25. Fernando Manuel Torres-Gil, "Age, Health, and Culture: an Examination of Health among Spanish-Speaking Elderly," in Montiel, ed., *Hispanic Families*, p. 85.

26. Margaret E. Kuhn, "New Life for the Elderly: Liberation from Agism," in *Enquiry, Studies for Christian Laity* (rev. ed.; Crawfordsville, Ind.: Geneva Press, 1974), p. 1.

27. *Ibid.*, p. 2.

28. Rosow, *Socialization to Old Age*, pp. 88–89.

29. Erik Erikson, *Childhood and Society* (2d. rev. ed.: New York: Norton, 1963), p. 232.

30. Robert Havighurst, Bernice L. Neugarten, and Sheldon S. Tobin, "Disengagement and Patterns of Aging," in Neugarten, ed., *Middle Age and Aging*, p. 161.

31. *Ibid.*

32. Kalish, *Late Adulthood: Perspectives on Human Development*, p. 64.

33. Havighurst, Neugarten, and Tobin, "Disengagement and Patterns of Aging," p. 172.

34. Melvin J. Krant, "Death with Dignity," in Mildred M. Seltzer, Sherry L. Corbett, and Robert C. Atchley, eds., *Social Problems of the Aging* (Belmont, Calif.: Wadsworth, 1978), p. 96.

35. Elisabeth Kübler-Ross, *On Death and Dying* (New York: Macmillan, 1969).

36. Kalish, *Late Adulthood: Perspectives on Human Development*, p. 93.

37. Krant, "Death with Dignity," p. 95.

38. Kalish, *Late Adulthood: Perspectives on Human Development*, p. 93.

39. Arthur Benjamin Downing, ed., *Euthanasia and the Right to Death: the Case for Voluntary Euthanasia* (New York: Nash Publishing Corp., 1969).

40. Zelda Samoff, personal communication, March, 1970.

41. Bernard Leibowitz, "Implications of Community Housing for Planning and Policy," *The Gerontologist* (1972) 18(2):138–43.

42. Uri Rueveni, *Networking Families in Crisis* (New York: Human Sciences Press, 1979).

43. Kuhn, "New Life for the Elderly: Liberation from Agism," p. 2.

44. Margaret E. Hartford and Mary M. Seguin, "Changing Approaches to Social Work with Older Adults," in Francine Sobey, ed., *Changing Roles in Social Work Practice* (Philadelphia: Temple University Press, 1977), p. 127.

45. Sandol Stoddards, *The Hospice Movement: a Better Way of Caring for the Dying* (New York: Stein and Day, 1977).

11. Summary and Reflections

1. Albert Memmi, *Dominated Man: Notes toward a Portrait* (Boston: Beacon Press, 1968).

Index